PENGUIN B

THE SHAPING OF MODERN GUJARAT

Achyut Yagnik is the founder-secretary of Setu: Centre for Social Knowledge and Action, an Ahmedabad-based voluntary organization which has been working with marginalized communities since the early 1980s. He was a journalist and has also taught development communication as visiting faculty in Gujarat University. He is co-author of the book *Creating a Nationality: Ramjanmabhoomi Movement and Fear of the Self.*

Suchitra Sheth studied visual communication at the National Institute of Design (NID), Ahmedabad. She is associated with Setu and has been visiting faculty at NID and the National Institute of Fashion Technology, Gandhinagar.

The Shaping of Modern Gujarat
Plurality, Hindutva and Beyond

ACHYUT YAGNIK and SUCHITRA SHETH

PENGUIN BOOKS

PENGUIN BOOKS

Published by the Penguin Group

Penguin Books India Pvt. Ltd, 11 Community Centre, Panchsheel Park, New Delhi 110 017, India

Penguin Group (USA) Inc., 375 Hudson Street, New York, New York 10014, USA

Penguin Group (Canada), 90 Eglinton Avenue East, Suite 700, Toronto, Ontario, M4P 2Y3, Canada (a division of Pearson Penguin Canada Inc.)

Penguin Books Ltd, 80 Strand, London WC2R 0RL, England

Penguin Ireland, 25 St Stephen's Green, Dublin 2, Ireland (a division of Penguin Books Ltd)

Penguin Group (Australia), 250 Camberwell Road, Camberwell, Victoria 3124, Australia (a division of Pearson Australia Group Pty Ltd)

Penguin Group (NZ), cnr Airborne and Rosedale Roads, Albany, Auckland 1310, New Zealand (a division of Pearson New Zealand Ltd)

Penguin Group (South Africa) (Pty) Ltd, 24 Sturdee Avenue, Rosebank, Johannesburg 2196, South Africa

Penguin Books Ltd, Registered Offices: 80 Strand, London WC2R 0RL, England

First published by Penguin Books India 2005

Copyright © Achyut Yagnik and Suchitra Sheth 2005

10 9 8 7 6 5 4 3 2 1

The international boundaries on the maps of India are neither purported to be correct nor authentic by Survey of India directives.

ISBN-13: 978-0-14400-038-8 ISBN-10: 0-14400-038-5

Typeset in Sabon by R. Ajith Kumar, New Delhi
Printed at Sanat Printers, Kundli, Haryana

This book is dedicated to

my granddaughter, Akshara
— Achyut Yagnik

my children, Ayesha and Aniruddh
— Suchitra

And all the children of Gujarat

Contents

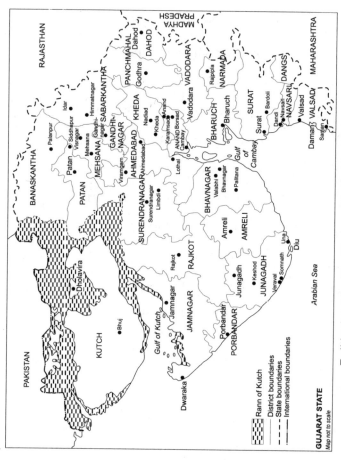

Political map with cities mentioned in the book

Acknowledgements

This book owes its existence to Kamini Mahadevan, our first editor at Penguin, and we would like to express our heartfelt thanks for her unwavering trust and support. Her comments and suggestions on early drafts forced us to think through many facets in a new way and greatly enriched our presentation.

In the early phase we were helped by Shalini Randeria, Shiv Visvanathan and D.L. Sheth, who gave us feedback on the outline of the book and encouraged us to take up this work as a challenge. We would like to thank Harsh Sethi and Vimal Balasubrahmanyan, who read several chapters and commented on them, and Jyotirmaya Sharma, who cheered us along throughout.

Many friends facilitated our search for books and references and we are thankful to Kirit Bhavsar, Gaurang Jani, P.M. Parmar, Ramesh Dave, Priyavadan Randeria, Raman Modi, Ravindra Vasavada, Hanif Lakdawala, Sheela Bhatt and Kavita Sivaramakrishnan. We are indebted to Jitendra Desai of Navajivan Trust and Amrut Modi of Gandhi Smarak Sangrahalaya for permission to reproduce material related to Mahatma Gandhi. We thank Jitendra Shah of L.D. Institute of Indology for permission to reproduce an illustration from a Jain miniature in the institute's collection.

We are grateful to our colleagues at Setu who supported us throughout the period we were at work on this book. Bhalubhai Desai not only encouraged us but went through early drafts of the book and made many suggestions. Even when he was in the United States, he learnt how to operate email just so that he could send us detailed comments. Ashok Shrimali helped with the research and also shouldered extra responsibilities in the organization to leave us free to write. Among other colleagues are Nina Haeems, Hina Patel, Parul Shah, Parvin Saiyad, Ramsinh Thakore and Udaysinh Thakore, and we appreciate their support as well.

We would also like to thank our copy editor Jaishree Ram Mohan, who worked meticulously on the prose and ironed out numerous wrinkles.

Finally, many thanks to the members of our families for their patience and encouragement throughout the writing of this book.

Preface

The idea of Gujarat and pride in Gujarati identity is pre-modern. Probably the earliest reference to Gurjardesh occurs in the eighth-century Apabhransh work *Kuvalayamala* by the Jain monk Udyotansuri. A glimpse of Gujarati pride can be seen in the fourteenth-century Sanskrit poem '*Nabhinandan-jinoddhar Prabandh*' by another Jain monk, Kakkasuri. He glorified Gurjardesh in the poem, describing in detail the flora of the land, its prosperous ports and the wealth of those who conducted business there. Interestingly, he indicated the boundaries of Gurjardesh through a catalogue of the religious places that were situated within the region, which corresponds roughly to Gujarat of today. About a hundred years later, poet Padmanabh used the word 'Gujarati' to refer to Gujarat in his historical poem '*Kanhadde Prabandh*'. Half a century after him, poet Bhalan of Patan took pride in his '*Gujar bhakha*' or Gujarati language. By the late seventeenth century, Premanand Bhatt, one of the greatest poets of the Gujarati language, proclaimed in his work *Nalakhyan*, '*Garvo desh Gujaratji*', Gujarat is majestic! One of the most moving expressions of identification with Gujarat is found in the poem '*Dar Firaaq-e-Gujarat*', On Separation from Gujarat, by Wali Muhammad Wali, a junior contemporary of Premanand's:

> Parting from Gujarat leaves thorns in my chest
> My heart-on-fire pounds impatiently in my breast
> What cure can heal the wound of living apart?
> The scimitar of exile has cut deep into my heart
> . . .
> And thank God's mercy, O Wali! He let that passion remain
> The heart's still anxious to catch a glimpse of my Gujarat again[1]

In fact, Wali Muhammad Wali, who is considered a pioneer of Urdu language and literature, was referred to by his contemporaries as Wali Gujarati.

We are neither poets nor historians and we have not even attempted to express our perception in the style of Kakkasuri or Wali Gujarati. What we have tried to present is a concerned citizen's understanding of the shaping of modern Gujarat.

Many aspects of modern Gujarati society and polity appear puzzling. A society which has drawn diverse people to its bosom can also be exclusive and excluding; Gujaratis, who have travelled to the corners of the world, can be inexplicably insular and parochial. In this industrially prosperous state one-fifth of the population lives below the poverty line; it is a place where women feel safe to move about unescorted and yet the female sex ratio is one of the poorest in the country. And most intriguing of all is that two Gujaratis rose to eminence in the twentieth century, one as the father of India and the other as the father of Pakistan.

In our attempt to explore and explain these paradoxes we have drawn from academic studies but have relied more on our field experiences and observations as well as conversations with old and young people of Gujarat during the last few decades. The two of us have diverse backgrounds. The senior of the two of us is a 'son of the soil', born and brought up in rural and small-town Gujarat. He has been a key participant in the public life of the state and has spent a long time as a journalist in an Ahmedabad-based Gujarati newspaper. The other has trained in visual communication at a design school in Ahmedabad, spent her entire adult life in the city and is married to a Gujarati. We are both associated with Setu, a voluntary organization which has been working with marginalized communities of Gujarat for the last two decades. This brief biographical digression is only to underline that our presentation in these eleven chapters is essentially an 'insider view' of the events and patterns in contemporary Gujarat.

Although studies on the history of Gujarat, in both Gujarati and English, have been published by other 'insiders', they focus on specific periods, areas and dimensions. For instance, M.S. Commissariat's *History of Gujarat* in three volumes, published in the mid twentieth century, covers the period from the fourteenth to mid eighteenth centuries and describes mainly political developments. The nine-volume *Gujaratno Rajkiya Ane Sanskrutik Itihas*, published by the B.J. Institute of Ahmedabad between 1972 and 1987, covers the period from the earliest times to the formation of Gujarat state. Each of these volumes devotes only a chapter or two to 'the social and economic situation'. As a result, the social dynamics and economic forces and their impact get less attention and the period after the formation of Gujarat state in 1960 is not presented. Nonetheless, we have greatly benefited from these historical works, which have given us meaningful insights into the past. For the more recent period, studies by a number of social scientists have contributed immensely to our understanding of social transformation.

The challenge before us was to look back and around to discern and weave together patterns as they have manifested themselves in the modern period. While we have used academic and scholarly sources as a backdrop, contemporary accounts and perceptions in the form of autobiographical accounts, letters and biographical studies have enjoyed a privileged position in our treatment of the subject. To capture the ethos of the time and expressions of collectivity, we have also turned to the vision of poets and the perceptions of common people as revealed through folksongs and folk literature. Sometimes, as in the material pertaining to the nineteenth century, it was difficult to demarcate the boundaries between literature, education, social reform and industrial entrepreneurship as many of the opinion-makers of the time were embodiments of all these activities and areas. In such a situation we have tried to distil the interplay of ideas and institutions and the manner in which they prepared the ground for what came next.

We would like to mention here that we have used the term 'modern' to mean the nineteenth and twentieth centuries in general. The first three chapters are in the nature of an introduction and provide an overview of Gujarat till the end of the eighteenth century. They do not take a strictly chronological view of the past but focus instead on specific events and themes which have a bearing on the present. The first of these chapters focuses on how Gujarati society came to be a synthesis of diverse peoples and cultures through waves of migration of people from Central Asia, its contact with West Asia and Africa through maritime trade and the resulting cultural synthesis in art, architecture, material culture, food and language. The second chapter looks at the development of the mercantile ethos and the way in which trading communities established their hegemony. They not only dominated the economy but also influenced and controlled politics, and their style and strategies infused the fabric of Gujarati society. The last of the introductory chapters chronicles Gujarat's encounters with the Turks (Muslims), Marathas and the Portuguese, which have had an indelible impact on the Gujarati collective memory. It explores the dimensions of these encounters to throw light on their implications for the present-day identity politics.

The next four chapters focus on the nineteenth century, culminating in Gandhi's return to Gujarat. The first of these looks at the impact of British rule. As a result of the combined plunder by the Mughal subas after Aurangzeb and the Maratha sardars during the eighteenth century, the British were welcomed in Gujarat as saviours and symbols of law and order. With the British came land settlement, modern legal framework, railways, modern technology and education. Barely 15 per cent of the area of the state was under direct British control, though a new order was also established in the more than 200 princely states in Gujarat, Saurashtra and Kutch. The next chapter explores how the introduction of modern technology set in motion the processes of industrialization, urbanization and the rise of an incipient middle class. A new working class came into existence, drawn mainly from Dalit, Muslim and other backward communities as well as migrants from within the state and outside. Parallel to this, from the 1870s, the idea of 'Swadeshi' also evolved, setting the stage for confrontation with the British.

The nationalist spirit took the form of active Congress politics dominated by Gujarati lawyers and economic nationalism dominated by Gujarati entrepreneurs and liberal princely states such as Baroda. Parallel to these two streams was militant nationalism in the first decade of the twentieth century. Gandhi entered the scene in 1915 and tried to respond to the changing scenario in Gujarat. We have looked at Gandhi from a Gujarati perspective rather than the perspective of the 'freedom struggle', presenting his attempts to mould society and politics through a synthesis of diverse Gujarati sources such as local syncretic sects, Jain traditions and elements from the mercantile ethos. He made a lasting impact on Gujarati language and literature, even systemizing and standardizing Gujarat spelling. He tried to transform Gujarati culture by emphasizing education in the mother tongue, unification of social and political action and inter-caste and inter-religious harmony.

The last four chapters concentrate on the developments in Gujarat after Independence, delineating forces which moulded the Gujarati society we see today. We have explored the polarization of the Hindus and Muslims of Gujarat, identifying the social and political developments which altered the relationship between these two religious groups and made them two antagonistic blocs. The chapter offers a glimpse of the transformation of Jinnah from a champion of Hindu–Muslim unity to a leader of Muslim nationalism, the evolution and articulation of Aryan identity, and the impact of the Shuddhi and the Tabligh movements in Gujarat. The next chapter commences with the movement for a separate state of Gujarat soon after Independence, drawing on older ideas of Gujarat and linguistic sub-nationalism. After the successful formation of a separate state, the expanding middle class changed the ethos of Gujarat, and a new kind of entrepreneurship replaced old mercantile value systems. It was held in place by development models based on unsustainable use of natural resources, rapid and widespread urbanization and the increasing marginalization of Dalits, Adivasis and minorities. This led to a phase of identity politics based on the Hindutva ideology, where the legacy of inter-community synthesis was made invisible and violence in multiple forms became increasingly visible in Gujarati society. The final chapter briefly looks at the communal violence of 2002 and reflects on its implications for the future course of Gujarati society and polity.

No doubt, a multitude of factors have contributed to the shaping of modern Gujarat and we have tried to indicate some of them. At times, lack of space forced us to treat some aspects briefly or even omit them altogether. We hope others will bring them to the fore in the future and a meaningful discussion and debate will follow.

Synthesis and Continuity

To the threshold of this land came the entire world,
from north and west, from east and south:
blessings showered from the heavens above
Mind–Might–Joy–Reason–Riches, beyond compare,
flowed in;
Like gems in a treasure trove were the people
Who blossomed from this confluence of the world.[1]

These lines are from the poem 'Gurjari Bhoo', The Land of Gujarat, written by Sundaram (1908–91), one of Gujarat's most eminent poets of the twentieth century. It was written in 1960 to celebrate the formation of a separate state of Gujarat, following the bifurcation of the bilingual Bombay state. Marking the same occasion, Umashankar Joshi (1911–88), an equally distinguished poet, composed 'Gujarat-Stavano', Odes to Gujarat:

A Gurjar resident of Bharat am I
I hope, each moment, for the prosperity of all
My heart full of joy
A Gurjar resident of Bharat am I

Between the Abu mountain and the Arabian Sea
This land of milk
folds in rapturous embrace
Diverse people from north, west, south and east
A Gurjar resident of Bharat am I[2]

Both Sundaram and Joshi presented Gujarat as a fertile land attracting and welcoming people and communities from all directions, a powerful sentiment shared by Gujaratis for centuries and also expressed in popular legends and folklore.

The cultural mosaic of present-day Gujarat is the amalgamation over centuries of a large number of communities who came over land from the north and the east, and both over land and by sea from the west, finding shelter and prosperity in Gujarat and eventually making it their home. They came as nomads, travellers, merchants, refugees fleeing persecution and even as conquerors. This intermingling of diverse people is borne out by an exhaustive survey carried out by the Anthropological Survey of India in 1980 in its *People of India* series, which, among other aspects, recorded 'people's memory of their movement, whether it was short distance or long distance'. The data on self-identity of communities, particularly on migration, revealed that in India, about 60 per cent of the communities are migrants. Gujarat topped the list among the larger states of India, with over 70 per cent communities indicating their migration to the present state or region. Of the 289 communities in the state, 124 Hindu communities (out of a total of 186) believe that they migrated to Gujarat, as do sixty-seven Muslim communities (out of eighty-seven). Among the thirteen Jain communities, twelve indicate that they came from outside. All hunter–gatherer communities, 70 per cent of fishing communities, 70 per cent of agricultural communities and 50 per cent of artisan communities believe that they migrated to Gujarat.

The ethnographic map of Gujarat suggests three patterns of migration: the interregional, interstate and the transnational. For example, when the Jain communities refer to their migration, they are essentially pointing to interstate migration, mostly from neighbouring Rajasthan or Madhya Pradesh. Many Brahmin and Vaniya castes use prefixes which suggest their place of origin, usually a town or region or even a direction as in the case of the Audichya Brahmins, where the prefix means 'northerner'. The Shrimali Brahmins and Vaniyas came from

Shrimal or present-day Bhinnmal, the Sanchora from Sanchor and the Jhalora from Jhalor towns of south Rajasthan. Similarly, the Mewadas came from Mewar and the Malwi from Malwa—regions which share their borders with Gujarat.

The *jamaat* names of several Muslim communities clearly indicate transnational migration to Gujarat. Many are endogamous jamaats with names such as Arab, Turki, Kabuli, Multani, Makrani, Baluchi, Pathan, Sindhi and Mughal indicating their origin in areas to the north or north-west. The Saiyyads, considered the highest stratum in Muslim society, mostly came from the north by land but a few of them entered Gujarat by sea and settled in coastal cities like Surat and Khambat (Cambay). *Mirat-i-Ahmadi*, an eighteenth-century Persian chronicle of Gujarat, lists eleven important families of Saiyyads with names such as Shirazi, Bukhari, Idrusi and Tirmizi, all of which refer to locations in West or Central Asia. Interestingly, the *People of India* survey reveals that Gujarat has the largest number of Muslim communities in India—more than Uttar Pradesh or Jammu and Kashmir.

It is not without significance that in the poems quoted earlier, after describing Gujarat as a confluence of various communities, both poets go on to venerate Lord Krishna, who is believed to have come to Gujarat from the north with his Yadava clan, settled in Dwarka and graced the land. This mythical past associated with Krishna is also a living past in the collective memory of Gujaratis. In fact, pastoralist communities like Rabaris and Bharwads claim to have descended from the Yadavas and count Krishna as one of their ancestors. Yet, their embroidery and jewellery tell an altogether different story, suggesting instead their movement from Central Asia, somewhere beyond the Hindukush. Similarly, the costume and embroidery of the Jats, a small pastoralist Muslim community of Kutch, also reflect the community's movement from beyond the mountains in Central Asia.

Apart from living memories of migration and mythical pasts is the historical past which connects Gujarat with the Indus Valley civilization. Numerous excavations at Lothal, Prabhas

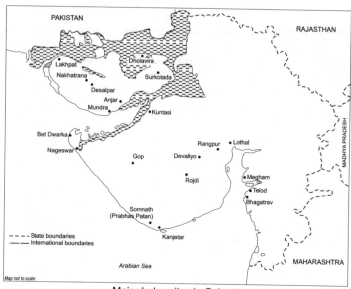

Major Indus sites in Gujarat

Patan (Somnath), Rojadi and Rangpur in Saurashtra and Dholavira in Kutch have firmly established that this region was part of an urban civilization going back almost 4000 years. Though no community traces its past to this era, it is nevertheless a living past. Contemporary pottery forms in Kutch and Saurashtra and bead-making techniques in Cambay bear close resemblance to excavated artefacts, and the maritime activity depicted on Lothal seals continues till today. Thus, Gujarat is a complex mosaic of interactions between the historical and mythical pasts which continue to shape the present.

OVERVIEW OF GUJARAT'S POLITICAL HISTORY

Clues to Gujarat's ancient history remained scattered and submerged for many centuries, and it was only in the early nineteenth century that they were explored and excavated, studied and deciphered. On the outskirts of Junagadh, towards Mount Girnar, stands a large granite rock with inscriptions in many 'strange' scripts which perplexed many a traveller for centuries. When deciphered, they completely transformed the way in which the region's history was perceived. The first inscription on the north-eastern side of the rock is composed in Pali, written in the Ashoka Brahmi script, and contains all the fourteen edicts of Emperor Ashoka (273–237 BC). Composed in poetic Sanskrit in AD 150, the second inscription on the western side narrates the history of lake Sudarshan (near present-day Junagadh), which was originally constructed on the order of the Mauryan emperor Chandragupta and renovated by Ashoka through his Yavan satrap Tushaspa. The inscription describes how the lake was subsequently destroyed by heavy rain and repaired soon after by a minister of Mahakshatrap Rudradaman. The third inscription in Sanskrit verse written in Gupta Brahmi script takes up the story of lake Sudarshan in AD 455-56, during the reign of Emperor Skandagupta, when it was damaged once again by heavy rain. The emperor's provincial governor Parnadatta promptly repaired it by reconditioning its embankments. Together, the three inscriptions throw light on 800 years of ancient Gujarat.

Equally interesting is the story of how these inscriptions came to be deciphered. It was James Tod, famous for his *Annals of Rajasthan*, who first reported the inscriptions of Junagadh in 1822 though he thought the script was Greek. After about fifteen years they were copied and sent to James Prinsep, who at the time was struggling to decipher the Brahmi script of Ashoka's edicts in Orissa. Prinsep realized that one of the Junagadh inscriptions was also inscribed in the Brahmi script and except for two extra paragraphs it was identical to the Orissa inscription. It was the first indication of the breadth of Ashoka's empire. Prinsep also deduced that the other two inscriptions belonged to a later period. For the next two decades these inscriptions on the Junagadh rock were the subject of intense discussions among Indologists, mainly at the Bombay branch of the Asiatic Society.

During the same period, far removed from the modern educational and research institutions, a young boy of Junagadh was trying to unravel the mystery of the scripts on the rock. For several years, he frequently visited the rock and made copies of every single letter. By the time he was sixteen, he became the talk of the town. His contemporaries believed that the mysterious letters represented a secret mantra which would lead to a hidden treasure and that the boy was the one destined to crack the code and find the treasure.

The boy, Bhagwanlal Indraji Bhatt (1839–89), attended traditional school in his childhood and learnt Sanskrit at home from his father and elder brother. By the time he turned twenty, Bhagwanlal was able to read the second and third inscriptions composed in classical Sanskrit and written in Gupta Brahmi. Colonel Lang, the British political agent in charge of native Kathiawad states during the 1850s, took great interest in the decipherment of the Junagadh rock inscriptions. When he came to know about young Bhagwanlal, he arranged to send him a copy of an article written by James Prinsep in 1838 which included Prinsep's 'copy' of the Junagadh inscriptions. Through friends in Bombay, Bhagwanlal was able to collect other articles published in scholarly journals and in 1856 prepared his version of all the three inscriptions, including corrections to Prinsep's transcription. Later he took to deciphering old coins in Junagadh, and his mastery over epigraphy and numismatics earned him the title of 'Little Antiquarian' from Colonel Lang.

Bhagwanlal was invited to Bombay in 1862 by Dr Bhau Daji, a well-known physician, social reformer and Indologist. He later travelled extensively throughout South Asia, read and copied hundreds of inscriptions, prepared notes on ancient monuments and collected a vast number of coins. His findings and efforts contributed to a more complete reconstruction of the ancient history of Nepal, Orissa, Andhra Pradesh and Maharashtra and the history of Jainism and Buddhism. In recognition of his work, he was made Fellow of Bombay university in 1882; two years later he received an honorary Ph.D. from Leiden university and was made an honorary member of the Royal Asiatic Society.

Yet, Bhagwanlal's name and his immense contribution remain virtually unknown. The main reason for this is that Bhagwanlal never wrote in English and his scholarly writing is available only in Gujarati. In the 1880s when he was invited by the editor of the Bombay Gazetteer to contribute a history of ancient Gujarat, he wrote it in Gujarati; this was later translated into English and published as Part I of Volume I of the Bombay Gazetteer. Bhagwanlal's history was essentially a political history of ancient Gujarat till the thirteenth century, reconstructed through his study of coins and epigraphs. Based on these, he described various dynasties that had ruled over the region and their chronological order and also an outline of the social history of how various communities entered Gujarat over the centuries from different directions by land and sea routes. As the Indus Valley civilization was not discovered till the early twentieth century, there was no question of Bhagwanlal considering its linkages to Gujarat.[3]

The Indus Valley civilization penetrated Gujarat from 2400 BC and remained vibrant till 1800 BC. After its decline, probably in 1500 BC, Central Asian people speaking Indo-European languages, and later known as 'Aryans', came to Gujarat from the north and spread Vedic culture. According to the Puranas three important Aryan tribes—the Sharyats, the Bhrigus and the Yadavas—arrived and left their imprint in mythology. Gujarat became part of the Mauryan Empire during the reign of Chandragupta Maurya in the third century BC and flourished under Ashoka. Buddhism was probably introduced during this period. Though we have no definite clues that explain how the Mauryan dynasty came to an end in the region, the Buddhist rock cut caves (c. third century AD) near Junagadh suggest that Buddhism continued to be vibrant even after the decline of the Mauryas. From the second century BC, Gujarat witnessed the arrival of the Indo-Greeks followed by the Shakas or Scythians and the Kushans in the early centuries of the Christian era. The rule of various dynasties of Kshatraps, who many scholars believe were Shakas, continued till the end of the fourth century AD in Gujarat. During this period two ports on the western coast—Bharuch or ancient Bhrighukachch and Sopara or Shurparak near Bombay—were famous as far away as the Roman Empire.

The Gupta emperor Kumargupta extended his empire till Gujarat in the early fifth century AD and after the reign of his son Skandagupta, the local Maitrak general declared himself the ruler of Gujarat. Around this time, the Hunas or Huns arrived and, either with them or following them, the Gurjars. Except for the southern areas, most of Gujarat was part of the Maitrak kingdom (c. AD 470–788). Their capital Valabhi was a famed centre of learning and according to the seventh-century Chinese traveller I-Tsing it was ranked with the celebrated Buddhist university at Nalanda. When Huien Tsang visited Gujarat in AD 614, it had more than 150 Buddhist monasteries, where 6000 monks resided. At Valabhi, there were two groups of Buddhist monasteries, one for the monks and one for the nuns. We do not know exactly how the Maitrak kingdom faded away but later Jain chronicles suggest that Valabhi was destroyed by the Arabs. In the eighth century AD, fleeing persecution by Arabs, the Parsis left Iran and received shelter from the local king at Sanjan in south Gujarat. It is believed that the Rabaris, now a prominent pastoralist community, also entered Gujarat from Sind and Rajasthan in the same period.

For the next three and a half centuries (AD 942–1299) Gujarat flourished under the Rajput kings of the Chaulukya or Solanki dynasty. Siddharaj Jaisingh and Kumarpal, 'Maharajadhiraj' of Gurjardesh, extended their sway up to Marwar, Mewar and some parts of Malwa and Konkan. Their southern frontier touched Vasai or Bassein and their northern frontier extended up to present-day Ajmer and Jodhpur. Gujarat acquired a political, cultural and geographical unity and identity under the illustrious Chaulukya rulers. Jainism spread widely and acquired prestige in Gujarat during this period. There was a great efflorescence of learning, art and architecture and Cambay emerged as a 'Gateway of Hind' in this era. Iranian, Arab and Armenian merchants and navigators frequented this thriving port, and Marco Polo, who visited Gujarat in the last phase of Chaulukya rule, called it the 'great kingdom of Cambay'.

The army of Sultan Alauddin Khilji defeated the last Chaulukya king, Karnadev (also known as Karan Ghelo), and

Gujarat became a province of the Delhi Sultanate by the end of the thirteenth century. A large number of Turks and Afghans came to Gujarat as soldiers and settled here in the following decades. A few Sidis of African origin arrived overland to join the army of the Sultans and many more were brought by sea as slaves. The North African traveller Ibn Batuta, who visited Gujarat in 1342, records being overwhelmed by the wealth of the Cambay merchants.

Timur Lane invaded India in 1394 and his plunder of Delhi started the process of disintegration within the empire of the Delhi Sultans. In this critical period the nazim (governor) of Gujarat declared himself independent in 1403 and laid the foundation of the Gujarat Sultanate. Though the sultanate was founded by Sultan Ahmed Shah's grandfather and father, this dynasty, which ruled for about 150 years, was always referred to as 'Ahmedshahi' in Persian and Arabic histories, though the people of Gujarat remember him as the founder of Ahmedabad. The later Sultans, Mahmud Begada (1459–1511) and Bahadur Shah (1526–37), once again expanded this kingdom up to south Rajasthan in the north, Junagadh and Kutch in the west, Malwa and Khandesh in the east and Vasai in the south.

It is important to note here that Gujarat is traditionally divided in four geographical, sociocultural subregions and the process of synthesis and homogenization in these subregions has followed different paths at uneven pace, merging with each other from time to time. These four sociocultural divisions are mainland Gujarat, extending from the southern tip of Aravali to the northern tip of the Western Ghats; the peninsula of Saurashtra or Kathiawad; Kutch; and the eastern Adivasi belt running from the Aravalli and Vindhya–Satpura range to the beginning of the Western Ghats. During the Mauryan and Gupta periods, Gujarat as we know it today was never regarded as a single political or cultural zone. Instead four distinct politico-cultural zones were identified: Anart (present-day north-central Gujarat); Lat (present-day south Gujarat); Saurashtra; and Kutch. The present-day Adivasi belt was referred to as the land of Nishad. The regional identity of Lat disappeared towards

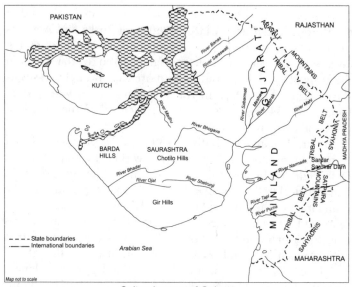

Cultural zones of Gujarat

the middle of the Chaulukya era and though 'Gurjardesh' as an entity was mentioned as early as in the eighth century, the name was applied to a small area consisting of present-day north Gujarat and the territory around Mt. Abu. The name 'Gujarat' gained currency from the fourteenth century onwards.

The fortunes of Cambay declined in the last phase of the Gujarat Sultanate due to problems caused by siltation, and Surat emerged as the major Gujarati port. European traders, beginning with the Portuguese, arrived in Gujarat for the first time during this period. Between 1505 and 1509 the Portuguese viceroy Francisco Almeida established a number of strategic posts on the western coast and his successors were more than eager to fortify them, particularly on the island of Diu off the coast of southern Saurashtra. When the Mughal emperor Humayun attacked Gujarat in 1533, Sultan Bahadur Shah entered into a pact with the Portuguese. In return for their support against Humayun, he first handed over Vasai to the

Portuguese and in 1535 Diu. Taking advantage of this climate of political turmoil, ambitious Rajput warriors with political aspirations entered Gujarat from Sind through Kutch. One of them, Jam Rawal of the Jadeja clan, captured the territory on the southern side of the Gulf of Kutch and established his kingdom of Jamnagar. Similarly, Sodha Rajputs arrived from Tharparkar and established small kingdoms in different parts of Saurashtra.

Akbar annexed Gujarat in 1572 and it remained a *suba* (province) of the Mughal Empire for the next 200 years. For administrative reasons, he reorganized the suba, detaching Khandesh in the south and some areas of Marwar in the north. Surat retained its position as the pre-eminent port and became the commercial hub of the Mughals during the reign of Jahangir and Shahjahan. It was referred to as '*Bandar-e-Mubarak*' and was the embarkation port for the hajj to Mecca. In the same period, European powers too engaged in an intense struggle for trade supremacy in Surat. Challenging the monopoly of the Portuguese, the Dutch established their factory (trading station) in 1606, and the British in 1613. The French were the last to enter the race, establishing their factory in 1668.

The developments of the fifteenth and sixteenth centuries played a crucial role in the shaping of modern Gujarat. Besides Ahmedabad and Surat, the first and second cities of today, other important cities in western Gujarat such as Jamnagar, Rajkot and Bhuj were established in this period. The bhakti movement and, following it, the Vaishnavism of Vallabhacharya developed, penetrated and empowered the common people. Saint poets, Hindu and Muslim, began to express themselves in the Gujarati language and laid the foundation of modern Gujarati literature.

The Mughal Empire disintegrated after the death of Aurangzeb in 1707 and was succeeded by Maratha rule. From the mid eighteenth century, the Peshwa and the Gaekwad of Vadodara shared the revenue of Gujarat between them. Later the Gaekwad became an independent ruler with his capital at Vadodara and territories spread over central Gujarat and Saurashtra. Most of the princely kingdoms accepted the supremacy of Maratha rulers but were constantly engaged in internal and external squabbles. It was in this scenario, of numerous princely kingdoms under Hindu and Muslim rulers and chieftains who were generally pompous and preoccupied with never-ending feuds, that the British established themselves in Gujarat in the latter decades of the eighteenth century. Following the defeat and decline of the Peshwas and the Treaty of Bassein (Vasai) in 1802, the British established their paramountcy in Gujarat in 1820.

It is clear that from the Mauryan era to the beginning of the British era, in political terms, Gujarat experienced cycles of centrifugal and centripetal forces. During the Mauryan, Gupta, Delhi Sultanate, Mughal and British eras there was a strong central power in the subcontinent and Gujarat remained a province within a larger empire, experiencing the connectedness to a larger political entity in its many dimensions. On the other hand, the Kshatrap, Maitrak, Chaulukya and Gujarat Sultanate periods represent the assertion of regional power at a time when the central power was weak, leading to the flowering of local languages and cultures and the strengthening of regional pride. At the same time, the expansionist approach of both the Chaulukya rulers and the Gujarat Sultans was resisted by the kings of Saurashtra, Kutch and Lat, as can be seen from local legends and proverbs. Thus, over the last thousand years, along with the development of peoples' self-identity as Gujarati, local and subregional identities as Saurashtrian or Kathiawadi and Kutchi were also asserted. These overlapping identities continue to play a significant part in public life. Yet, a common language and shared patterns of everyday life—in agriculture and architecture, food and textiles, trade and commerce, arts and crafts—bind the people together.

SYNTHESIS AND CONTINUITY

Echoes of the Indus Valley civilization in the rhythm of everyday life in rural Gujarat were apparent till the mid twentieth century. The practice of two-crop agriculture—rabi and kharif—bullock carts, brick-lined wells and the way of lifting water from wells with *dhenkvo* (lever lift based on stone counterweights) reflect continuity over the last 4000 years. The potter's wheel, the designs on the pots and the craft of bead-making show similar continuities. In daily food, the preference for millets—bajra and jowar—has continued since the Indus era: in both the arid areas of Kutch and Saurashtra and the fertile area of central Gujarat, the preference for bajra is still widespread. In southern Gujarat, not only the poor and marginal farmer but the rich farmer too prefers jowar over wheat. Sesame and linseed were used in the Indus era and sesame oil remained the principal medium of cooking till the mid twentieth century.

After the Indus era, Gujarat must have continued to receive new crops, grains, fruits and vegetables but no definite record is available for the Mauryan and Gupta periods. From AD 1000 onwards numerous literary works directly or indirectly throw light on the history of agriculture and food. *Dwayashray* by the Jain savant Hemachandracharya (1084–1173) has scattered references to *modak (laddu), shashkuli (sankli), khaja, urnayu (sutarfeni)* and *vadi*, sweets and savouries which are popular in Gujarat even today. The V*arnaksamuchchaya* of the sixteenth century is a mine of information and lists about 900 food preparations which include thirty-six types of laddus. It also mentions the names of famous Gujarati savouries like dhokla and khandavi. Idli is mentioned as *idari*, and *idada*, its adaptation in south Gujarat, is also referred to in this interesting Gujarati text written in the Devnagari script.

After the establishment of the Delhi Sultan's rule, the increasing interaction with Turks, Afghans, Iranians and Arabs made a deep impression on everyday life. New food preparations like jalebi, biranj and halwa became popular. We find references to jalebi in the *Varnaksamuchchaya* too. Persian words for dry fruits such as *badam, pista* and *jardalu* are so commonly used by Gujaratis that their Persian origin comes as a surprise to them. Similarly, among common fruits, *khadbuj* and *tadbuj* (watermelon), *narangi* and *ananas* are local adaptations of Persian words.

Following the arrival of the Portuguese in coastal Gujarat,

New World crops like potato, tomato, tobacco and maize made their entry in the sixteenth century. The Portuguese words for potato—*batata* and *bataka*—have been assimilated into Gujarati. Curiously, maize or *makkai* has replaced traditional millets only in the Bhil Adivasi area north of the river Narmada. Though the cultivation of groundnut (another contribution from the New World) as a cash crop began only in the early twentieth century, today Gujarat produces two-thirds of the total groundnut production in India and the crop plays a vital role in the political economy of Saurashtra. In fact, in the past fifty or sixty years, groundnut oil has become the most popular cooking medium throughout Gujarat, replacing the sesame of Indus times.

Imprints of synthesis and continuity are clearly visible in various architectural forms, particularly in public architecture. The oldest reference to a man-made lake is in the Junagadh inscription describing lake Sudarshan. The construction of lakes by the state continued over the centuries, and lakes constructed over the last thousand years are extant in many towns. Two lakes of the Chaulukya era—Mansar of Viramgam and Malav of Dholka towns—are associated with Minal Devi, mother of Siddharaj, and are in use today. The most famous lake of this era, Sahasraling, was constructed by Siddharaj but except for a few remnants nothing has survived. The Kankariya lake at Ahmedabad was constructed during the rule of the Gujarat Sultans and the Khan lake of Patan was built by Mirza Aziz Koka, governor of Gujarat during the reign of Akbar. All these lakes incorporated elaborate systems for water harvesting, channels for water transportation, filtering arrangements and outlets. In keeping with this great tradition, the Sursagar lake of Vadodara and Ranjitsagar lake of Jamnagar were built during the nineteenth and twentieth centuries.

A new wave of constructing decorative city and village gates has gathered momentum in Gujarat in the last few decades. Even small villages in the interior now have 'Gandhi Gate' and 'Sardar Gate' at their entrances. Gujaratis living abroad have also contributed by funding the construction of modern gates in their native villages in the memory of close relatives. This wave is essentially a modern incarnation of an age-old tradition of constructing decorative city gates, started by kings and sultans. Unlike recent times, city gates were then an intrinsic part of fortification and not independent entities that merely marked the entrance to the city. The oldest surviving city gates of Gujarat belong to the Chaulukya era and the most famous among them are the gates of Dabhoi and Jhinjhuvada. The exquisite carving on both gates represents the finer elements of Chaulukya architecture and sculpture. City gates of the Gujarat Sultanate period, such as the 'Three Gates' and other gates of Ahmedabad, are elegant but with hardly any carving. The 'Three Gates' of Cambay, constructed in the memory of Akbar's visit to the city, and 'Lal Gate' built by the Nawab of Surat in the early eighteenth century are weak imitations of the older city gates of Gujarat. After the advent of the British, the princely states continued the tradition of building city gates, where the European influence is distinctly visible. The city gate of Morbi in Saurashtra has a clock tower above it and the one in Dharampur in south Gujarat is decorated with sculptures of women in the Grecian style.

The element that binds the people of Gujarat, across differences of religion and region, caste, communities or creed, is the Gujarati language. Evolved during the Chaulukya era on the foundation of Sanskrit, Prakrit and Apabhransh, Gujarati acquired its distinct character in the Sultanate era. During the Mughal era, it was further cultivated by saint poets on the one hand and merchants on the other. As the court language of both the Gujarat Sultanate and the Mughals was Persian and because merchant communities had extensive linkages with Arabic-speaking West Asia, the influence of Persian and Arabic is immense and pervasive. It would not be an exaggeration to say that it is impossible to write good Gujarati without using Persian or Arabic words. In addition to administrative and legal words like *zilla* (district), *taluk* (block), *jamin* (land), *jaydad* (property), *faujdari* (criminal), *diwani* (civil), *adalat* (court) and *insaaf* (justice), Persian and Arabic words related to human existence like *dil* (heart), *dimaag* (mind), *jindagi* (life), *lohi* (blood), *jaban* (speech), *hayati* (existence) and *khud* (self) have been internalized by Gujarati.

Several compound nouns in Gujarati are made up of two synonyms, one of which is Persian or Arabic and the other Sanskrit–Gujarati, for example, *kagal-patra* (letter), *naukri-dhandho* (service-business) and *bhet-sogaad* (gift). Similarly, there are compound nouns consisting of component words with different meanings where one word is Gujarati and the other Persian such as *meva-mithai* (sweet), *nafo-toto* (profit and loss) and *dana-pani* (food). It is remarkable that hundreds of Persian and Arabic words have been incorporated into Gujarati merely by adding Gujarati prefixes and suffixes to them. For example, the Gujarati word for 'wilful' is *aapkhud* (aap+khud), 'autocrat' is *aapakhatiyar* (aap+akhatiyar), an 'intelligent person' is *akkalvan* (akkal+van) and the 'fortunate one' is *naseebvan* (naseeb+van).

We can add numerous examples to show the penetration of Persian and Arabic in Gujarati but what is surprising is the replacement of Sanskrit–Prakrit words by Persian-Arabic words even in the core aspects of Gujarati society, navigation and trade. The common word for 'port' is *bandar* (as in Por*bandar*) and *khalasi* is 'mariner', both originally Arabic-Persian. Similarly, in the realm of trade and commerce, many basic words such as *bajar* and *dukan* for 'market' and 'shop' respectively are Persian and Arabic in origin. Though 'usurer' and 'broker' are ancient categories among merchants, the Gujarati words for them are *sharaf* and *dalal*, both Arabic in origin. *Keemat* (price), *nafa* (profit), *nukshan* (loss), *namu* (account) and *jama* (credit) are also drawn from Arabic and Persian.

A number of Portuguese words have also entered the Gujarati lexis. In common parlance 'salary' is *pagaar*, 'bread' is *pao*, 'key' is *chavi*, 'stable' is *tabelo*, all Portuguese contributions. The Christian priest is still known by the old Portuguese word, *padri*. It is little wonder then that with British rule, thousands of English words were assimilated into Gujarati. By the mid nineteenth century, resistance to the large-scale influx of English words in Indian languages took the form of a campaign by the educated elite in Hindi- and Marathi-speaking areas. Even in the process of standardization of Indian languages, the first generation of Indian educationists tilted in favour of Sanskrit equivalents. They tried to introduce Sanskrit equivalents not only for English words but also for a large number of Persian-Arabic words in their respective languages. Similar 'purification' was attempted by a few eminent Brahmins in Gujarat, a process that met with strong opposition from the liberal, reformist elite. This generated a bitter war of words between the two contesting camps—conservative and reformist—which were mainly divided on sociocultural issues. In 1900, one reformist leader, Sir Ramanbhai Nilkanth, who was also a renowned literary figure, wrote a powerful satire, *Bhadrambhadra*, where the main character had changed his name from Dolatshankar to Bhadrambhadra to avoid the Arabic word *dolat* (wealth) in his name. On his way to Bombay he asks for a *mulyapatrika* instead of a railway ticket and, by always insisting on using Sanskrit words and Sanatani practices, he picks up quarrels which ultimately land him in jail.

Today, a century after the publication of *Bhadrambhadra*, the spoken Gujarati of urban centres exhibits a greater inclination towards the use of English words. Urban trading centres in the Mughal era displayed a similar tendency for Persian-Arabic words when the entire vocabulary relating to trade and commerce was replaced by words derived from Persian and Arabic. In addition to mercantile castes and communities, other Hindu castes associated with government service such as Nagars and Kayasthas systematically studied Persian to improve their chances of getting into the Mughal bureaucracy. By the seventeenth century, a number of Nagars, Kayasthas and Brahmakshatriyas succeeded in securing key posts of diwan, vakil, bakshi and munshi in the Mughal administration. Even today, many families from these upper castes use these bureaucratic designations as their family surnames. It is not a coincidence that the same upper castes, with administrative and mercantile traditions, were the first to attain proficiency in the English language during the nineteenth century and secure influential positions in the new order.

While describing this synthesis between diverse communities, we have to acknowledge that diversity also results in conflict. Against the backdrop of absorption and intermingling is an equally long history of interreligious, interregional and intercaste conflict, of which we have recorded evidence since Chaulukya times. In response to this friction, institutions, attitudes and traditions emerged from within Gujarati society to preserve the social order and create conditions for balance and continuity. The most powerful of these is the mercantile ethos, which we shall discuss next.

2

Mercantile Ethos

It is not mere coincidence that the three Gujaratis who played a critical role in shaping the Indian subcontinent—Dadabhai Naoroji, M.K. Gandhi and M.A. Jinnah—belonged to mercantile communities. Naoroji was a Parsi and himself a businessman; Gandhi was a Modh Vaniya whose father and grandfather had held important administrative positions in the princely states of Saurashtra; and Jinnah belonged to the trading community of Khojas. For almost a thousand years merchant communities—Hindus, Jains, Muslims and, later, Parsis—not only dominated the economic sphere but also wielded influence in Gujarati society and power in political affairs. They set the norms for 'high culture' and became representatives of Gujarat for the outside world.

Geography played a crucial role in giving merchants their prominent position. Gujarat's strategic location within Asia and its ports along the northern centre of the Indian Ocean placed it at the intersection of a number of trading systems and proved propitious to Gujarati merchants. They profited from the overland interregional trade of Asia across the subcontinent and within the western region. But their greatest wealth came from maritime trade, both along the coast and across the seas in ships propelled eastwards and westwards by the monsoon winds. One quarter of India's coastline is in Gujarat and the string of harbours and ports from Sind to Konkan served a vast hinterland. Silk from China, horses from Arabia, ivory and slaves from Africa, cloth and indigo from Gujarat itself, opium and grain from the north, spices from southern India and the Far East, to name just a few commodities, passed through these ports for centuries. Local communities of skilled shipbuilders, navigators and craftspeople contributed to the prosperity of enterprising merchants and traders. The sweep of this maritime network is summed up by Tomé Pires, a fifteenth-century Portuguese traveller: 'Cambay [i.e. Gujarat] chiefly stretches out two arms, with her right arm she reaches out towards Aden and with the other towards Malacca . . .'[1]

Gujarati merchants travelled to West Asia, Africa, South India and the eastern edges of the Indian Ocean, creating a diaspora consisting of kith and kin networks in the ports of the Indian Ocean littoral. Gujarati cuisine responded to the demands of long sea voyages and overland trips with a wide variety of dry snacks, chutneys, pickles and sweets which could keep fresh for long periods.

Maritime trade activity goes back almost four millennia to the days of the Indus Valley civilization. Whether or not Lothal was a dockyard is a subject of archaeological controversy, but the excavation of Indus Valley seals, weights and etched carnelian beads in the Persian Gulf and Mesopotamian lands, representations of boats on terracotta seals found at Lothal and the discovery of artefacts of Persian Gulf provenance at Indus sites in Saurashtra and Kutch point to commercial contacts between these regions. This contact continued and, apart from numismatic evidence, we have indications from the Buddhist Jataka stories (c. 400–100 BC), which mention the ports of Bhrighukachchh (Bharuch) and Supparaka (Sopara). The importance attached to maritime mercantile activity is reflected in the *Supparaka Jataka* where the Bodhisattva is born as an accomplished blind navigator who steers a ship of 700 merchants to safety and in the *Kundaka-Kuchhi-Sindhava Jataka* where he is born into a trader's family.

Next we have *Periplus of the Erythrean Sea* (variously dated between AD 100 and 300), a marine guidebook which is believed to be the record of a Greek sailor who navigated the Red Sea, Persian Gulf, Malabar and Coromandel coasts and who resided in Barygaza (Bharuch) for many years. According to Periplus, Bharuch was the principal distributing centre of western India from where the merchandise brought from abroad was carried to the inland countries. One route went south to Paithan and then on to other towns of central India towards Bihar. The other route went northwards towards Ujjain and Mathura. Goods were also sent along these routes to Bharuch for export. Bharuch thus emerged at the junction of the Silk Route and the Spice Route.

The earliest glimpse of the traders themselves is found in a vivid description of a marketplace in *Kuvalayamala* written in AD 778 by a Jain monk, Udyotansuri:

> A prince enters the hattamagga [market] and sees deshvanik [traders from various regions] speaking different languages. The traders of Marudesh [western Marwad] were crooked, indolent, fat, fun loving, firm and puffy limbed. He sees another group from Gurjardesh—well fed on ghee and butter, religious and diplomatic. Next he sees traders—bathed, bodies smeared with sandal paste and hair parted, handsome traders from Lat. Then the prince sees traders from Malwa—thin, dark skinned, handsome, quick tempered and arrogant.[2]

Traders were called *Vanik* or *Vanijah*, which evolved over the centuries to Vaniya, a caste term which today refers to both Hindus and Jains. Till the fifteenth century Hindu and Jain Vaniyas were referred to as Meshri (from Maheshwari, indicating their Shaivite faith) and Shravak respectively. With the rise of the Vallabhacharya Sampraday, many Meshris adopted Vaishnavism and thereafter Hindu traders were referred to as Vaishnav Vaniya and Jains continued to be called Shravak. The commonly used 'Baniya' is a corruption of Vaniya used first by the Portuguese and then by the Dutch and English as a collective noun for all Gujarati traders irrespective of religion. *Baneane* was the Portuguese corruption and *Banyan*, the English one. Other variants were *Benjan* and *Bunyan*.

The social status of merchants began to rise in Gujarat with the spread of Buddhism followed by Jainism (which were the faiths of many merchants) in the Maitrak and post-Maitrak periods from the fifth and sixth centuries AD onwards, and Kshatriyas were increasingly replaced by the appointment of Vaishyas to high offices of the state. The first clear mention of this practice comes in the eighth century when Vanaraj, the founder of the Chavada dynasty and the city of Patan, made the merchant Jamba his *mahamatya* or chief minister, the merchant Ninnaya his prime counsellor, and Ninnaya's son, Lahara, the general of his armies. This trend continued and strengthened during Chaulukya times and it is noteworthy that the scholar Amarchandrasuri (thirteenth century) suggested that ministers be enrolled from the merchant class. Other Jain colophons describe many ministers and generals who were from the merchant community.[3]

The most famous merchants during the Chaulukya period were the Jain brothers Vastupal and Tejpal, who held important posts at the court of the Vaghela kings Lavanaprasad and Virdhaval. Many Jain biographies have been written about their lives and, even though such accounts are often hagiographic, it is clear that they played a critical role in the political and economic consolidation of the Chaulukya kingdom in the first half of the thirteenth century. They belonged to a family of merchants from Patan and all their ancestors appear to have held ministerial positions. Vastupal was chief minister and later appointed governor of Cambay, where he put an end to piracy, created a congenial atmosphere for business, recovered arrears of revenue from recalcitrant officials and filled the state treasury. Tejpal succeeded as chief minister after his brother's death and continued to manage the financial affairs of the state with great dexterity. He is credited with the victory over Ghughula, chief of Godhra who used to plunder merchants, pilgrims and caravans going to and from Gujarat. Tejpal thus extended Gujarat's eastern borders and made trade routes safe and secure.[4]

Thus, by the end of the thirteenth century, there was a considerable increase in the power and status of merchants in Gujarat. The extent to which merchant–ministers were transformed, acquiring skills well beyond their traditional role, is revealed by Vastupal's reaction on being provoked by Samkha, the ruler of Lat:

> It is a delusion to think that kshatriyas alone can fight and not a vanik . . . I am a vanik well known in the shop of battlefield. I buy commodities, the heads of enemies, weighing them in the scale of swords. I pay the price in the form of Heaven.[5]

This combination of economic and political power set in motion a hegemonic order where merchants called the shots.

EXPANSION OF SOCIAL BASE

From the early Chaulukya period, two simultaneous processes contributed to the creation of the mercantile ethos of Gujarat. The first was a social process which resulted in the expansion of the merchant community itself. The second was the conversion of several communities to Muslim sects under the influence of pirs and preachers and their subsequent shift to trade and commerce.

Traditionally, trading was the occupation of the Vaishya section of society. But around the seventh and eighth centuries northern Gujarat and southern Rajasthan witnessed two transformative processes which resulted in the expansion of the social base of the merchant community. Analysing names of persons appearing in epigraphic material of the Chaulukya period, the archaeologist–historian H.D. Sankalia indicates that in the first phase some Shaka, Gurjjara tribes from Central Asia entered the Hindu *Chaturvarna* fold as Kshatriyas. Post-Chaulukya bardic traditions also suggest that four Rajput clans—Parmar, Parihar, Chaulukya and Chauhan—were *agnikul* or fire-born clans. According to these mythological accounts Rishi Vasishtha performed a yajna at Mt Abu to eliminate demons and from this yajna emerged four warriors who became the progenitors of these Rajput clans. Scholars believe that this myth is an allegory for the absorption of 'foreign' tribes into the Hindu fold. Sankalia suggests that in the second phase some of these Kshatriyas or Rajput families became Vanikas and shifted to trade and commerce. While many Vanik families practised Shaivism, some of them embraced Jainism. For instance, the bulk of the Osval Jain merchants were Rajputs before they adopted Jainism, which according to Jain sources took place around the mid eighth century.[6] Since their new faith precluded them from violence and taking life, they gave up warfare and agriculture, opting instead for trade and commerce, thus increasing the numbers of the traditional Vaishya community.

In the post-Chaulukya period, some sections of the Brahmin community, notably Nagar Brahmins, were also prominent businessmen, particularly as financiers and moneychangers, as indicated by the incidence of the surname 'Nanavati' (moneychanger) in this community. There are numerous references to Brahmin businessmen in the seventeenth-century khatpatras, which are quasi-legal documents pertaining to transactions in real estate. One of these mentions that in 1642 one Trikamlal Bhatt, a Brahmin, sold his shop at Mangrol in Surat district to a utensil manufacturer. Another Brahmin businessman is mentioned in a khatpatra of 1656, which records that Kalyan Joshi of the Shrimali Brahmin caste sold his shop in the Manek Chowk area of Ahmedabad to a Jain businessman.[7] The Mirat-i-Ahmadi offers a glimpse of the wealth and prestige of Brahmin businessmen in the eighteenth century:

> [Vadnagar] was a wealthy town where rich people and wealthy moneylenders resided and where eminent traders of the Nagar Brahmin community who transacted business worth lakhs of rupees in many cities and regions lived.[8]

The most eminent Nagar Brahmin business house in the eighteenth century was the pedhi of Arjunji Nathji Travady of Surat. He had a wide subcontinental network of trading and banking activities with branches in Dhaka, Madras and Banaras and financed the trade of the East India Company to the tune of lakhs of rupees. Along with business activity, due to their proficiency in Persian and, later, English, Nagars held high administrative positions in the court of the Mughal governor, princely states and British government.

Beginning in the twelfth century around the reign of Siddharaj (1094–1143), several communities in Gujarat peacefully converted to Muslim sects.[9] The three important Muslim sects of today are the Bohras, the Khojas and the Memons. The Bohra faith was embraced mainly by the Vaniya community, though, under the influence of pirs, many Brahmins too converted and after their conversion took to business. Most of today's Khojas were originally Lohanas of Kutch and Saurashtra who considered themselves Rajput. The Memons, prominent traders in both India and Pakistan, are mainly from the Lohana community of Saurashtra, Kutch and Sind. This suggests that communities who were not traditionally associated with trade took to it after their conversion to Islamic sects.

After conversion to Islam, these communities were released from the restrictions on upper-caste Hindus against crossing the sea. They took to maritime trade in a big way and became the first non-Arab/Persian traders in the Indian Ocean countries. It is believed that these traders took Indian Islam to the Far East. After the opening up of East Africa in the nineteenth century, they became pioneers of trading activity there, dominating not only the financial world but also the political affairs of the region. Interestingly, it was these Gujarati Muslim traders along with Kutchi Bhatias who provided equipment, rations and financial services to European explorers such as Stanley, Livingstone, Burton and Cameron and thus facilitated the 'discovery' of Africa.[10]

After the Jains, Bohras, Khojas and Memons, the Parsis joined the expanding fold of trading communities during the Mughal period. Upon their arrival in the eighth century they took up farming and weaving. In the sixteenth century, they entered trading, and played a significant role in the rise of Surat and Bombay. The last to enter business, and what we could call the 'Vaniya fold', were some sections of the Patidar community who were traditionally farmers and cattle rearers. In the nineteenth century, they began trading in agricultural products such as tobacco, edible oils, jeera and isabgol, and later moved to other commodities. Large numbers of them went as indentured labour to east and south Africa and, after their period of indenture was over, took up petty trade and hawking and rose to control vast commercial enterprises there. Thus, over the last thousand years, members of the Hindu Chaturvarna, the newly introduced Islamic sects and Parsis joined to form the expanding business community of Gujarat.

MERCHANTS AND THEIR INSTITUTIONS

As trade activities expanded and intensified, commercial communities got stratified and specialized. *Vepari* was a general term for traders; other specializations were *sharaf* (banker or financier), *nanavati* (moneychanger), *dalal* (middleman or broker to traders and bankers as well as between traders and artisans), *marfatia* (agent) and *adatia* (commission agent). Along with these specializations evolved supporting systems such as *hundi* (letters of credit) and *angadia* (courier service which transported cash, documents or precious goods such as diamonds). As the number of business groups grew and as trade expanded, traders and artisans organized themselves into autonomous organizations to regulate trade and traders.

Traders' organizations have existed for over a thousand years. Jain texts of the Chaulukya period refer to *shrenis*, which were groups of artisans and craftsmen. Another institution was *panchkula*, a board of five members, nominated by the state and which included government officers and influential merchants of society. The *Prabandhachintamani* indicates that the panchkula performed various tasks such as the collection of pilgrimage tax, supervision of construction work and enforcement of non-slaughter measures. The Anavad inscription from Patan reveals another institution, the *pancha-mukha-nagara* or city council, which was composed of the local panchkula, the priest and *Mahajans* which included *sadhu* (merchant), *sreshti* (moneylender), *thakura* (variously thought to refer to feudal chief, landowner, merchant), *soni* (goldsmith), *kansara* (utensil manufacturer), *vanijyaraka* (travelling merchant) and *nau-vittaka* (shipowner). According to the inscription, this group met to discuss the issue of additional taxes on locals by buyers and sellers.[11]

In pre-Chaulukya and Chaulukya times, *Mahajan* was used both in the sense of 'great man' and also as a body representing a group of people engaged in the same commercial occupation, a governing council with an elected or hereditary leader. The institution of the Mahajan as we know it now first appeared in the Mughal period. It was a regulatory body which functioned for the higher economic strata of merchants, bankers, agents and so on, and usually different commodities had separate Mahajans, for example, the cloth merchants' Mahajan or the grain merchants' Mahajan. The head of the Mahajan was the *sheth* and, as the commercial class of Gujarat was diverse, Mahajans could have a varied membership of Hindus, Jains, Sunni and Shia Muslims of local and foreign origin, and Parsis. These Mahajans were usually concerned solely with commercial matters, regulating prices, adjudicating disputes within the occupational group and representing its members in disputes with other Mahajans or artisan groups. Such Mahajans existed only in the large cities of Gujarat while in smaller towns and villages people in the same occupation tended to belong to the same caste and the caste panchayat regulated commercial matters.[12] The regulatory body for artisans was called *Panch*, whose head was the *patel*. The membership of a Panch was usually coterminous with the jati or occupational caste subdivision as people practising a craft or skill were invariably of the same caste. Thus in such situations, the jati panchayat or caste council regulated commercial affairs. We can get a clear idea of the relative authority of the caste panchayat of the Panch and the Mahajan from this instance:

> Some years ago, the carpenters' rate of wages was six annas nine pies in the city of Baroda. The carpenters' caste panchayat raised it to 14 annas. The Mahajan interfered

and directed the carpenters to keep the old wages. But they would not agree and the Mahajan therefore ordered that no one should employ their services. This lasted for a month when the carpenters had to give in, and the Mahajans fixed their wages at 8½ annas, and the working hours from 8 a.m. to noon and from 2 to 6 p.m. It also prohibited them from working overtime in morning though they were allowed to do so at night.[13]

Conflict resolution was thus a combination of coercion and compromise, with the Mahajan invariably having the upper hand.

In the large cities, notably Ahmedabad, Surat and Baroda, was another sort of Mahajan: a city council headed by the Nagarsheth who was usually a Vaniya, Jain or Hindu. This was a citywide body on which, theoretically, sat representatives of all the occupational Mahajans and occasionally a few Patels of the artisan communities as well. In practice only the Vaniya and other upper castes formed the Mahajan and the lower castes such as Luhars (blacksmiths), Suthars (carpenters), Golas (threshers) and Ghanchis (oilpressers) were ignored. This citywide Mahajan fixed rates of work, working hours and wages, decided holidays and so on. Town feasts were organized by the Nagarsheth; he gave the call for strikes and ordered the closing of shops on the death of a member of the ruling house or eminent person. Through the Mahajan, merchants of these big cities negotiated with their government in matters of trade. For instance, in July 1616 the officer of the Surat customs house was dismissed after, according to a contemporary English source, 'some violence done by him to a chief bannyane, the whole multitude assembled shut up their shops and (as their custom), after a general complaint to the Governor, left the city . . .'[14] The governor dismissed the officer of the customs house and the merchants returned. Later in the 1660s, under Aurangzeb, there were several cases of forced conversion to Islam in Surat and a particular qazi was tyrannizing the Vaniyas. In 1669, they struck back. All the heads of Surat's Vaniya families, numbering some 8000, left Surat en masse for Bharuch, and from there petitioned the emperor:

> In the interim the people of Surat suffered great want, for the Bannians having bound themselves under severe penalties not to open any of their shops without order from their Mahager or generall Councill, there was not any provisions to bee got; the tanksell [mint] and customeshouse shut; no money to be procured, soe much for house expences, much less for trade, which was wholy at a stand; and it will continue till their returne.[15]

They returned to Surat only after getting an assurance from the emperor and normalcy was restored. The eight-month-long *hadtal* and the accompanying *hijrat* or exodus reflect the collective strength of the Mahajan and their capacity to mobilize and organize. The word *hadtal/hartal*, which is now used to mean 'strike', is derived from the act of putting a *tala* (lock) on the *hatt* (shop or market).

While the citywide Mahajan was primarily intended as the highest authority in matters of trade only, as far as Hindu and Jain traders were concerned it became an authority in matters of caste also. A person dissatisfied with the order of his caste could appeal to the Mahajan. The appellant would neither eat nor drink nor move from the Mahajan Sheth's house until his complaint was heard and he was given relief. Appeals over the decision of the Mahajan were made to the ruler of the land and, if he found it unjust, he could set it aside. The diverse membership of Mahajans also meant that on occasion tensions along social lines had to be resolved. In 1927, in the cloth Mahajan in Ahmedabad, Vaishnav Vaniyas refused to contribute their share to the Mahajan's common fund to maintain a Jain *panjrapole* (home for disabled and aged animals). They insisted that a part of the common fund be transferred to their own temples. Often the Nagarsheth was also the religious head of his community, as in the case of Virji Vora, who was the head of the Jains of Surat in the seventeenth century, and Shantidas

Jhaveri, who was the head of the Jain community of Ahmedabad.[16]

The Mahajans and Panchs became organizations through which merchants and artisans carried out collective bargaining to protect their interests. Since the artisans supplied basic necessities, they wielded some amount of power. In 1895, when an Ahmedabad banker developed differences with a tilemaker his roof remained uncovered for months. The tilemakers' Panch stood by him and the banker had to settle his differences amicably on terms acceptable to the other party. Though the Panchs were much weaker than the Mahajans, they showed their strength in dealing with the authorities too. In 1846, when the Ahmedabad municipality decided to levy one 'pie' tax on each donkey-load of bricks entering the city walls, the brickmakers' Panch refused to deliver goods except at the kilns, thus shifting the cess as well as the cost of transportation on to the customers.[17]

MERCHANTS AND RULERS

Parallel to the sociological process that contributed to the creation of a Vaniya fold was a cultural process which began to crystallize the Vaniya world view and its relationship to the state. The first significant development was the rise of Jainism as a result of which ahimsa became central to everyday life. Siddharaj's successor, Kumarpal (AD 1143–73), was practically converted to Jainism and aspired to make Gujarat a model Jain state. His *amarighoshana* (proclamation of non-violence) enjoined citizens to abstain from taking animal life, prohibited animal sacrifice by Brahmins, hunting, alcohol, animal combat and betting.[18] Whether such legislation had much practical impact on the bulk of the population is debatable but Kumarpal's decree introduced a new value system revolving around the idea of non-violence which became a code of ethics for all the 'upper' castes and was later adopted by the emerging modern Hindu sects.

The Chaulukya period also saw the development of a code of ethics for business practice. Jain preachers and teachers exhorted traders to follow truthful and peaceful means of earning wealth. In the eleventh century Jinesvarasuri, in his *Satsthanakaprakarana*, described the code of conduct a merchant was expected to follow and ways to deal with political power and resolve conflicts peacefully. A merchant was advised to neither cheat on weight nor charge more. He was to deliver the goods of the same quality as seen and approved by the customer, and never indulge in adulteration. Since a king could be of great service or disservice to merchants, a merchant was to call on the king frequently and flatter him by reciting his good qualities; a merchant was to refrain from refuting the king or keeping the company of his opponents. Jinesvarasuri advised moneylenders to never advance a loan for the sake of greed and the creditor was not to use pledged items such as carriages and bullocks for his personal benefit without making a payment. If a wicked debtor refused to return the loan or turned violent, the creditor was advised to forgo his money rather than fight with the debtor. In *Trisastisalakapurusacarita*, Hemchandracharya (the guru of Siddharaj and Kumarpal) advised merchants to remain calm and peaceful when provoked, pointing out that a merchant should not display his heroism even though he may be heroic. Since peace is essential for the promotion of commercial activity, merchants at large were advised to avoid all strife, strain and provocation in the interest of their profession.[19]

The Vaniya fold internalized this combination of ethics and realpolitik built around the ideals of fair business practice and maintaining working relationships with the power of the day. Ethical business practices based on fair trade and honest dealings gave Gujarati traders a reputation of being trustworthy and they received great acclaim from foreign travellers. For instance, Marco Polo bestowed generous praise on the merchants of Lat, calling them 'the best merchants in the world, and the most truthful' adding that 'if a foreign merchant who does not know the ways of the country applies to them and entrusts his goods to them, they will take charge of these, and sell them in the most loyal manner, seeking zealously the profit of the foreigner and asking no commission except what he pleases to bestow'.[20] This of course does not mean that all merchants were truthful but, in a world with no written contracts, it would have been impossible to conduct large-scale business across the seas without such a value system. And while merchants generally stayed on the right side of the state, we have seen that they did, on extreme provocation, show their displeasure with those in power.

The real test of the trading communities' relationship with power came after the advent of 'Muslim' rule in Gujarat. In 1313, when Alauddin Khilji's Turkic troops passed through Saurashtra, they desecrated the Jain temples of Shatrunjaya. The account of the anguish caused by the sacrilege and the restoration of the sacred temples by Samar Shah, a rich merchant of Patan, is found in two Jain accounts: *Samra-Rasu*, a contemporary Apabhransh account by the Jain monk Amradevsuri, and *Nabhinandan-jinoddhar Prabandh*, written about two decades after the event by Kakkasuri in Sanskrit. The two accounts describe how Samar Shah took it upon himself to rebuild the temples. To secure royal permission for this he waited upon the general Alp Khan with lavish gifts and not only procured permission for repairs and rebuilding but also a contribution from him. The Turkic rulers and the Jain business community were thus able to come to a working relationship even though the Turks simultaneously engaged in warfare with the Vaghela kings. The merchants for their part quickly realized the shifts in power equations and set about making space for themselves and their interests in the new dispensation.[21]

This incident was not an exception and merchants repeatedly displayed the skill of winning over invading armies and imperial powers. In the mid seventeenth century, Shantidas Jhaveri, a wealthy banker and jeweller of Ahmedabad, was able to use his financial influence with Shahjahan to get permission to rebuild the Chintamani temple, which was razed by Aurangzeb when he was governor of Gujarat. In the eighteenth century, when the Maratha hordes rampaged through the cities and towns of Gujarat, their merchants paid them money to save their cities from being ransacked. According to one account, merchants of Ahmedabad city paid 60 lakh rupees, Ahmedabad district 39 lakh, Baroda 2.5–9 lakh, Surat 5 lakh, Bharuch, Jambusar and Amod together 13 lakh, and Vadnagar, with the richest sharafs, 100 lakh.[22] In 1725, to save the city of Ahmedabad from the loot and plunder of the Marathas, the Nagarsheth Khushalchand (who was the grandson of Shantidas) 'with his own money and at the risk of his life' bought off the invaders. Grateful citizens, through their Mahajans, pledged to pay Khushalchand, in perpetuity, four annas for every hundred rupees worth of goods on all commodities entering or leaving the city. Hindus and Muslims as well as the Dutch, English and French merchants residing in Ahmedabad during that period paid the grant to Khushalchand. Their sons and heirs continued the payment to the heirs of Khushalchand for almost a hundred years till the government of the East India Company commuted this payment in 1820, replacing it by a small annual political pension.[23]

Since the Gujarat coast had long been hospitable to foreign traders, the Europeans when they first appeared were treated as just another group of traders. Gujarati traders— Hindus, Jains, Muslims, Parsis— became brokers, bankers and agents to the Portuguese, Dutch and English traders. With the decline of Mughal power following Aurangzeb's death, the merchants entered into shifting alliances with all the contesting powers:

Merchant ship with British flag, 1831

Mughal governors, local nawabs, Maratha sardars as well as Portuguese, Dutch and English governors and officials. It was not as if they could save their future on all occasions but, with great resilience, they tried to protect their economic interests and even tried to expand them by taking advantage of the new opportunities presented by the changing circumstances.

VANIYAS AND SOCIETY

How was this Vaniya culture viewed by the rest of society? Accounts of the maritime history of the west coast of India reveal that, apart from the merchant class, many other groups traded at their own levels. In lieu of a salary crewmembers on ships took small quantities of goods which they traded in the ports of call along the way. Similarly, those who left for hajj from Surat carried goods to trade along the way and at Mecca, with the profits made helping to subsidize their pilgrimage. Kings and queens and members of the court, including the Mughal emperor and his family, traded and financed ships even though they were not formally considered part of the Vaniya fold. But the view of the bulk of the society is best revealed by Gujarati proverbs related to the 'Vaniya'. The *Bhagvadgomandal*, a standard Gujarati lexicon, lists the following:

Vaniyani moochchh nichi: the Vaniya is ready for compromise
Vaniya Vaniya fervi tol: the Vaniya always changes allegiance according to circumstance
Vaniya mugnu naam pade nahi: the Vaniya will not commit himself to anything[24]

The standard Gujarati–English dictionary lists:

Jaate Vaniyabhai, etle todjod karvaman kushal: Being born a merchant, he was possessed of tact and was good in settling quarrels[25]

In the rural areas, the common people interacted with the Vaniya in his role as shopkeeper and moneylender. Farmers borrowed money at the onset of the agricultural season and artisans and craftspeople took advances so that they could buy their raw materials and support themselves while they worked. In some crafts, the sharaf would supply raw materials and give an advance and collect the finished goods and, as we have seen, craftspeople were relatively well protected by their Panch. The small farmers and the poor, who borrowed money and took food and other daily necessities on credit, experienced the worst exploitation of the village Vaniya usurer and shopkeeper. The system was one where the Vaniya was supported by the village power structure and is revealed in the following extract from a prize-winning essay written in 1852 by a newly literate student belonging to a farming community:

> The three powerful people in villages—the village revenue officer, the village headman and the village Vaniya—all of them loot the farmer in many ways . . . When there is a wedding in the family, the farmer goes to the Vaniya and borrows seventy-five or hundred rupees and signs for hundred and twenty-five rupees. This is because the Vaniya lends money at high rates of interest and there is no one else to borrow from. So he [the farmer] has no choice but to pay about 3 or 4 rupees per hundred every month. He has no choice but to accept these terms. He mortgages his cows, buffalos, bullock carts, goats, fields and the grain in the fields and virtually signs away his life. With such a loan he happily celebrates the wedding. Then when it is time to pay the annual tax to the government, he again takes a loan. Then come household expenses—his wife takes jaggery, turmeric, coconuts, chillies etc. on credit from the Vaniya's shop. The Vaniya gives goods worth one paisa but writes a credit of two paisa in his books . . . To repay the loan, the farmer gives grain from his fields to the Vaniya who does not record it in his books. After some days the Vaniya goes to the farmer

to collect his money and the farmer says that to clear the principal loan he had been sending grain and all that remains is the interest which he would pay. To this the Vaniya replies that no grain has reached him and demands to see the proof that the farmer had indeed sent grain. And of course the farmer has no proof because he does not know how to read or write or keep accounts. So he is not in any position to show accounts; all he can give is a verbal account. The situation soon comes to blows and the Vaniya complains to the headman who issues summons to the farmer and begins an inquiry into the matter. The farmer describes how he has been sending grain to the Vaniya every year, towards repayment of the loan. Then the Vaniya presents his books and shows that no grain has been received. Based on this, the headman rules in favour of the Vaniya and issues orders to confiscate the farmer's house, fields, household goods, plough, bullocks and all his goods. The Vaniya auctions these and recovers his money. And in this way, thousands of farmers and their families are reduced to beggars and forced to migrate. [26]

The Vaniya's single-minded focus on generating profits had another outcome: a gradual but steady decline of the intellectual tradition nurtured by Jain and Brahmin poets and scholars in the Chaulukya era. Gujarat has not seen another towering personality since the twelfth-century scholar Hemchandracharya, who was known in his time as *kalikalsarvagya*—the omniscient one of the Kaliyug—in recognition of his immense contribution in the fields of grammar, poetics and philosophy. Although a number of Jain monks continued the tradition of knowledge and preserved thousands of manuscripts with religious zeal in their *bhandars*, the mercantile climate scarcely encouraged free thinking or fundamental research; on the contrary, studies in the areas of philosophy, poetics, grammar, logic or the arts were discouraged. By the mid eleventh century, Jinesvarasuri described a merchant who persuaded his son to give up 'unproductive' and 'uneconomical' activities of dance and drama, and got him trained instead in metallurgy and alchemy.[27] As a result of the ascendancy of Jainism, the Brahminic tradition of knowledge lost its pre-eminence and during the Gujarat Sultanate–Mughal times, Brahmins attached greater importance to the study of Persian than to the study of Sanskrit. It is not surprising that the Gujarati word *vediyo*, which literally means 'a person who has studied the Vedas', has become synonymous with 'bookworm' or 'a learned fool'. In addition to the Brahminic tradition, the Sufi tradition, which developed in Gujarat from the twelfth century onwards, also lost respectability in society. The Gujarati adjective *sufiyani* has come to refer to 'superficial' or 'high-sounding but impractical' instead of the original associations with the mystical or spiritual.

This tendency to neglect knowledge traditions is summed up in an address delivered by Muni Jinvijayji,[28] when he was head of the historical research section of the Gujarati Sahitya Parishad in 1936. Commenting on the lack of historical and scientific research in Gujarat he said:

Since Gujarat is a land dominated by trade, the vaishyavritti [mercantile ethos] supersedes all other influences. The main aim of the people here is to figure out ways to make the most amount of money. That knowledge which enables them to achieve this aim is considered useful knowledge. All other knowledge, according to them, is useless. This pervades society—from the most ordinary, rustic person in Gujarat to the highest, intelligent and cultured section. And because of this, intelligent persons work very hard to be successful in disciplines such as law, medicine and engineering and they also achieve the highest expertise in these disciplines. But there is no special scope to make money in disciplines like history and science. And therefore, intelligent people do not choose to explore these subjects. Talented people engaged in other professions can write poetry, stories, plays or such light compositions in their free time. But research in history and science are not born of relaxed and leisurely time. They are not born during brief vacations in the cool atmosphere of the hills of Matheran, Mahabaleshwar, Nilgiris or Nainital. They are born mostly in old dilapidated libraries located in dusty lanes of crowded cities or stinking, dark rooms of dilapidated laboratories and after many years of sleepless and hungry nights. The wise Gujarati would obviously not like to plunge into such meaningless activity where, after such monumental labour, there is no practical gain.[29]

3

Oppressive Encounters

From very early times, Gujarat came into contact with a variety of people and cultures, both peaceful and aggressive. The mercantile ethos with its emphasis on diplomacy and peaceful conflict resolution offered one mechanism of coping with these diverse encounters. However, when it came to the unease of memory, it could not offer any durable way to put the past to rest. Some of these encounters were transformed into powerful symbols through which a whole range of politics related to culture and identity was articulated and contested in the following centuries.

When Mahmud Ghazni stormed into Gujarat in the early eleventh century, he must not have imagined that his visit would unfold a new phase not just in Gujarat but in the whole of the subcontinent. Entering from the north, the Turkic army of Mahmud Ghazni first sacked the city of Chandravati near Mt Abu and then marched towards the Chaulukya capital of Patan. King Bhimdev I fled without offering any resistance and the great city was plundered. Before destroying Prabhas Patan, the port city of Somnath, Mahmud razed a number of towns en route, including

Somnath temple ruins

the temple city of Dilwara near the Gir forest. After breaking the *jyotirling* of Somnath and taking away a booty of two crore dinars, Mahmud returned by a westerly route through Kutch and Sind.

For the contemporary populace Mahmud's incursion was, at most, like a devastating cyclone or a nightmare and appeared to have no further connotations. Bhimdev soon returned to his capital and, according to an inscription of 1169, also rebuilt the Somnath temple 'with excellent stone and studded it with jewels'.[1] Significantly, the inscription does not mention Mahmud's destruction but says instead that 'the temple which was rebuilt by Bhimdev was decayed due to time'.[2] Neither inscriptions of the Chaulukya period nor important Jain chronicles of Gujarat from that period, such as *Dwayashray* and *Prabandhachintamani*, refer to Mahmud's aggression or the destruction of Somnath. However, a contemporary Apabhransh work of Dhanpal, court poet of King Bhoj of Malwa, refers to this event in the following words: 'the Turushkas destroyed Shrimaladesh, then Anhilvad Patan, Chandravati and Sorath were destroyed and then Dilwada and Someshwar were also destroyed.'[3] In *Vividhatirthakalpa*, composed in the late thirteenth century, Jinaprabhasuri informs us that 'after destroying Gujjar, Mlechchharaj, the Lord of Ghazni, turned towards Satyapur in the year 1081 [of the Vikram era].' In both the contemporary work of Dhanpal and in the Jain work written 150 years after the event, the aggressors were identified as Turushka or Turks and Mahmud was described as 'Mlechchharaj' and 'Lord of Ghazni'. They do not highlight the religious identity of the aggressors and simply refer to them in terms of their ethnic identity and geographic origin.

GUJARAT'S ENCOUNTER WITH 'MUSLIMS'

It is historically significant that Gujarat, particularly coastal Gujarat, witnessed the coming of 'Muslims' since the early seventh century. The first raid took place only four years after the death of the Prophet in AD 635 when the governor of Bahrain sent a naval expedition against Thana (near Bombay) and

Bharuch. Several similar naval expeditions followed. After the conquest of Sind by Muhammad bin Qasim in AD 712, Arab invasions started through land routes as well. Between AD 724 and 738 Al Junaid, the governor of Sind, attacked a number of kingdoms in western India, including north Gujarat and Lat. Two inscriptions, one in Kavi near Bharuch dated AD 736 and another in Navsari also in south Gujarat dated AD 739, describe attacks by Tajiks. The Navsari plate of the Chaulukya king Pulakeshiraj provides a graphic description of the devastation caused by the Tajik army. In both records, the term Tajik is used to describe the Arabs. Like the later references regarding Turushka for Turks in the eleventh century, the aggressors are identified by their ethnic origin.

We do not have contemporary local records about the subsequent raids of the Arabs on Gujarat but al Bilazuri/ Baladhuri, an Arab writer of the ninth century, recorded a raid made on Gandhar port near Bharuch around AD 760 by Hisham ibn Amru, the governor of Sind during the reign of Caliph al Mansur. According to al Bilazuri, Hisham destroyed the 'budd' temple at Gandhar and built a mosque in its place to commemorate his victory. This was probably the first mosque erected in Gujarat on the ruins of a temple, though no further details are available. During the rule of Caliph al Mahdi, another Arab expedition was sent to Gujarat in AD 777 when the larger part of the troops succumbed to an epidemic. Among the dead was Abu Bakr Rabi, who was the first commentator on Hadith; thus, the first traditionist in Islam lies buried in Gujarat.[4] The death of Rabi on the Gujarat coast suggests that Muslim theologians and scholars accompanied the Arab armies on their early expeditions to India.

While these Arab invasions were going on, Arab merchants and navigators, who in the pre-Islamic period merely traded and returned to their place of origin, started flocking to the west coast of India and settling down. The earliest recorded settlements on the Gujarat–Konkan coast date back to the seventh and eighth centuries AD. Their numbers increased by the ninth century. The conquest of Sind followed by the founding of Baghdad and its emergence as the new capital of the Arab empire in the eighth century changed the focus of Arab polity and economy. They turned their back on the Mediterranean and, along with the newly converted Persians, concentrated more on Indian Ocean trade.

A number of Arab travellers, geographers and scholars visited India during the ninth and tenth centuries. The merchant Suleiman of Basra, who landed at Thana in AD 851, noted that the ruler of Jurz (Gujar Pratihar) was unfriendly to Arabs while the Balhara (Rashtrakut), who ruled further south, was more friendly. In his words, 'no Indian king loves the Arabs more than the Balhara. Like him, his subjects too, love the Arabs.' At the time of Suleiman's visit the coast from Bharuch to Chaul (or Saymur) was part of the Rashtrakut kingdom of Amoghavarsha Vallabhrai. The first mention of locals taking to Islam appears at the end of the ninth century in the account of Buzurg bin Shahryar, an Arab captain who made frequent trips to the west coast. He mentions that on one of his trips he met a newly converted Muslim from the Hindu fold who was a shipmaster and a rich trader. The geographer and historian Abul Hasan Masudi reached Cambay in the early ninth century and, after an extended stay at Cambay, Bharuch, Sanjan, Sopara, Thana and Chaul, he wrote that in the cities of the Balhara kingdom Muslims were 'honoured and protected' and were allowed to erect their own mosques. According to him the largest settlement was that of 10,000 Muslims at Chaul, whose ancestors had come from Siraf, Basra, Baghdad and other cities in West Asia.[5] In a map drawn in AD 967, the Arab geographer Ibn Hauqal mentions four cities of Gujarat with mosques situated in Hindu kingdoms: Kambaya (Cambay), Sindan (in southern Kutch), Saymur (Chaul) and Qamuhul or Mamuhal or Famuhul (Patan).[6]

The descriptions of Arab travellers and geographers suggest thriving Arab-Muslim communities scattered over the coastal cities of Gujarat–Konkan which were protected and respected by the Rashtrakut kings and their subjects. The list of cities with mosques indicates the religious freedom enjoyed by the

Arabs not only in the Rashtrakut kingdom but also in the smaller Rajput kingdoms of Patan and Kutch. Since the Rashtrakut kings were friendly with the Arabs, they appointed Arab merchant princes as governors and administrators in their vast kingdom extending from the river Sabarmati in central Gujarat to the source of the Kaveri in Karnataka. From the Chinchani copper plates (found at Chinchani village, Thana district in present-day Maharashtra) belonging to the Rashtrakut king Indra III, we learn that Madhumati (the Sanskritized form of Muhammad) was governor of Samyana mandal[7] in the early tenth century. Muhammad was son of Sahiyarhara of the Tajik community and was also known as Sugatipa. The Chinchani plates, which are records of religious gifts, mention several provisions made by Madhumati. He established a free ferry service on the streams of Sanjan, a feeding house where rice, curries and ghee were distributed free of cost (sadavrat) and made a grant of land (with the permission of the king) to a 'mathika' or small monastery for Brahmin students. The Chinchani record is a testament to the Arab community's socio-political eminence under the Rashtrakut kings, the socio-religious milieu of the west coast of India at that time and the attempt of Arab merchants to meld with local cultural traditions.

From the mid tenth century onwards, the Chaulukya dynasty ruled Gujarat for 362 years. They continued the religious policy of their predecessors and even after the cyclonic invasion and destruction of Somnath by Mahmud Ghazni the Chaulukyas did not abandon their 'rajdharma'. Neither Bhimdev I nor his successor retaliated along religious lines against local Muslims. They made a clear distinction between the Turkic invaders and the peaceful Arab-Iranian merchants. By the time of Karnadev (son of Bhimdev) the southern Gujarat coast—Cambay, Bharuch and Sanjan ports—was under Chaulukya rule and maritime trade had come to play a vital role in the political economy of the Chaulukya state. In such a scenario, political wisdom also demanded a tolerant and just policy towards the powerful merchant-navigator community of Arabia and Persia which occupied a commanding position in the 'Arabian' Sea.

The *Mirat-i-Ahmadi* notes that by the end of the eleventh century a number of Sufi saints had established their *khankhah* or monastery and madrasas in Patan, the capital of Gujarat, and propagated Islam peacefully. The Sufi Haji Hud arrived in Patan during the reign of Karnadev (AD 1064–94) and many Hindus embraced Islam under his influence. It is said that when Karnadev came to know about him and his teachings, he went to meet him and granted him permission to establish his khankhah and madrasa. Another famous Sufi, Sheikh Ahmad Dehalia, settled in Patan during the reign of Siddharaj and in his successor Kumarpal's time, two other Sufi saints, Syed Muhammad or Sheikh-e-Jahan and Sheikh Ahmad Arafati, spread their religious message.

Siddharaj was generous and just to the Muslims in his kingdom and was acknowledged as such not only in Jain chronicles but also by the Turkic chronicler Muhammad Ufi who expressed fulsome praise for this exceptional ruler. Ufi relates the story of how, incited by a group of 'fire-worshippers' (probably referring to Parsis or Hindus), a mob attacked a mosque and razed it. A *khatib* managed to escape and reached Siddharaj's court and complained about the attack. Siddharaj went in disguise to Cambay and investigated the incident. Convinced of the guilt of his own people, he punished them and also ordered the rebuilding of the mosque at royal expense.

Ufi recounted the incident in 1211, about a hundred years after it happened, and went on to say that the mosque rebuilt by Siddharaj was destroyed again during an attack by the king of Malwa and renovated by a rich merchant of Cambay. This is borne out by the Cambay inscription which is the earliest 'Muslim' inscription in the whole of northern India. It records the construction of a Jami mosque in Cambay by the merchant Said in 1218.[8] The date of this inscription falls during the reign of Bhimdev II (1186–1242), who had on more than one occasion come into armed conflict with Turkic invaders, indicating that the commercial relationship between 'Muslims' and 'Hindus' was not affected by the armed hostility between their rulers. Muhammad Ufi describes how Muhammad Ghori, after his defeat at the hands of Bhimdev II, turned down the advice of his ministers to replenish his exhausted treasury by confiscating the property of Wasa Abhir (a merchant of Patan) in Ghazni. Yet, when the same Said (supported by the neighbouring Hindu king Samkha) challenged Vastupal's authority, it led to armed conflict; Said was defeated and his property confiscated by Vastupal. The conflict revolved around control over the revenue of Cambay and was unrelated to the religion of the parties involved. In fact the brothers Vastupal and Tejpal are known to have earned the goodwill of a Muslim sultan by protecting his preceptor/mother who had come to a port of Gujarat while proceeding on a pilgrimage. [9]

The acts of generosity and religious tolerance were not limited to kings and nobles and this is borne out by the story of Jagadu, a famous merchant of Bhadreshwar on the Kutch coast. Jagadu controlled a vast maritime trading empire and had extensive contacts with merchants of West Asia and according to the *Jagadu-charita* he was a pious Jain too. Two gestures made by Jagadu clearly indicate that there was interaction and mutual regard between traders which transcended business relations, religious affiliations as well as political animosity between their respective states. The first gesture was the benefactions made by Jagadu when a great famine afflicted the whole country. From his 700 granaries, grain was distributed to:

Visaldeva	8000 mutakas (measure)
Hammira, ruler of Sind	12,000
Madanavarman, ruler of Avanti	18,000
Garjanesa,[10] Mojadina, ruler of Delhi	21,000
Pratapasimha, ruler of Kasi	32,000
Skandhila,[11] famed as Emperor	12,000[12]

As is clear from the list above, there was no religious distinction in providing relief during the famine. Jagadu was also a patron of religious shrines and built not only Jain temples but also a *masiti* or mosque called Shimli at Bhadreshwar. The author

uses the term *mlechchhalakshmi karanatah* while referring to
the reason for him building the mosque, indicating that trade
with the *mlechchh* (foreigner) was Jagadu's source of wealth
and building the mosque was an acknowledgement of this and
his way of thanksgiving.[13]

A bilingual inscription of 1264 from Somnath Patan records
in both Arabic and Sanskrit the endowment of a mosque by a
wealthy shipowner of that city. This inscription reveals some
of the complexity of 'Hindu'–'Muslim' relationships at all levels
of society by the thirteenth century. The Sanskrit part is more
comprehensive and detailed than the Arabic and its adaptation
of Arabic phrases to Sanskrit terminology indicates the linguistic
synthesis which was in evolution within this cultural milieu.
Equally interesting is the attempt to translate Arabo-Muslim
concepts using Sanskrit vocabulary. The real importance of the
inscription however lies in the information it furnishes regarding
the Muslim communities of Somnath Patan. The inscription is
about the shipmaster Nakhuda Nuruddin Firoz, who came to
Somnatha-deva-nagara from Hurmujadesa (Hormuz) for
business. Firoz purchased land just outside the town (it is also
possible that he received it as a gift from the local chief Raja
Chhada), in the presence of all the leading jamaats and with
the support and permission of the local Panchkula headed by
Shaiv Pashupat Acharya Parvirbhadra. The devout Firoz built
a mosque and made a number of bequests for its maintenance,
purchase of daily necessities and provision of staff for
conducting worship in the mosque. With these resources the
mosque was to be properly maintained 'so long as the moon,
the planets and the stars endure, for the salvation of Firoz'.
Any surplus which remained was to be sent to Mecca and
Medina. Firoz instructed that responsibility for administering
the money and maintaining the mosque was to rest jointly with
the jamaats or congregations of the *nakhuyaorika*, owners or
commanders of ships and sailors; *ghamchikas* or oil-men
belonging to the towns; together with their *khatib* or leader of
the prayer; Muslim *chunakaras*, lime-workers or masons; and
the Muslims among the *patrapatis*.

This Sanskrit text has a shorter Arabic version which gives the date and details regarding the acquisition of the land and the construction of the mosque by Firoz; it also contains the customary prayer which has been omitted from the Sanskrit text: '. . . In the city of Somnath, may God make it one of the cities of Islam and (banish) infidelity and idols . . .' The Arabic text is silent about the administrative arrangements and only mentions that surplus funds be sent to the holy cities. The inscription indicates that by the thirteenth century the Muslim community had expanded beyond trading and maritime activities to include occupations such as oil pressing and masonry. The jamaat as a social structure had already evolved and was differentiated by occupation.[14]

The last Chaulukya king, Karnadev II or Karan Ghelo, was defeated by the army of Alauddin Khilji under the leadership of his brother Ulugh Khan and Nusrat Khan in 1299. The capital Patan fell into the hands of the invaders without much effort and among the captured women was Queen Kanwala Devi or Kamala Devi. After plundering Patan, the Turkic army marched towards Saurashtra and repeated Mahmud Ghazni's deed. This was the second sack of the Somnath temple, and its significance for us is that the incident and its description in later Persian sources supplied the elements for the subsequent image of Muslims in the nineteenth and twentieth centuries.

The first element was the description of the invasion. The contemporary historian Barani wrote, 'the treasure, elephants and womenfolk of Raja Karna fell into the hands of the army of Islam'. In the 273 years between Mahmud's assault and Ulugh Khan's, Persian historians had raised Mahmud Ghazni's iconoclasm into the ultimate role model for a devout Muslim king. Now invaders were no longer referred to by the region they came from but by the religion to which they belonged.

The second element was the humiliation of Hindu women by Muslim invaders, embodied by Amir Khusro's composition *Ashiqa* which describes the love affair between Alauddin Khilji's son and Karan Ghelo's daughter. For the Hindu reader, Kanwala Devi's capture stands for Muslim abduction of Hindu women and the subsequent 'love affair' a second humiliation. Implicit in this story is also the 'masculinity' of Muslims and the vulnerability of Hindu women.

The third element, the desecration of Hindu sacred places by Muslims, was supplied by Ulugh Khan's trail of destruction. After destroying Somnath he went eastwards and sacked and plundered Cambay and destroyed a temple. More importantly, he used the material to build a Jami mosque at the same site.

The fourth element was the perception that the victory of Alauddin Khilji marked the end of a glorious era in Gujarat. The *Dharmaranya Puraan*, written around the thirteenth and fourteenth centuries, says that with the coming of Alauddin Khilji's army 'kshatryia rajya was destroyed and replaced by mlechchha rajya'.[15] In the nineteenth century, when it became customary to classify Gujarat's history into Hindu and Muslim periods, this perception was reinforced and became the fulcrum on which the Hindu–Muslim engagement was balanced. These four elements were woven and rewoven from the nineteenth century onwards in the politics of identity and culture.

The impact of the march of Alauddin Khilji's army is also revealed in the *Kanhadde Prabandh* (1456), an Apabhransh composition by Padmanabh, the court poet of the kingdom of Jhalor. He says, 'They burned down villages and devastated the countryside. Many cities were destroyed and they looted the property of people, enslaved Brahmins and women and children of all eighteen varnas.' He describes in detail the destruction of Somnath, revealing that even after 150 years the event continued to have a powerful impact on the mind of the vanquished. It ends with the lament, 'Oh Lord Somnath! Where then was your trishul?'[16]

Later accounts such as Padmanabh's overshadowed contemporary descriptions such as that of Kakkasuri in *Nabhinandan-jinoddhar Prabandh*, written about two decades after the event. Kakkasuri focussed on the adjustment and accommodation in the interaction between the newly established regime and local merchants. Describing how Samar Shah was able to gain Alp Khan's permission to rebuild the Shatrunjaya temples, Kakkasuri showers praise on both the Sultan and his deputy: Alauddin is compared to Indra and Alp Khan to Brahma, as both the destroyer and renovator of temples.[17] Obviously, this aspect never featured in later accounts nor became part of the collective memory.

The Somnath temple was destroyed for the third time in 1395 by Zafar Khan, the last governor of the Delhi Sultans, after which he ruined the temples of Diu and Idar. Zafar Khan belonged to a family of recent converts to Islam (his Rajput father had converted) and was zealous in his efforts to spread Islam.

> He made efforts at the proclamation of the word of god (confession of the Muslim faith). He led an army for plundering the temple of Somnat, that is Pattan dev. He spread Islam at most of the places.[18]

His grandson Ahmed Shah became Sultan in 1411 and is remembered as one of the most intolerant rulers of Gujarat. Ahmed Shah destroyed a number of temples and replaced them with mosques. He appointed an officer for the spread of Islam and enforced jiziya, a tax that had not been systematically or vigorously collected in Gujarat in the 125 years of Muslim rule before him. The administration was handed to Malik Tuhfah, with instructions to quell turbulent non-Muslim elements and enforce jiziya strictly. He is reported to have suppressed many Rajput chieftains, enforced both salami and jiziya on them and secured a number of converts to Sunni Islam. These converted Rajputs turned into a distinct community called Molesalam and Malek and are now scattered in central Gujarat. A number of artisan communities and cultivators also converted, some by force, others since they were too poor to pay jiziya and still others who were oppressed because of their low status in the Hindu ritual order and were attracted by the egalitarian message of Islam. The forceful imposition of jiziya was a watershed in the social history of Gujarat. Even though Muslims had been a constituent element of society since the seventh century and a large number of mosques were already a part of the landscape, for the first time, the state distinguished between its citizens along the lines of religion. In one stroke, Gujarati society was divided into two religious blocs not only in the cities but also in rural areas.

Hindus were not the only community at the receiving end of Ahmed Shah's religious orthodoxy. Since he was a devout Sunni, he considered it his religious duty to punish the heterodox Shia Bohras, who were a wealthy and sizeable community in Gujarat. Throughout the Chaulukya period, for about 250 years, Shia missionaries had spread their faith without any political interference. Ahmed Shah not only forced them to convert to the Sunni fold but also sentenced to death the Mullahji or religious head of the Shia Bohras in Ahmedabad as he did not approve of their religious calendar and timing of Id. According to Shia Bohra practice, the month started with the first day of the waxing moon, just as in the Hindu calendar. Considering this practice heretical, Ahmad Shah ordered the execution of the Mullahji. Subsequently the entire community was persecuted by the later Sultans.

Mahmud Begada, under whom the Gujarat Sultanate reached its apogee, also continued Ahmad Shah's policy and converted a number of Rajput kings, destroyed the temple of Dwaraka and desecrated the temple at Somnath. It is said that Mahmud got the sobriquet 'Begada' when he won the two *gadh* or forts of Junagadh and Pavagadh and forced both the vanquished kings to accept Islam. He also forced the Sodha and Sumra chieftains of south Sind to convert. The distancing between the two communities was accentuated during the reign of Sultan Mahmud III (1537–54) after he decreed that Hindu subjects should wear red armbands, prohibited public celebrations of Holi and Diwali, prohibited Hindus from riding horses and ordered that no instruments be played in Hindu places of worship.[19]

Though Ahmad Shah and his descendants zealously followed Islamic injunctions, they also appointed Hindus to senior positions in their administration, unlike the governors of the

Delhi Sultans before them. Two Vaniyas, Manekchand and Motichand, were members of Ahmad Shah's council of ministers.[20] Rai Raichand, who led the battle against Rana Kumbha of Mewar, was general in the army of the next Sultan, Qutbuddin (1451–59). Two Hindu amirs, Rai Rayan and Malik Gopi, became very influential at the court of Mahmud Begada. Malik Gopi, considered one of the founders of the city of Surat, played an important role in tilting the Sultan's policy in favour of the Portuguese.

Following the political upheaval in West Asia caused by the Mongol invasions, a large number of Muslim theologians, scholars and some eminent Sufi saints came to Gujarat from Iran and West Asia in the fourteenth and fifteenth centuries. Gujarat was regarded as a safe haven and the Sultans welcomed theologians as they enhanced their reputation as good Muslim kings. One of the earliest scholars who came to Gujarat was al Damamini. He came from Egypt and was appointed professor of Arabic grammar in one of the madrasas of Ahmedabad. Another celebrity was Baharaq from Hadarmut, who was appointed tutor of the prince. During the reign of Mahmud Begada, the philosopher and mathematician Haibatullah Shah Mir arrived from Shiraz. The most famous among these immigrant scholars was Abul Fazl Ghazaruni, who came from Persia. One of his disciples, Sheikh Mubarak of Nagor, was the father of Abul Fazl, the philosopher-historian of Akbar's court. In *Ain-i-Akbari*, Abul Fazl wrote that his father learnt the intricacies of mysticism and philosophy from al Ghazaruni and was introduced to a number of books on metaphysics and speculative theology. The presence of these intellectuals in Ahmedabad made it a great centre of Islamic learning and education.[21]

GUJARAT'S ENCOUNTER WITH THE PORTUGUESE

The Portuguese arrived during the last phase of the Gujarat Sultanate. They were the first European power to land on the western coast with the ambition to control the Indian Ocean trade by acquiring and controlling key ports and taxing the trade passing through them. They tried all means to make this possible—diplomatic channels, bribes and inciting factionalism, and when these were not successful, they resorted to loot, plunder and burning of entire port cities. The coastal people suffered the most and no one was spared, whether they were Hindu, Jain or Muslim, Brahmin or Baniya, Arab or Abyssinian.

Beginning with Bassein in 1546, where they killed a large number of Muslim traders, the Portuguese went northwards and slaughtered the entire population of Magdalla near Surat and burnt down all houses. Only one man 'whose hands were ordered to be cut off was left alive to carry the news of this atrocious victory'.[22] Similarly Hansot near Bharuch was also set on fire. Then they went to Diu, where they sacked the city and routed the army of Sultan Muzaffar Shah. They continued their reign of terror and in the second round they burnt down a number of towns on the Saurashtra coast, including Una, Mahua and Gogha. The prosperous port of Gandhar was also destroyed. The famous port city of Prabhas Patan-Somnath was also sacked and Hindu temples and mosques were destroyed. This destruction was made possible by their naval strength and facilitated by the waning power of the Gujarat Sultanate.

The Portuguese agenda was twofold: economic and religious. They set out from their country to control the spice trade to Europe, which was till then controlled by Muslims. Recently free from Muslim domination, the Portuguese wished to strike at their economic strength and simultaneously propagate the Christian faith.[23] So once they were in control of the ports of Bassein, Daman and Diu they set about converting the local population in these towns. This was Gujarat's first encounter with Christianity.

> Temples and mosques were destroyed, and Hindu and Muslim public worship forbidden within the Portuguese settlements. Only Christians could hold public office, and various kinds of pressure were used to persuade people to become Christian . . .[24]

The pillage, plunder and religious persecution of the Portuguese lasted for many decades, though their impact was restricted to the coastal towns of Gujarat and Saurashtra. Their power waned and, finally, they were restricted to Daman and Diu on the Gujarat coast as a result of rising Mughal power.

GUJARAT'S ENCOUNTER WITH THE MUGHALS

Gujarat was annexed to the Mughal Empire by Akbar in 1573 and the next hundred years saw peace and prosperity. Akbar abolished jiziya and pilgrim tax, earning the goodwill of the Hindu populace. The persecution of Shias also ended and thus the equation of the state and its subjects was altered after 269 years. Respecting the sentiments of a number of denominations of Vaishnav, Jains and Parsis, Akbar granted many farmans to them to enable them to practise their religions peacefully. For instance, on the request of Jains, animal slaughter was banned during their holy period of *paryushan*.[25] Akbar commenced a process of interfaith dialogue in 1575, which resulted in his Din-i-Ilahi.

The cultural synthesis which evolved during the Mughal era is reflected in myriad facets of the Vallabhacharya Vaishnav sect, one of the most popular and powerful religious sects of Gujarat:

> The age of Viththalnathji [Vallabhacharya's son who spread Pushti Margi Vaishnavism in Gujarat] was the pinnacle of the Mughal era. The arts and crafts as well as luxurious lifestyles also reached their high point. And we see that the best of this style was reflected, nurtured and matured in the adornment of Shri [Krishna as addressed by Pushti Marg devotees], His robes, the food offered to Him, articles for His decoration, music, literature and so on. In the attire of Shri and food offered to Him too we find an echo of the Mughal era. We immediately experience this when we gaze at the images of Shrinathji and Shri Yamunaji, their robes and ornaments. Several sweets and fried foods among the items of chhappan bhog

Shrinathji

[fifty-six food articles offered to Shrinathji] reflect the Iranian lifestyle gifted to India, which we can both see and relish.

This glorious absorption of Iranian culture within Indian culture has become such a part of our lives that to say the above would be regarded as heresy by our Vaishnav brethren. But this is a fact which we are not in a position to negate. The reflection of Mughal–Rajput style in the attire of the great Vaishnav acharyas, from Viththalnathji to Shrihariraiji-Shripurushottamji, confirms this reality.[26]

Jahangir and Shahjahan continued this liberal policy to a great extent and this phase was rudely interrupted when Aurangzeb became governor of Gujarat in 1645. He desecrated the Chintamani Parshwanath Jain temple built by the wealthy merchant Shantidas and converted it into a mosque. Shantidas sought the intervention of Shahjahan and by a farman of 1648 the emperor ordered that a wall be built between the temple and the mihrab and the fakirs occupying the temple premises be evicted. However, the Jain temple was never used for worship again.

In 1658 Aurangzeb became emperor and reintroduced jiziya. Through his farman of 1665 he prohibited Jains and Hindus from closing their shops on 'Pachusan' (paryushan), last day of the month and eleventh day; ordered that arrangements be made to ensure that Kolis of Himmatnagar do not disturb Muslims when they recite their Friday prayers; instructed that action be taken against those who have repaired and resumed worship in temples demolished in Ahmedabad and other districts; and prohibited Hindus from lighting lamps in the marketplace during Diwali.[27]

If Aurangzeb was intolerant of the 'idol-worship' of his Hindu subjects, he was not less severe on those Muslims whom he regarded as schismatics. He appointed Sunni imams and muezzins in Shia Bohra mosques at Ahmedabad. In 1703 it was reported to the emperor that two Bohras, Isa and Taj, were spreading their 'heretical' doctrines. They were arrested and sent as prisoners to the court. Some time later, news reached the emperor that one Mulla Khanji, the leader of the Ismaili Bohras, was preaching heresy with twelve others, and that they had collected over one lakh rupees at Ahmedabad to secure the release of the prisoners, and were in the possession of about sixty of their religious books. The diwan of the province was ordered to arrest the mullah and his associates and send them to the court along with the money and the heretical books. But Aurangzeb did not rely on repressive measures alone for the purpose of weaning the Bohras from the Shia faith. He sent orders to the local authorities that the children of the Bohras, as also illiterate adults, should be given religious instruction on orthodox Sunni lines both in the city of Ahmedabad and in the parganas, and that the cost of their education was to be recovered from this community.[28]

In the last phase of his reign Aurangzeb ordered the destruction of the Hatkeshwar temple of Vadnagar and decreed that Hindus other than Rajput should not carry arms or ride elephants, palkhis, or Arab and Iraqi horses.[29] In 1702 Aurangzeb called for information about the temple of Somnath, which had been destroyed on his orders earlier in his reign. He instructed that if Hindus had revived worship there the temple was to be demolished completely.[30] In 1706, a year before his death, he ordered the demolition of the temple at Dwaraka but we do not know if this order was carried out.

Aurangzeb's intolerance and bigotry eclipsed from people's memory the liberal and peaceful reign of three Mughal emperors before him. The dominant imprint in the collective consciousness was of the discrimination against Hindus and their cruel persecution by Muslim rulers.

GUJARAT'S ENCOUNTER WITH THE MARATHAS

Maratha incursions into Gujarat began soon after Aurangzeb became emperor. Led by Shivaji, they plundered the cities of Gujarat, solely for booty to finance their expansion in the Deccan. Shivaji's first plunder of Surat took place in 1664. Pitching his tent outside the city, he sent two messengers with a letter requiring the governor and the three most eminent merchants in the city—Haji Said Beg, Virji Vora and Haji Qasim—to come to him immediately and negotiate the ransom, failing which he threatened the whole town with destruction. When he received no answer, Shivaji's army entered the city, started looting the houses and then setting them on fire.

> Throughout Wednesday, Thursday, Friday and Saturday, this work of devastation continued, every day new fires being raised, so that thousands of houses were consumed to ashes and two-thirds of the town destroyed. As the English chaplain wrote, 'Thursday and Friday nights were the most terrible nights for fire. The fire turned the night into day, as before the smoke in the day-time had turned the day into night, rising so thick that it darkened the sun like a great cloud.'[31]

The mansions of Virji Vora and Haji Said Beg were ransacked and the Marathas carried away jewels and money and destroyed the buildings and warehouses. The English chaplain wrote, 'His desire of money is so great that he spares no barbarous cruelty to extort confessions from his prisoners, whips them most cruelly, threatens death and often executes it if they do not produce so much as he thinks they may or desires they should;— at least cuts off one hand, sometimes both.'[32] Shivaji repeated the devastation again in 1670 and this time he set fire to two-thirds of the town. An echo of Shivaji's misdeeds was heard at the time of his coronation in 1674:

> Two of the learned Brahmans pointed out that Shiva, in the course of his raids, had burnt cities 'involving the death

of Brahmans, cows, women and children.' He could be cleansed of this sin, — for a price. It was not necessary for him to pay compensation to the surviving relatives of the men and women who had perished in his sack of Surat or Karinjia. It would be enough if he put money into the pockets of the Brahmans of Konkan and Desh. The price demanded for this 'pardon' was only Rs 8,000, and Shiva could not have refused to pay this trifle. (Dutch Records, Vol. 34, No. 841)[33]

However the real loss of Surat was not the booty which the Marathas carried off but the destruction of trade of this richest port of India. For several years after Shivaji's raids, the town used to throb with panic every now and then, whenever any Maratha force came within a few days' march of it, or even at the false alarms of their coming. On every such occasion the merchants would quickly remove their goods to the ships, the citizens would flee to the villages and the Europeans would move to the adjacent port of Swally. Business was scared away from Surat and inland producers hesitated to send their goods to this the greatest emporium of western India.[34]

During both the attacks of Shivaji, the English traders resisted the Maratha army and their ransom demands. During the second attack, while the local governor abandoned the city and left the people to their fate, prominent merchants of the city took shelter with the English. The encounter with Shivaji left the local population traumatized but the role of the English created a favourable impression on them. After Surat, Bharuch became the next target. In 1675 the Maratha army crossed the Narmada for the first time and took ransom from the people of Bharuch. After ten years, Shambhaji's army again plundered Bharuch. During the reign of Chhatrapati Rajaram, his senapati Dabhade collected regular payments from various towns in return for sparing them from plunder. In the beginning of the eighteenth century, Surat was attacked and ransacked for the third time and, as a result of the recurrent plunder, the Marathas came to be known as *Ganim*. The word Ganim means 'guerrilla' in Marathi and has positive connotations, while in Gujarati it came to mean 'Marathi plunderer'. When Baroda was attacked and looted, an unknown poet composed a prayer to Goddess Ambika to protect Gujarat. In this famous *'Ganimno Ladaino Pavado'* we can see the expression of the anguish of the common people of the time:

> The city of Baroda was burnt to ashes
> And all the villages around were laid waste
> Such is the terror of Ganim
> Not a rag nor a penny was spared
> Oh Mother Goddess Ambika! Protect Gujarat!
> …
>
> If you kill the Ganim
> The world will be saved
> And you will be called Life-giver[35]

In 1707, the year Aurangzeb died, Balaji Vishwanath entered Gujarat from Malwa, looted Godhra, Mahudha and Nadiad and camped on the outskirts of Ahmedabad. The Mughal subedar gave a ransom of over two lakh rupees. In this declining phase of Mughal power, Mughal officials fought with each other to secure power and ruled different parts of Gujarat in partnership with various Marathas sardars. Between 1737 and 1743 the Mughal Momin Khan and Damajirao Gaekwad established diarchy and divided Ahmedabad between them, each assuming control over six city gates. After this, the Mughals were pushed out and Maratha supremacy was established. The Marathas fought with each other for control and by 1758 Ahmedabad witnessed diarchy for the second time when eleven gates belonged to the Peshwa and one to the Gaekwad. Through all this time, they continued to plunder and harass the people of mainland Gujarat and Saurashtra.

Maratha rule was marked by widespread corruption, torture and exploitation. If a merchant was seen to be wearing good clothes, the spies of the Maratha sarsuba (officer in charge of a district) would report it and he would be summoned to court and compelled to pay several thousand rupees. If he refused, a boulder would be placed on his chest and pressure applied till the merchant, gasping for breath, paid up the money. As a result, except for the Nagarsheth, merchants gave up wearing good clothes or maintaining horse carriages. Common people were also tortured in similar ways by the subordinate officers. In 1760, to meet the expense of his son's thread ceremony, the sarsuba Santoji fixed a lump sum to be collected from the various classes of citizens, which came to be known as *janoi vero* or sacred thread tax! He also imposed other taxes on social events, such as marriage among Hindus and remarriage of widows as practised by innumerable lower castes. To obtain permission to remarry, a widow now had to pay a rupee and four annas. Four rupees had to be paid by anyone taking a marriage party outside the city limits and a marriage party coming from outside had to pay ten annas.[36] Ratnamanirao Jote comments in his history of Ahmedabad, '. . . the Marathas asphyxiated Ahmedabad, the prosperous city of eight lakh people, and when it was handed over to the English the city was little better than a corpse'.[37]

An overview of 800 years, covering three oppressive encounters, suggests that the invasion of Gujarat and destruction of Somnath by Mahmud Ghazni in the early eleventh century and the annexation of Gujarat by Alauddin Khilji were not considered turning points by contemporary Gujarati accounts. Nevertheless, the large-scale destruction left them in great shock and fear of the unknown intensified. Later, in the sixteenth century, the coastal population of Hindus, Muslims and Parsis experienced the oppressive presence of the Portuguese but extensive economic relations between them continued for the next 200 years. For more than 150 years Maratha armies plundered the cities, towns and villages of Gujarat without making any distinction on religious lines and turned this fertile land into a wretched province. But amid such oppressive encounters, the process of sociocultural synthesis at the grassroots continued as saints, bhaktas and bhakti poets and the auliyas and pirs preached love and tolerance. Gujarat witnessed the rise of a number of communities which followed both saints and pirs as well as sects, such as Pirana and Pranami which amalgamated the teachings of the established religions and occupied a space in the twilight between Hinduism and Islam. The evolution of Gujarati language and literature, the emergence of Indo-Islamic and later Indo-European architecture, the development of classical Hindustani music and introduction of new musical instruments from western Asia and Europe give us a clear indication of cultural synthesis during this period.

A range of pertinent questions around identity, memory, politics and culture evolved in the colonial period, generating 'new chapters' in the history of Gujarat and fresh tensions engulfed Gujarati society. In the Great Revolt of 1857, one section of Hindus, Muslims and Marathas in Gujarat jointly fought against the oppressive Raj while another section of rajas, maharajas and new elite, irrespective of religious persuasion or provincial distinction, supported the Raj. In the fourth quarter of the nineteenth century, new equations emerged between Hindus and Muslims and this politics of culture and identity intensified in the twentieth century. We shall attempt to understand the changing and contesting perceptions and articulations about self and society in a separate chapter.

4

Welcoming the British Raj

Gujarat was the first region in the Indian subcontinent to encounter the English East India Company when the flagship *Hector* under the command of William Hawkins dropped anchor at Surat in 1608. Within ten years, the English had defeated the Portuguese and established their first factory at that prosperous port of the Mughal Empire. For the next seventy years trade flourished between the merchants of Surat and the Company and when the Company transferred their headquarters to Bombay in 1683 many merchants relocated themselves to the new city. For the next two centuries and even afterwards, not just merchants but scores of enterprising Gujaratis followed the footsteps of the Company and made Bombay their new home.

John Company's new avatar as the British Raj at Bengal had but a faint echo in Gujarat. Parallel to the ascendancy of the English in the east coast after their success at Plassey, the Marathas were establishing their ascendancy in Gujarat with their capture of Ahmedabad in 1758. Surat was still under the nawab, the last vestige of the Mughal Empire, who was sandwiched between the rising power of the Peshwas and the English. Taking advantage of the fluid political situation, the English established de facto control over Surat in 1759. The poet Narmad, one of the pioneers of modern Gujarati literature, described the event in his history of Surat: 'Two flags were flying on the castle of Surat, the red flag of Mughals on the south-east tower and the English one on the south-west tower of the castle.' The diarchy of the nawab and the English continued till the close of the century when the English forced the last nawab to take a pension and thereby established full control on the cities of Surat and Rander and the surrounding countryside.

Apart from the political situation in western India the English were aided in their final takeover of Surat by the Surat merchants, who gave them their active support. The East India Company's main trade at that time revolved around cotton cloth. In this trade, a complex web of relationships interconnected the Company, the merchants, and big and small artisans divided into castes and subcastes, each associated with a specific craft in the production of cotton cloth. The Company procured cotton cloth from big merchants—Hindu, Muslim and Parsi. In turn, these merchants operated through local subagents or mukadams, who collected the fabric from the weavers. In this three-tier operation the weavers were always worst off as they worked under conditions of debt bondage. The English did not face serious impediments till the third quarter of the century, but by the 1780s Dutch, Portuguese and French companies entered the trade in a big way. The weavers took advantage of the situation and began producing coarse cloth and selling it at higher prices to these competing companies. The English responded by putting pressure on the weavers through the merchants and mukadams, even prohibiting them from leaving Surat without the written permission of English officials.[1] The oppressed weavers and artisans reacted with a violent protest targeting Hindu, Parsi and Bohra merchants.

Surat witnessed two riots, one in 1788 when Muslims, mostly exploited weavers, attacked Parsi merchants and another in 1795 when Muslim weavers, along with sepoys and servants of the nawab, targeted Hindu and Bohra merchants. They destroyed a market, injured several merchants and damaged many houses and temples. The second riot unnerved the entire community of Hindu and Bohra merchants of the city. The partisan role of the nawab's sepoys and servants led the merchants and Mahajans to view the English East India Company as their last hope. In their perception, while the Marathas and their periodic raids for chauth were a constant external threat, the decadent nawab with his ever-increasing demands was an internal threat. As a way of ensuring their collective safety and security, they turned to the English.

The Shroffs, Mahajans and the 'Dai' (the chief priest of Bohras who also controls the community) of Surat city submitted petitions to the Company in 1795. The merchants pleaded that they were 'unarmed and unguarded, relying wholly for their safety and protection on the English flag'. The Dai similarly argued, 'I have ever considered myself under the protection of the flag of the hon'ble English company' and urged that he be granted a guard for the 'protection of my life and property'. They reviewed the history of the Company in Surat, suggesting that it had attained control of the castle in 1759 'at the request and advice of the inhabitants for the general good and quiet of the place' and that the English at that time had promised to provide the merchants with protection against local governors (nawabs) in return for their cooperation.[2]

The Company also carried out large-scale trade from Bharuch through their factories till the end of the seventeenth century. But by the mid eighteenth century, they had withdrawn their establishment here though they continued to import cotton and cloth through this port city. After taking over Surat the English set their eyes on Bharuch to further their trade and expand their power in Gujarat. Bharuch was also very attractive because of its lucrative customs income and large cotton-producing countryside. By raking up an old dispute with the Nawab of Bharuch regarding an excessive levy of duties on cloth and clubbing it with certain claims of the Nawab of Surat, the English attacked Bharuch in 1771 but failed to capture it. The next year they stormed the port city by land and sea and captured it along with a large territory of the nawab extending to 162 villages. The personal secretary of the nawab, Munshi Abbas Ali, wrote a metrical composition in Urdu, *Qissa-i-Ghamgin* or 'A Tragic Tale', which focussed on the events leading to the tragic end of the Nawab of Bharuch. He indicated that the betrayal by the nawab's diwan, Sheth Lallubhai, and instigation by a leading Parsi merchant of Surat, Dhanji Shah, played a critical role in the downfall of the nawab.[3] Although the English records of Bombay and Surat do not suggest any complicity on the part of these two leaders of the mercantile community, other local sources indicate that a large number of Hindus and a section of the Parsi merchants of Bharuch were eager to welcome the English. Seven years after the annexation of Bharuch, as part of their political calculations, the English contemplated handing over the territory to the powerful Maratha sardar Scindia. When the elite of Bharuch came to know about the negotiations they prayed to God that the 'Maratha' would not occupy their city. By 1779 the English–Maratha negotiations broke down and the city elite celebrated the continuation of English rule by performing many yagnas and offering *naivedya* in the temples.[4] Nevertheless, the Bharuch area was transferred to Scindia in 1783 as part of a negotiated settlement and remained with him till 1803, when the English recaptured it by force.

With the decline of the Peshwa in the early nineteenth century, the English moved ahead with their designs to capture power in western India. They established their paramount power in Gujarat by the Treaty of Bassein with the Peshwa in 1802 and with treaties with the Peshwa and Gaekwad in 1817-18. Since Surat and Bharuch along with their countryside had been taken over earlier and Ahmedabad had been annexed by 1818, the English carved out four 'districts'—Surat, Bharuch, Kheda and Ahmedabad—out of 'khalsa' (conquered) territory and allowed the remaining areas to be ruled by princely states under the close supervision of English Residents. Throughout their rule of 150 years or so, first as Company Bahadur and then as British Raj, barely one-seventh of the combined area of Gujarat, including Saurashtra and Kutch, was under the direct rule of the British.

Colonel Walker, the Resident at Baroda, entered Saurashtra for the first time in the early nineteenth century to settle the claims of the Gaekwad and the Company. He had initially planned to enter into pacts with twenty-nine princes and finalize the amounts they would pay as tribute. But he soon realized the tangled complexity of the political setting of Saurashtra

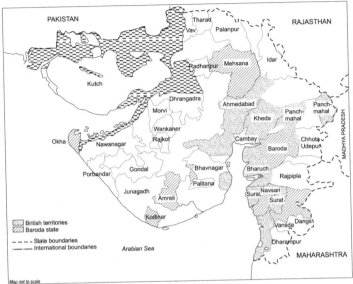

British territories and major princely states

and, by 1807, entered into pacts with 153 princes. Some of the princes were sceptical in the beginning but most of them were eager to get rid of the Marathas, who had been oppressing them for tribute for more than a century. The diwans and karbhaaris—administrators of princely states—were Nagar Brahmins and Vaniyas and some of them also undertook *ijaaro*, that is, lease to collect revenue from specific *mahals* or block of villages. Colonel Walker assured them of the continuation of their leases and other privileges and his conciliatory approach succeeded in winning them over. Similarly, property conflicts between local Rajput chiefs and rajas were also settled in favour of the chiefs and they became great supporters of Company rule. However, the rajas and chiefs of the Jadeja and Jethwa clans of Rajputs were, from the outset, reluctant to deal with Colonel Walker because he insisted on adding one 'indispensable article' in his pacts, which was a prohibition of the practice of *doodh peeti* (female infanticide) in their communities and territories. Although they agreed under duress, the practice continued in northern Saurashtra and Kutch in one form or another till the end of the nineteenth century.

Diwan Ranchhodji, a contemporary Nagar Brahmin statesman, in his history and memoirs, *Tarikhe Sorath va Halar*, written in Persian, credited Colonel Walker with the successful settlement of Saurashtra and praised him for his 'vision, courage and diplomacy': 'he has purchased people with his sweet tongue . . . he subdued the enemies of the state by force as well as persuasion'. Fourteen years after Colonel Walker's 'settlement' and a year after the English achieved overlordship over the whole of Gujarat, the governor of Bombay Presidency, Mountstuart Elphinstone, visited Gujarat. He invited Diwan Ranchhodji of Junagadh for discussions at his camp in Ghogha port. The Diwan described their meeting as follows:

> The Governor was very kind to me and when I reached there he came forward about forty steps from his tent to receive me and when I left he came out for about hundred steps to say goodbye. He arranged seven chairs for my brothers and vakil and on three occasions, each time for three hours, he discussed with me in private with full attention and courtesy. The entire discussion was carried out in Persian. I have no words to praise him for his hospitality. I have not seen in my life a person with such great foresight, such unique courage, carrying out the work of his master with such competence. At the time of departure, promising me the support of the English government, he said that there would not be any trouble to me from any king of the area.[5]

This description of the meeting between the new master and the traditional aristocracy encapsulates the diplomatic approach and accommodating attitude of both sides at the beginning of the British era in Gujarat.

ESTABLISHMENT OF A NEW ORDER

Mountstuart Elphinstone played a critical role in the downfall of Maratha rule and the establishment of Company rule in western India. He was appointed commissioner of Deccan in 1818 and became governor of Bombay in 1819. During the eight years of his governorship he laid the foundation of British administration in present-day Maharashtra and Gujarat. Romesh Chandra Dutt, historian and diwan of Baroda state, observed:

> His [Elphinstone's] fame as a liberal administrator rests mainly on his work in three dimensions. His first endeavour was to codify the law. His second great object was to confer on the people of India as large a share in the work of administration as was then possible. His third and last purpose was to spread a sound education among the people, so as to enable them to take a higher and more responsible share in the future in the management of their own concerns.[6]

Elphinstone formed the whole of the Bombay Regulations into a Code in 1827. This code, also known as Elphinstone's Code, consisted of twenty-seven regulations, subdivided into chapters and sections. By this code he established a juridical system in Gujarat and the Deccan where the munsif or native commissioners tried cases at the lowest level, above whom were assistant judges, then the District Diwani and Faujdari Adalats and, finally, the Sadr Diwani and Nizamet Adalat. The Bombay Regulation IV laid down the legal system by which the presidency, including Gujarat, was to be governed. Under the provisions of the new legal system the acts of the British Parliament would remain supreme, followed by regulations of the governor in council. Then the customs and usage of the place where the case arose would be employed to decide the case. Only after these were found to be unavailable would the personal law of the defendant and justice, equity and good conscience prevail as law.[7] Before finalizing the code,

Elphinstone arranged for the compilation of laws of place and personal laws of the 'natives'. Since he considered caste as the real locus of customary laws, caste rules of Surat, Bharuch and Kheda districts were compiled by organizing assemblies of the entire castes in question.

Elphinstone's model differed significantly from Bengal, where the colonial juridical administration of disputes between the natives was the oldest. Lord Hastings and William Jones assumed that Indian subjects already possessed their law of marriage, inheritance and other practical custom in their religious texts. As a result, under Lord Hastings's direction, a digest of indigenous laws for Hindus based on the *Dharmashastra* or Sanskrit religious texts and a detailed code of Muhammadan laws based on Persian-Arabic texts were compiled in the last quarter of the eighteenth century. Elphinstone, however, was not convinced about the overarching application of the *Dharmashastra*. 'What we call Hindu law,' he wrote, 'applies to Brahmins only, each caste has separate laws and customs.'[8] Caste rules compiled and made effective as customary laws under Elphinstone gradually lost their legal significance. After the 1857 Rebellion, under the Crown's imperial rule, the Bengal model was applied throughout India and the Bengal premise that all castes and groups possessed either unified Hindu or Muslim law was accepted. Nevertheless, the approach of compiling caste rules and their application made a deep impact on caste governance in Gujarat. Most of the upper castes in Gujarat, and their subcastes, published their 'caste constitution' in the latter half of the nineteenth century and even today many 'backward' castes, including Dalits and Adivasi groups, publish their caste constitutions with periodic amendments.

Following the example set in Madras by its governor Sir Thomas Munro, Elphinstone opened the door to the employment of Indians in judicial and revenue works of Bombay Presidency. The first generation of munsifs and mamlatdars—lower civil judges and revenue officers—was inducted into the British administration in Gujarat in the second quarter of the nineteenth century. Almost every one of them was from the Hindu higher castes and Parsi community. Among Hindu castes, Nagar Brahmins, Kayasthas and Vaniyas got selected because of their knowledge of Persian and their family tradition in administration. During Lord Bentinck's time, positions of sadr amin and munsif were given wider powers, a new and higher post of principal sadr amin was created and the salaries of all offices were raised. In the executive branch, Indians were placed as deputy collector and by mid-century they were made eligible for the post of deputy magistrate where they obtained limited criminal jurisdiction for the first time.

This early generation of 'native' officers enjoyed great prestige among the local population and it was through them that British rule and western values penetrated the cities and towns of Gujarat. A few of these officers emerged as pioneers of the social reform movement. Bholanath Sarabhai, who belonged to Nagar family of Persian scholars is a fine example. The first to join the British judiciary as munsif in 1844, he rose to the post of principal sadr amin and finally retired as first class subordinate judge. By establishing the Dharma Sabha and later the Prarthana Samaj, he challenged the religious orthodoxy of his time and also contributed significantly to the advancement of women's education. It is not surprising therefore that the first two women graduates of Gujarat, Vidyaben Nilkanth and Sharadaben Mehta, were his granddaughters.

INTRODUCTION OF MODERN EDUCATION
In the spread of western ideas and values, a pivotal role was played by the colonial education system initiated by Elphinstone in Bombay Presidency. Among all the presidencies of the time, Bombay was probably the most backward in the field of new education. Elphinstone called a public meeting in 1820 and a 'society for the promotion of the education of the poor' was formed. He obtained a grant of 5000 pounds for this society for printing textbooks and purchasing prizes. For the spread of general education Elphinstone proposed to improve and increase the native schools; to supply them with schoolbooks; to

encourage the lower classes to obtain education; to establish new schools for the teaching of European sciences; to prepare books of moral and physical science in the vernaculars; to establish new schools for teaching English; and to hold forth encouragement to the people. To conciliate the directors of the East India Company Elphinstone pointed out that the cost of the school to the Company would be small and would be largely borne by villages. Nevertheless, his scheme did not receive sanction before he left India.[9]

In 1823, with meagre funds at his command, Elphinstone established a new agency called 'Bombay Native School Book and School Society' which opened primary schools and prepared the first textbooks in Gujarati and Marathi languages in the presidency. By 1826 the first ten schools were established in Gujarat: three in Surat, two each in Ahmedabad and Bharuch and one each in Kheda, Nadiad and Dholka. Over the next twenty-five years the spread of education was sluggish and uneven. There were forty Gujarati schools in the British area with less than 3000 students and in the princely states, excluding Baroda state, not more than four schools were opened.[10] Most of Kathiawad and Kutch and rural Gujarat remained untouched by colonial education till the middle of the century. Traditional indigenous schools continued to impart elementary education throughout Gujarat and a survey conducted by Bombay government in 1842 in the three districts of Surat, Ahmedabad and Kheda revealed that almost 70,000 children received elementary education from traditional teachers. Gradually, these Gamthi Shala or traditional schools lost their importance and by the end of the nineteenth century the few remaining schools were struggling to survive.

English-medium education received a powerful stimulus in India after the triumph of 'Anglicists' over 'Orientalists' in 1835. For Lord Macaulay, who was not only the new law member but also president of the Committee of Public Instruction, 'a single shelf of a good European library was worth the whole native literature of India and Arabia'. The new education policy initiated by him and approved by Governor General Lord

Bentinck did not find favour with the administrators of Bombay Presidency, who followed Elphinstone's policy of spreading education through local languages. For them the medium of instruction was the basic issue and not the 'promotion of European literature and science' as suggested by Lord Bentinck. Like James Mill, they believed that general enlightenment could be brought about more quickly and efficiently by the translation of European books into local languages. But both Bentinck and Macaulay were convinced that the vernaculars were too poorly developed to become the vehicle of liberal education.

Colonel Jervis, head of the Bombay Board of Education, had been associated with educational work since Elphinstone's time and in his Minute of 1847 he pointed out that unless vernacular education was given greater encouragement the fruits of education would be restricted to 'a number of scribes and inferior agents for public and private offices and a few enlightened individuals isolated by their very superiority from their fellow countrymen'. The governor of Bombay endorsed Colonel Jervis's position in a letter to the Board of Education. Thus the opposition of the Bombay government to English-medium education resulted in the very slow expansion of English schools in the presidency. The first government English school in Gujarat was established in 1842 in Surat, and Ahmedabad had to wait for another four years to have an English school. Even in 1856, twenty years after Bentinck's new education policy, there were only eight English schools in Gujarat with less than 900 students.[11]

English education received a boost when the famous Education Dispatch of Sir Charles Wood was sent out in 1854. After this a new, comprehensive system of education, from primary level to university, was established in all the three presidencies. This dispatch envisaged an educational system built in collaboration with private organizations and financed by a system of grants-in-aid. A 'payment by result' system was introduced in Bombay Presidency and grants were paid out on the basis of students' success in examinations. Within ten years of Sir Charles Wood's dispatch, about 35,000 students, including about 2000 girls, were receiving primary education in British areas and princely states of Gujarat. Predictably, almost 70 per cent of these students belonged to the Brahmin or Vaniya castes, other Hindu castes formed about 20 per cent, and Muslims accounted for almost 6 per cent.[12]*

IMPACT OF MODERN EDUCATION

Statistics of schools and students may not illuminate the changing contours of sociocultural life in Gujarat but within twenty years of the introduction of colonial education in Surat the conflict between old and new world views started taking various forms. Durgaram, a Nagar Brahmin who was the first teacher in the newly established Gujarati schools, started teaching geography and astronomy according to the modern understanding of these disciplines while his colleague Pranshankar, another Brahmin teacher, continued to teach Puranic geography and astronomy. Even after undergoing a special ten-month training at Bombay in 1837, Pranshankar continued to instruct his students that 'the earth never moves around the sun' but that they should answer otherwise in order to pass their examinations.[13]

Durgaram went a step further: he began to challenge Brahminic rituals and practices and advocated widow remarriage. In 1844, along with Dadoba Pandurang, headmaster of the first English school, he formed an association called Manav Dharmasabha in Surat and a new chapter began in the cultural history of not only that city but Gujarat as a whole. Members of the association discussed social, religious and cultural issues in their weekly meetings and vigorously propagated the idea of unity and equality of all human beings. The caste system and untouchability were condemned by all the founding members of the

Durgaram

sabha, who became famous as the 'Five Daddas' as their names started with the letter 'd'. When Durgaram issued an open challenge to the practitioners of mantra, tantra and jadoo (chants, spells and magic) the entire city was electrified. For five weekends, thousands of people assembled to witness the contest but no tantric could prove his point.

In August 1844 the authorities raised the duty on salt from 8 annas to one rupee per *maund* and the agitated people of Surat responded with a general strike. Not a single shop was opened and Durgaram wrote in his daftar—register of the sabha:

> On the first day thirty thousand Hindus marched to the office of the magistrate and some sepoys and civilians were injured in the melee. On the second day, Muslims also joined and all of them marched towards the fort where some of them even threw stones. On the third day similar protests continued peacefully and the English judge and Collector called a meeting of the city leaders for consultation and withdrew the increase in duty.

On the fourth day, there was a heated debate on the entire episode at a meeting of the sabha. Some of the members preferred petitioning to agitation and strike. Summing up the debate, Durgaram made this historic statement:

> It is proper for the people to petition the king, but only when the king seeks the opinion of the people before taking action. But if the king does not follow this and instead oppresses his subjects, then the people should fight the king and punish him and hand over the kingdom to another king. A good human being is one who supports such a process. One should not worry about dying for such a cause because the protection of one's fellowmen is a great good in itself. Please listen! A king must rule in the best interests of his people, he must empathize with his people. But instead of doing this if he oppresses people, pauperizes them and favours the subjects in one area so

that they may become wealthy at the expense and pauperization of subjects in another area, the people must rise against such a king and the kingdom must be handed over to another king who follows the path of righteousness. This does not apply only to the English but to all the kings on earth. Till today, we have seen a number of tyrannical kings both in the world and in our own country. All such kings have been ousted by their subjects. So a petition to the king is appropriate when one is oppressed by one's fellowmen but if the king himself oppresses his people, then the people, praying to the almighty for guidance, must resist him with their collective strength.[14]

Such a radical and bold statement, where the primacy of people is asserted in unequivocal terms, was scarcely repeated in the next fifty years in Gujarat. Even Mahipatram, a biographer and student of Durgaram from whose account these lines have been excerpted, and who himself was a leading social reformer, commented thirty-four years later, 'Durgaram would have been sent to the Andamans if he had made such a statement today.'

While Durgaram attacked the old order and simultaneously challenged the new order when it turned oppressive, Dadabhai Naoroji, sixteen years his junior, was studying mathematics, chemistry, philosophy and political economy from European professors at the Elphinstone Institute in Bombay. After a few years he was appointed assistant teacher at the same institute and, along with other teachers and students, he formed the Students' Literary and Scientific Society in 1848, which initiated a new discourse in western India. An important rule of the society was that political and religious subjects would not form part of the discussions and the most important objectives were social reform and spread of knowledge. The medium of discussion at the society was English but Gujarati and Marathi branches of Gnan Prasarak Mandali (Society for the Diffusion of Knowledge) were formed to spread awareness and knowledge among common people. Dadabhai took the lead in the Gujarati mandali and edited its Gujarati periodical, *Gnan Prasarak*.

To translate their ideas into action, the leading members of the society decided to open schools for girls. Within two months forty-four Parsi girls and twenty-four Hindu girls were enrolled in seven schools started by the society. Compared to Hindus, both Gujarati and Marathi, the Parsi community extended greater financial support and encouragement to girls' education. By 1855, 740 girls attended nine schools run by the society: 475 were Parsi, 178 were Marathi Hindu and only eighty-seven were Gujarati Hindu.[15] As Gujarati was their mother tongue, both Parsi and Hindu Gujarati Elphinstonians were active members of the society and the Gujarati Gnan Prasarak Mandali. However by 1851 differences arose between them, and the Hindu members formed a separate association called the Buddhivardhak Hindu Sabha. The first pamphlet published by this new sabha was on women's education. The attitude of the community was revealed by the first secretary of the sabha, Mohandas Ranchhoddas, when he wrote in an autobiographical piece, 'Among Gujarati Hindus, the section opposing women's education was very powerful and to convince them the subject was discussed again and again.'[16]

Printing had already been introduced in 1812 by a Parsi named Fardunji Marzbanji. The first Gujarati newspaper, *Mumbai Samachar*, was started by him in 1822 and is today the oldest surviving daily in India. In early 1857 Parsi social reformers of Bombay took the lead in establishing the first women's magazine in

Cover of *Streebodh*, March 1972

Gujarati, *Streebodh*. Although, for the first two years, the editors were eminent Parsis like Behramji Gandhi and Sorabjee Bengallee, Hindu social reformers later contributed to its development.[17] For the next five decades, the magazine made a vital contribution to Parsi and elite Hindu women's education and empowerment.

Three Elphinstonians, all members of Buddhivardhak Sabha, Narmadashankar Lalshankar, popularly known as Narmad (1833–86), Mahipatram Rupram (1830–91) and Karsandas Mulji (1832–71), came to the fore as catalysts of the new era. In the early 1850s in Bombay they received European knowledge

Narmad

and values from their British teachers and inspiration for socio-religious reforms from their Indian teachers. They perceived themselves as patriots and apostles of a new era. For them the spread of new education and technology, changes in age-old socio-religious practices and development of Gujarati language were significant dimensions of *swadeshabhiman* (pride in one's own country), a word coined by Narmad. While two of them, Narmad and Mahipatram, were Nagar Brahmins from Surat, Karsandas was a Kapol Vaniya from Bombay. Their strong advocacy for widow remarriage invited the wrath of their families and communities. Twenty-one-year-old Karsandas and his wife were thrown out of the home by his aunt. Narmad was expelled from his caste when he married a widow in the next decade.

The year 1860 turned out to be milestone for all of them when Mahipatram left for England for further studies, leaving behind a storm of protest from the Nagar community. Narmad entered into a public debate with the Vaishnav acharya Jadunathji on the issue of widow remarriage and Karsandas wrote an acidic article attacking the misdeeds of Vaishnav acharyas. Sea voyage or foreign travel was taboo for the Gujarati upper castes, and Brahmin and Vaniya caste councils were most sensitive on this issue. As a result, Mahipatram was expelled from the Nagar caste. When his father died two years later, not a single Brahmin in the city of Surat was ready to perform the last rites. This forced him to submit to caste diktats and observe prayashchit for re-entry into the caste. Mahipatram's submission to caste decrees was severely criticized by the social reformers of his time and even his old friend Narmad ridiculed him publicly. Reacting to the criticism, Mahipatram wrote an article declaring that his conviction about foreign travel had not changed. He was expelled again and, after four years of struggling against Brahmin orthodoxy, he was forced to yield for the second time. The caste council gave him limited re-entry after he observed prayashchit for the second time. Foreign travel remained a contentious issue for many more years and, thirty years after Mahipatram, even Gandhi was forced to observe prayashchit by his Vaniya caste.

Karsandas Mulji joined the Buddhivardhak Sabha with an essay on *deshatan* or the needs for foreign travel and its benefits. He advanced a number of arguments in support of foreign travel but his most striking argument was his suggestion that the large-scale import of machine-made goods had ruined Indian artisans and therefore the younger generation should visit foreign countries to learn new techniques. In 1853 the sabha published this essay as its second booklet and Karsandas became a welcome addition to the young Bombay circle dedicated to sociocultural reform. For the next two years he contributed regularly to *Rast Goftar* (Herald of Truth), a Gujarati newspaper started by Dadabhai, and in 1855 he founded his own weekly Gujarati newspaper, *Satyaprakash* (Light of Truth), where he attacked Hindu upper-caste rituals, customs and practices. Like most of his contemporaries, Karsandas directly addressed caste leaders in his articles, whether it was the issue of girls' education or social practices such as excessive expenditure and display of wealth during wedding celebrations, singing of obscene songs at marriages and ritual beating of chest at funerals. Infuriated, the leaders of Karsandas's Kapol Vaniya caste initiated steps to debar him but they could not muster enough support from the community.

What precipitated the crisis was an article by Karsandas in *Satyaprakash* of October 1860, where he criticized Vaishnav acharyas, popularly known as Vaishnav Maharaj, for their licentious and immoral behaviour. He specifically named Jadunath Maharaj of Surat, who was then camping at Bombay, as the one who should put a stop to such practices. Jadunath charged Karsandas and Rustomji Ranina, the publisher of *Satyaprakash*, with libel and this became famous as the Maharaj Libel Case. Almost all social reformers, Hindu and Parsi, Gujarati and Maharashtrian, openly supported Karsandas and Ranina. Elphinstonians and some rich Gujarati merchants and traders too joined the reformers' camp. However, the opposite camp was very powerful. Vaishnav Maharajs enjoyed great prestige and exercised power over their Kapol Vaniya and Bhatia followers, who came out in defence of their gurus. Both these communities dominated a number of commercial activities in western India, and they controlled many important Mahajans in Bombay. The relationship between Sampraday, Panch and Mahajan—in this case the Vallabhacharya Vaishnav sect, the caste council of Vaniyas and Bhatias, and the trade councils—was intricate and all of them derived authority from each other. With the support of Kapol Vaniya and Bhatia caste councils and the trade councils dominated by them, Jadunath Maharaj put enormous pressure on his followers during the trial. After many twists and turns in the case, Karsandas was vindicated. Although this case raised a number of ethical and legal issues, for the newspaper-reading public of the period the spotlight was on the immoral lifestyle of the maharaj and it became a sensational case throughout India. The verdict was hailed as a victory for the reformists and thirty-year-old Karsandas was acknowledged as a hero in India and England. For the Vallabhacharya sect, caste councils and trade councils, it set into motion a downturn in their power and prestige.

In 1862 Karsandas went to England as the representative of a Vaniya merchant. On his return after seven months he wrote his famous travelogue, *Englandman Musafari* (Travels in England), where he described various facets of British life. His caste council, already perturbed by the libel case, expelled him and asked other Vaniya castes to expel those friends of Karsandas who dared to continue social interaction with him. Fearing caste authorities, most of his friends declined to have any social ties with him. Even the leading members of Buddhivardhak Sabha who had earlier organized a send-off party for Karsandas declined to dine with him. Narmad wrote a long poem on this turn of events and asked, 'Has the Buddhivardhak Sabha gone into hiding?' Only two friends, both leading Vaniya merchants, stuck to their principles and continued social interaction with Karsandas. One of them was a Nagar Vaniya and, when his caste council failed to expel him from the caste, the Mahajan expelled the entire Nagar Vaniya caste from the membership of the Mahajan.[18] Karsandas refused to bow down to caste dictates and remained debarred from his caste till his death in 1871, at the age of thirty-nine.

The most famous among the young Elphinstonians was the poet Narmad. With his vivacious personality, he became a legend in his lifetime. Celebrated as a pioneer of modern Gujarati literature, he started writing poetry in 1855 and within three years he became a celebrity among the Gujarati-speaking elite of Bombay, Hindu as well as Parsi. In his autobiography, the first one in the Gujarati language, he says, 'From the year 1859 I became free from religious superstition [and] turned into a cultural reformist.'[19] Because of his skilful articulation in prose and verse, he led the reformist group for the next ten years.

In that critical year of 1860, Narmad distributed handbills where he openly challenged Jadunath Maharaj to a public debate on the issue of widow remarriage. He asserted that the Hindu shastras approved of widow remarriage. Jadunath agreed to a public debate but on the appointed day not a single reformist accompanied Narmad to face the hostile crowd of followers of the maharaj. Only his close friend Karsandas Bawa, a wrestler, went with him. During the debate, instead of discussing the main issue, the maharaj asked him a direct question about whether or not the scriptures were inspired by God. The discussion that followed revolved around the divine origin of the scriptures, while the issue of widow remarriage, which had prompted the debate, remained unsettled. The episode left Narmad bitter, as not one of his reformist friends had even accompanied him to the debate. Nevertheless, he continued his crusade, first from Bombay and then from Surat but his disenchantment with the reformers as well as with the idea of reform intensified over the years. In the late 1860s, more than his words, his actions alarmed the upper caste of Surat. First he gave shelter to a widow and later, even while his first wife was alive, he married Narmadagauri, a widow belonging to his own caste. Narmadagauri's parents filed a case of kidnapping against Narmad but, with the support of eminent lawyers of Surat and Bombay, he fought the case successfully. No wonder a number of popular songs were composed about this marriage at the time!

In the midst of this controversy, Narmad gave the final touches to his *Narmakosh*, the first systematic Gujarati lexicon, modelled on the Webster dictionary. He prefaced this dictionary with an invocatory poem, '*Jai Jai Garvi Gujarat*', which came to acquire the status of an anthem. In this visualization of Gujarat he included mainland Gujarat as well as Saurashtra and the invocation of a proud Gujarat inspired the following generations. During this period, Narmad focussed on the study of history, trying to compare various civilizations, ancient and modern, and published his *Rajyarang* in two volumes. In the preface, he underlined the word 'rajya' and said:

The etymology of the word 'rajya' suggests that it is derived from the root raj, 'to illuminate' and thus rajya, state, refers to a luminous association of people [janamandal] which respects authority or authority which illuminates the janamandal . . . Religion wields authority over the people of some regions; in others, religion and force are both employed and in still other regions, only force wields authority.

. . .

Many states flourished and declined—how they were established, how they flowered and why they declined—and how new states took their place, shone and disappeared—Rajyarang offers glimpses of these transformations. I have presented this spectrum of transformation so that at least an impression of these changing colours remains constantly in our memory.[20]

Narmad's comprehensive history of civilizations spanning 5000 years was a landmark. With all the limitations posed by the fact that he wrote from existing material available in English, *Rajyarang* presented a philosophy of history and time. In the closing lines of the book he drew on the Hindu concept of *mahakaal* and suggested that it appears in the forms of dharma, artha and kama. He denounced reformists and reform as well as the 'European' world view for the last ten years of his life and became an ardent believer of Vedic religion. This U-turn left a deep mark on the intellectual life of Gujarat in the last quarter of the nineteenth century. In this period of intense intellectual churning a junior contemporary of Narmad's, Govardhanram Tripathi (1855–1907), put forward his idea of the synthesis between East and West, conservatives and reformists, through his epic Gujarati novel, *Saraswatichandra*. The debate continued as university-educated Gujaratis were divided into three streams of thought: reformers, conservatives and those who believed in a synthesis of the two.

SOCIAL REFORM IN AHMEDABAD
Parallel to the social reform movement in Bombay, another movement inspired by British officers was initiated in

Ahmedabad in the mid eighteenth century. Prominent among the reform-minded officers was Alexander Forbes, who came to the city in 1846 as assistant judge. Within two years he established the Gujarat Vernacular Society (GVS), an association for the 'promotion of Gujarati language and literature, diffusion of useful knowledge and growth of general education'. To translate these ideas into action he chalked out a programme including the publication of a newspaper, establishment of a library, compilation of a Gujarati dictionary, collection of manuscripts and setting up schools for boys and girls.

For Forbes the work of establishing the GVS and activities conducted by it was a 'religious duty'. In the first annual report of the GVS he wrote:

> We are under a religious obligation not only to do the work for which we are responsible to human masters and which for the most part they alone can turn to the good of the country; but (beyond that) to employ ourselves and our faculties and means in some measure (what measure is a question left to every man's own decision, but in some measure) to the benefit of India and the glory of our Lord Jesus Christ therein.
>
> Now we acknowledge this at Ahmedabad by some social enterprises in which many are partners together. When we contribute to a Christian Mission we acknowledge the call. When we try to lift up the language of the province from its present ignoble condition and encourage the more gifted fancies among those to whom it is vernacular, to enlarge, refine and regulate it by manifold application, that it may become fitter to convey from mind to mind and from generation to generation both the beautiful and the true, then too we acknowledge the same call to benefit those among whom for the present we are sojourners.[21]

Within a year of its establishment, the GVS published the first newspaper of Gujarat, the weekly *Vartmaan*. Since it was published every Wednesday, the weekly was popularly known as *Budhvaaryu* (the Gujarati equivalent of that day). The city elite found this first taste of public expression bitter; Nagarsheth Himabhai regarded the publication as one that 'generated disunity and conflict'.[22] The first 'native' library of the city was established soon thereafter. It was the second library to be set up in Gujarat; the first one had been founded in Surat a decade earlier. Another historic development was the first girls' school, with twenty girls, started by the GVS in 1849. The following year, Harkunvar Shethani, the widow of Nagarsheth Kesarisinh Hutheesinh, donated money for the school and accepted full financial responsibility for its further development. Inspired by the success of the girls' school, another rich merchant, Sheth Maganlal, donated funds to start two other girls' schools in the next year. Just as in Bombay, access to education for girls opened up new vistas for Gujarati women. For the first few years the number of girls in these three schools was limited; in 1855 barely 275 girls received primary education in Ahmedabad.

After serving the city for four years, Forbes was transferred to Surat. By then, the GVS had set up new institutions through which it implemented its agenda for reform. Forbes left behind a Gujarati friend who not only developed all these institutions but also nurtured Gujarat with his creative genius. This friend of Forbes was the poet Dalpatram. Forbes had planned to write a history of Gujarat modelled on Colonel Tod's *Annals of Rajasthan*. He needed someone to assist him in his study of written and oral Gujarati sources and Bholanath Sarabhai suggested the name of Dalpatram, an upcoming poet who was well versed in Gujarati, Sanskrit and Vrajbhasha. On receiving Forbes's invitation, Dalpatram walked about 130 kilometres from his native Wadhwan to Ahmedabad. Dalpatram preferred to compose in Vrajbhasha but Forbes encouraged him to use Gujarati instead and the friendship between them enriched Gujarat and Gujarati literature.[23]

Though Dalpatram was deeply rooted in the culture and religion of his soil, with his discerning eye and sharp mind he was able to perceive the change in the times and the arrival of a new order. Working with Forbes and studying historical material with him helped him develop a keener sense of history. In spite of not having any formal education in the English school system or in the English language, he could grasp the critical importance of Western education and Western science and technology in shaping the future of both Gujarat and India. Being a poet, his first love was his language, Gujarati, and, conscious of its predicament as a language of the bazaar, he took on the challenge of transforming it into a language of knowledge and adorning it with grace and beauty. Unlike Narmad, he was not directly exposed to Western literature but close interaction with Forbes gave him some idea about different genres of English literature as well as the varied themes explored by Western writers. Till 1849 Dalpatram expressed himself in verse but wrote his first essay to enter a competition sponsored by the GVS. This essay was the prize-winning *Bhootnibandh* on the topic of superstitions about ghosts and witchcraft, which Forbes translated into English. Inspired by his success, Dalpatram continued to write both prose and verse. A year later, he wrote the first play in Gujarati literature, *Lakshmi Natak*, which was an adaptation of the Greek play *Plutus* by Aristophanes. Forbes had described the storyline of the original play and Dalpatram replaced the Greek god of wealth with Lakshmi, the Hindu goddess of wealth, and for the dialogue style drew heavily from the Bhavai folk tradition of Gujarat. In 1851 he wrote *Gnyatinibandh*, an essay on caste. Given the times he was writing in, Dalpatram's treatment of the subject was revolutionary. Underlining the basic unity and equality of mankind in the introductory prayer, he pointed out that caste was a social arrangement and not divine in nature. Discussing the Vedic conception of the origin of the four varnas, he suggested that God created four types of human beings with four different attributes and not four varnas per se and asserted that the story of the origin of the Brahmins from the head and Shudras from the foot of the supreme being was nothing more than poetic imagination! To contest, even mildly, the divine origin of the Vedas in those days required not only firm conviction but also great courage.

From 1855 onwards Dalpatram became the driving force behind the GVS and its monthly, *Buddhiprakash*, and through both the institution and its publication he gave direction to Gujarati literature and public life for the next twenty-five years. When Mahipatram left for England Dalpatram wrote a booklet endorsing the voyage and strongly advised Brahmin and Vaniya castes to transcend religious dogma regarding foreign travel. In *Vencharitra*, a fourteen-act play in verse, based on the story of the Bhagwat, he communicated a clear message supporting widow remarriage and rejecting child marriage. He retired from the GVS at the age of fifty-eight because of ill-health. The next year he published a collection of his poems, *Dalpatkavya*, and secured forever the title of 'Kavishwar' in Gujarati literature.

Dalpatram in Ahmedabad and Narmad in Bombay and Surat represent a prototype where commitment to literature, education and social reform fuse within one persona. Mahipatram, Karsandas and others were also similar except that they tended to concentrate their attention on one or the other of these facets. In the third quarter of the nineteenth century, all of them worked relentlessly towards social reform and the refinement of the Gujarati language and in this they received the support of the British rulers. As a result, most of them regarded British rule as divine dispensation. Though their area of influence was limited to the upper sections of society, each one of them emphasized the unity of Gujarat, where Hindus, Muslims and Parsis enjoyed equal status. Significantly, the voice of rural Gujarat or an articulation of the problems of the poor is scarcely found in the writings of this first generation of British-educated intellectuals. Narmad's realization of the limits of social reform is expressed in his autobiography, where he described his visit in the mid 1860s to Chanod-Karnali, two minor tirthas on the bank of the river Narmada in Bharuch district:

There is nothing like a reform movement in these villages. The word 'reform' has spread far and wide but has not reached these villages . . . The reformists in Bombay are shouting but it is mere lip service. I thought that I should write an essay outlining a Reform Mission and then youngsters representing this Mission would reach every village and propagate good ideas. Some reformists think that reform is limited to changing traditional dining and clothing habits. They feel ashamed to mingle with the poor and illiterate. They do not travel out into the districts. What is the use of their tall talk?[24]

Unlike Narmad, Dalpatram visited rural areas frequently when he accompanied Forbes to collect old texts and gather folk literature. Despite this, the voice of the oppressed sections is missing except for a powerful condemnation of *veth* (forced labour) perpetuated by the bureaucracy of the Raj.

IMPACT OF A NEW LAND REVENUE SYSTEM

It was through the land revenue system, evolved from the time of Elphinstone, that the Raj penetrated deep into rural Gujarat. Before the governorship of Elphinstone, posts of patel (village headman) and talati (village accountant) created by the Raj had already disturbed the local power structure and was vehemently opposed by hereditary revenue officers. Farming of revenue collection was an integral part of the political system, first under the Mughals and from the mid eighteenth century, under the Marathas. The Maratha rulers appointed a *kumavisdar*, generally from among the Maratha sardars, at the zilla or district level, with a fixed amount of revenue. In turn he appointed desais and amins at mahal or block level, who raised revenue and collected various taxes with the assistance of *mazumdars* or revenue accountants. Since power and prestige was derived primarily from land, all the hereditary officers, desai, amin and mazumdar, enjoyed high social status. The appointment of patels and transfer of police authority to them and the appointment of talatis directly accountable to the English collector reduced the authority and affected the position of this powerful section of society.

Like Thomas Munro in Madras, Elphinstone rejected the zamindari land settlement and opted instead for the ryotwari settlement. He saw the number of small peasant proprietors in the Deccan and recognized their importance as a source of rural stability. He established the ryotwari system after a proper survey to establish what each ryot or peasant proprietor should pay to the state. Further, he wanted that the state should realize this payment from each village headman. In 1823, in his Revenue Letter to the Court of Directors, he said, 'The Survey will fix the rights and the payment of each ryot, after which the village may be farmed for a certain number of years to Patil.' Elphinstone thus tried to combine the principle of the ryotwari system with his notion of a village system where the village council and its Patil or Patel maintained peace and stability. But such a combination was contrary to the spirit of the Company's rule. The Company wanted to deal individually with each land tax payer and levy as much tax as he could pay. The Company did not favour collecting land tax through village headmen and, consequently, the ryotwari system was implemented without any additional feature recognizing the village council.

The Survey Settlement recommended by Elphinstone was put into effect by Pringle, an officer of the Bombay Civil Service from 1824 to 1828. The survey took the Company's officers to every village of the Company's territory in Gujarat. The settlements were conducted on unrealistic and exaggerated estimates of the produce of the soil and, as the Bombay Administrative Report of 1872-73 itself admitted, it led to disastrous results:

His [Pringle's] assessment was based on a measurement of fields, and an estimate of the yield of various soils, as well as the cost of cultivation; the principle adopted being to fix the Government demand at 55 per cent of the net produce . . . The preliminary work of measurement was grossly faulty, and the estimates of produce which formed such an important element in the determination of the assessment, and which had been prepared in the most elaborate manner, were so erroneous as to be worse than useless. But meanwhile the settlement had been introduced, and with the result of aggravating the evils it had been designed to remove. From the outset it was impossible to collect anything approaching to the full revenue. In some district not one half could be realised. Things now went rapidly from bad to worse. Every year brought its addition to the accumulated arrears of revenue, and the necessity for remission or modification of rates . . . Every effort, lawful and unlawful, was made to get the utmost out of the wretched peasantry, who were subjected to torture, in some instances, cruel and revolting beyond all description, if they would not or could not yield what was demanded. Numbers abandoned their homes, and fled into the neighbouring Native States. Large tracts of land were thrown out of cultivation, and in some Districts no more than a third of the cultivable area remained in occupation.[25]

Pringle's system was abandoned in 1835 and a re-survey was initiated. The first Regular Settlement was carried out the next year and the process continued for many years. In 1847 a Joint Report was finalized, which formed the basis for the Bombay Land Revenue System. Romesh Dutt summarized the main features of the system:

It recognised the transferable and heritable right of the cultivator to his field . . . It also made an elaborate scale for the distribution of the District revenue demand among a million of fields contained in the District but it prescribed no limit to the demand . . . The Company retained the power to shape the demand, to vary it, to increase it, at each recurring settlement, according to condition of the people. No system could be devised by human ingenuity better calculated to keep an agricultural nation permanently poor and resourceless than the system which left to revenue officials the absolute and unrestricted power to increase the revenue demand at each recurring settlement. The cultivator had no voice in the settlement of the land tax; he was not consulted in fixing the tax; he was called upon after the demand was settled to pay it or quit his ancestral land and starve.[26]

The Company directors and Elphinstone wanted to abolish revenue farming but in the *mehwasi* or turbulent areas of Gujarat it was difficult to follow the revenue system of *rasti* or peaceful areas. The political circumstances of the times compelled the new rulers to recognize the existing agencies of revenue collection and village administration like Talukdars, Jagirdars, Bhagdars and Narwadars. The last two agencies were not overlords like Talukdars and Jagirdars; they were known as Manotidars, who extended surety for individual proprietors and villages in matters of land tax. Most of these agencies were recognized by Regulation XVII of 1827 and farming of revenues continued in at least 10 per cent of the area of Gujarat under Company Rule as well as Crown Rule. Yet, the power and prestige of these traditional authorities were greatly diminished in the new dispensation.

The word 'Talukdar' was coined by Company officers. Earlier, they were known as *Garasia* in Gujarat and historically they were identical with the ruling princely families of Saurashtra. With the exception of a few Muslims, they were Rajputs and Kolis or of mixed Rajput–Koli descent. During the early years of Company rule they were not included in the list of tributaries like the chiefs of Saurashtra and Kutch. As a result, they lost the prestige accorded to princely families. Furthermore, for the first few years, the Company collected annual payment from them but very soon the nature of payment was altered and instead of a tribute it was considered to be rent or revenue. This change resulted in a greater loss to Talukdars. In 1821 the rental was increased by 50 per cent. Subsequently, Elphinstone introduced annual leases and also fixed the payment at 70 per cent of the produce. This large share, which was expected without remission of any kind, barely admitted a livelihood to Talukdars. The decline of the status of Talukdars under Company rule was graphically described by a British officer called Reeves in 1862:

> We have thus seen the ancient chief, actual proprietor of his domain and once powerful enough to resist Mughal invasion of his rights, sword in hand, converted by British mismanagement founded on error, but not the less most unrighteous into an annual leaseholder or mere tenant-at-will of Government and reduced to extreme degradation.[27]

The Talukdars, known among contemporary Gujaratis as Thakors, resisted not only the higher land revenue demand of the Company but also the erosion of their kingly authority. In the 1830s many Thakors offered armed resistance to Company rule in north Gujarat. Some of them, including a queen of Amiliara, engaged in guerrilla warfare against the British army for years. The most stubborn resistance came from the tribals of eastern Gujarat such as Bhil Nayaks of Godhra, Chhota Udepur, Baria and Jambughoda, who revolted against the new rulers. It was only after getting military support from the Gaekwad and Scindia that the Company was able to re-establish its authority. The period between 1849 and 1857 was comparatively peaceful for the English but with the onset of the Great Revolt of 1857, a large number of Talukdars and Jagirdars in north, central and eastern Gujarat challenged the Raj, taking swords into their hands. Their kinsfolk, Rajputs and Kolis, also joined them. The Bhil Nayaks again rose in revolt against the 'Topiwalas' who were destroying their forests as well as their way of life.

THE GREAT REVOLT OF 1857

Bholanath Sarabhai wrote in his diary of 23 May 1857:

> Today I heard that a powerful mutiny has broken out in Delhi ... God willing, there will be peace soon. Everyone

is agonized by the news that the unfortunate English people, their innocent wives and children were killed by cruel people . . . Recently we have heard that the mutiny has spread to many places . . . Compared to other rule the British rule is far better and may God continue it for ever.[28] [ellipses in the original]

Bholanath was not the only member of the elite of his time who sided with the Raj and prayed for its continuation. In the aftermath of the Revolt, Narmad welcomed the Queen's Raj:

Victory! Victory! Victory to the Queen;
May your fame spread far and wide
Quick! Quick! Quick may your enemies flee
Now we sincerely pray
That rid of all obstacles,
May the Queen have a glorious reign[29]

Even more than the new elite literati, social reformers and educationists, it was the maharajas and rajas of Gujarat as well as prominent merchants who supported the British. The princely states extended military support while merchants actively helped the rulers in more ways than one. For instance, the Nagarsheth of Ahmedabad, Premabhai Himabhai, allowed the British to use his private mail network between Indore and Ahmedabad to gather intelligence for their military campaigns. He and other merchants jointly established a hospital for wounded soldiers in Ahmedabad. The Gaekwad, who was the most powerful among the maharajas of Gujarat, along with the rajas of Idar and Rajpipla, extended military support throughout the Revolt. Complimenting the Gaekwad, Colonel Richmond Shakespeare, the Political Agent in Gujarat at that time, said, 'If the Gaikwad had not helped the British government it would have been very difficult for the British government to hold Gujarat. It was entirely because of the support of Maharaja Khanderao of Baroda that the government was able to preserve peace in Gujarat.' For a long time an erroneous impression was created in Gujarat that the impact of the revolt was very limited and that the 'government was able to preserve peace'.

Compared to North India the uprising was limited to certain areas and no prominent king or queen revolted against the Raj, but it is little known that a large number of chieftains of smaller principalities of Mahi Kantha and Rewa Kantha as well as various arms-bearing communities in Gujarat challenged the Raj. The Thakors and Jagirdars of north and central Gujarat, the Kolis and Bhils of hilly regions and the Vaghers of coastal Saurashtra also rose in revolt. In fact the Bhil chieftains of eastern Gujarat continued their guerrilla warfare till early 1859 and the Vaghers of Dwaraka fought relentlessly for almost a decade. Written records about the resistance offered by the Kolis, Bhils and Vaghers are meagre and as evidence contained in oral traditions and those expressed in folklore have not been collected, our knowledge of what happened in 1857 in Gujarat is limited to information derived from British accounts and Baroda state records, which naturally do not emphasize the struggles of these communities.

In the British territory of Gujarat, Ahmedabad cantonment was the first to join the uprising. After receiving the news of the revolt by the Indore-Ratlam sepoys and cutting of the mail link to Ahmedabad by them in June 1857, the 7th regiment under the leadership of a subedar prepared a plan to capture the city first and then proceed towards Baroda. The plan misfired and General Roberts, the commanding officer, quietly disarmed the regiment and punished the subedar. In July the Gujarat Irregular Horse attempted to rise against the British, followed by the Grenadiers in September. Their efforts failed and their leaders, along with about twenty uniformed persons, were put to death.

In the latter half of 1857 a serious plan to uproot the British and dethrone the Gaekwad was drawn up by Bapu Gaekwad, half-brother of the ruling maharaja. For his anti-maharaja activities, Bapu Gaekwad was expelled from Baroda and he came to Ahmedabad. He received support for his plan from two leading merchants of Patan, Maganlal Shroff and

Nihalchand Jhaveri, and encouragement from Raja Bhonsle, a sardar of the Gaekwad. Although Bapu Gaekwad failed to muster support from Ahmedabad cantonment, his friends were able to collect an army of 2000 Kolis in north Gujarat and to persuade a few Jagirdars and village chiefs of central Gujarat to rebel. Their strategy was to first attack Baroda during Diwali on 16 October and, after overthrowing the maharaja, proceed towards Ahmedabad for the final assault. With the fall of Delhi on 20 September, a wave of despondency swept across Gujarat and a number of supporters started withdrawing from the struggle. As if this was not enough, someone leaked the plan to the maharaja on 10 October as he was celebrating the British victory with British officers in his palace. The combined army of the Gaekwad and the British swung into action and within no time all the rebel leaders were arrested. With the exception of Bapu Gaekwad and Raja Bhonsle, all the other leaders were tried. Three were blown from guns, three were hanged and the rest were sent to the penal colony at Andamans. Two villages on the banks of the river Mahi, Pratappur and Angadh, were burnt down for sheltering the rebels.

Earlier, in July, two cities on the eastern border of Gujarat, Dahod and Godhra, witnessed open revolt by Muslim Jagirdars and their small armies. For five days, Dahod remained under the control of the rebels and, with the support of defiant sepoys arriving from Indore, they attacked Godhra and captured government offices. Within a week the combined army of the British and Gaekwad overpowered them and the leaders were punished. In north-west Gujarat, around the southern tip of the Aravali, a number of Koli Talukdars revolted against the triumvirate of the British, Gaekwad and Raja of Idar. Together, these three forces burnt down two Koli villages towards the end of 1857. The Koli chieftains collected an army of 2000 Koli-Bhil soldiers and attacked Gaekwadi villages near present-day Gandhinagar. Adopting guerrilla tactics, they continued their resistance till the end of 1858. While Koli chiefs fought around the river Sabarmati, the Bhil chiefs challenged the British around the Mahi and Narmada rivers.[30]

In sum, unlike in North India, the events of 1857 in Gujarat were not a 'Sepoy Mutiny' except for the early stirrings by sepoys of Ahmedabad cantonment. It was a revolt sustained by Thakors, Jagirdars and Talukdars of north and central Gujarat with the support of arms-bearing communities such as Kolis, Bhils, Arabs and Pathans. Almost all the Talukdars of north and central Gujarat, numbering 140, were against the domination of the Gaekwad and the British and they participated in the revolt, directly or indirectly. Their main grievance was against the Inam Commission appointed by Lord Dalhousie, which was formed to take over land without 'proper' entitlement. The Talukdars viewed the commission as one more step to dispossess them of what was rightfully theirs. They were also aggrieved because the British sided with rajas and maharajas who were undermining their authority and traditional rights. Unnerved by their discontent, the British settled most of the claims of the Talukdars in their favour in the aftermath of the revolt.

Further west, in the region near Dwaraka known as Okhamandal, the Vaghers rose in revolt in 1858. They came to know about the events of 1857 through pilgrims and also heard rumours about the overthrow of the British Raj. All the clans of Vaghers assembled on 1 January 1858 and resolved to uproot British-Gaekwad rule from Okhamandal and the encounter, which was not less than a small war, took place near Dwaraka and Bet Dwarka. By July 1859 the Vaghers practically ruled the entire Okhamandal area and their leader, Jodha Manek, assumed the royal title and addressed letters to the rajas of Jamnagar and Porbandar asking them not to support the British and Gaekwad. Between September and October the British and Gaekwad carried out a large-scale anti-Vagher military operation by sea and land routes. Bet Dwarka was recaptured first and then Dwaraka and, during this operation, the British under the command of Colonel Donovan demolished some temples of Dwaraka and Bet Dwarka. They broke images, looted temple treasures, destroyed many houses and killed cows and other animals. Agitated by such barbarous acts, the rajas of Jamnagar, Porbandar and Kutch as well as the Mahajans of a number of cities of Kutch and Kathiawad lodged their protest before various British authorities.

The Vaishnav merchants of Bombay too joined the protest and their Mahajan decided to register their disapproval by not celebrating Diwali. The *Times of India*, published from Bombay, took note of this event in its issue of 26 October 1859:

> Sensation. The destruction and plunder of the idols and temples of the Hindoos by the British force while engaged in storming the fort of Beyt, seems to have produced the utmost sensation in the minds of the Hindoo community. Their feelings have been so greatly hurt by the excesses of the British soldiers at Beyt, that they have resolved to pass these Dewali holidays in mourning as it were. Not only that, but a great majority of them are trying every means in their power to dissuade the other communities, such as the Parsee and the Borah, from lighting as usual their shops and establishments.[31]

The merchants demanded the restoration of temples and images and return of looted temple treasures. The British Political Agent of Kathiawad also made a representation to the Bombay government and ultimately the matter was taken up at the highest level at Calcutta. Only on the promise of restoration of temples and return of properties did the issue subside.[32] Under the leadership of Jodha Manek, the Vaghers continued their resistance from the Gir forest and after his death his nephew Mulu Manek led the fight till 1868. The heroic struggle of both these Vagher leaders was celebrated in a number of folksongs composed during their lifetime.

Gujarat witnessed greater commotion when people were disarmed in early 1858. The government of Bombay ordered that people be disarmed in the princely states as well as in British territory. In most of north and central Gujarat, Thakors and Jagirdars vehemently opposed the move in the beginning but finally submitted. In many villages British officers used brute force and, to terrorize people, burnt down entire villages. Four villages in north Gujarat—Kanaria, Dubar, Anodia and Agdol—which were just 50 or 60 kilometres from Ahmedabad, were burnt to ashes. Villages Pal in Panchmahal and Khanpur near Anand were also destroyed. The lone voice against this brutal policy was that of J.P. Willoughby, former Political Agent of Kathiawad who later became member of the British Parliament. He severely criticized the government of Bombay and authorities in Gujarat for burning villages like outlaws and punishing the innocent with the guilty.[33]

For a long time the legends of Nana Sahib Peshwa, Tatiya Tope and Maulvi Liaquat Ali, three eminent leaders of the revolt, reverberated in Gujarat in different forms. It was believed that the three of them spent their last days in Gujarat: Nana Sahib as Swami Dayanand in Sihor near Bhavnagar, Tatiya Tope as Taheldas in Navsari and Maulvi Liaquat Ali, before his arrest and deportation to Andaman, in Sachin near Surat. The circulation of these legends, chiefly the ones about Nana Sahib, continued even after Independence and popular Gujarati magazines and research journals published articles offering 'evidence' regarding the final years of the life of the last Peshwa.

The Kolis, Bhils and Vaghers paid a huge price for their resistance to British rule. They were not only defeated in battle and punished for having dared to resist but, in the aftermath, these communities were marginalized by the rest of society as outlaws. Being arms-bearing communities, they too were disarmed in early 1858 and also forced to practise agriculture. A majority of them were unable to adapt to the lifestyle and norms of settled agriculture and were forced to give way to agriculturalist communities like Kanbi or Patidar in the latter half of the nineteenth century. Their predicament was intensified in the early years of the twentieth century when these communities were classified as 'criminal tribes' and further stigmatized. This marginalization and stigma has continued to this day and is the reason for their peripheral status as 'backward' communities and for their being invisible in mainstream Gujarat even today.

Thus, the coming of the British transformed the polity of Gujarat, altering legal and administrative structures and agrarian relations. The British education system led to the questioning of traditional customs and practices and a new view of the past emerged as history began to be rewritten. But the impact of the new order on the everyday lives of common people of the region is reflected in this excerpt from a folksong sung by the fisherwomen of coastal Saurashtra, probably composed in the 1880s:

From far off lands came Lely[34]
And very enthusiastically
Took over our king's fort

He swept aside our measuring cups
And brought instead, his weighing scales
And took over our king's fort

He cast away our silver and brass coins
And brought instead his rupees
And took over our king's fort

. . .

He discarded our mashru and kinkhab
And replaced them with thin satin
And took over our king's fort

He got rid of our milk and curds
And filled the pitchers with liquor
And took over our king's fort

In place of our bullocks and carriages
He brought his iron vehicle
And took over our king's fort

All our grains and cereals are gone
And with them our vitality
He took over our king's fort.[35]

5

Industrialization and Swadeshi

Mussalmans and Hindus, people of my country!
Make the trade route your rope-snake, the ship your churn,
Do 'sagar-manthan', bring forth Lakshmi.
Be bold and act, there is no other way.

'King Industry' rules, your wealth is gone
To foreign hands. The fault is yours
You did not unite.
Do not idle the days away
Awake, educate yourselves and overcome.

Fight not with your own people,
Fall not into debt again.
Give up superstition and wasteful customs,
Farm fallow lands, grow more crops,
Make work for idle hands.

Learn new skills, bring industry and new machines,
Wake up! Heed Dalpat's plea, people of my country![1]

In 1851, when the poet Dalpatram wrote '*Hindustan Upar Hunnar Khanni Chadhai*' (Attack of King Industry on Hindustan), Western technology had already made its presence felt in Gujarat. Dalpatram not only recognized the tremendous challenge before traditional manufacturing and business methods but shrewdly realized that the only way to triumph over modern technology was to adopt and master it. His 170-stanza allegory described the march of Hunnar Khan (King

Industry) and his general Yantra Khan (General Machine) and exhorted the Muslims and Hindus of India to come out of their stupor and vanquish the invader by uniting and reforming their communities, acquiring modern education and becoming proficient in the use of new skills and machinery.

Dalpatram

Though the British were preoccupied with cementing their political power in Gujarat, they had also begun setting up research stations for improving local cotton varieties, holding exhibitions and demonstrations of the latest English machines and tools, conducting scientific explorations for iron ore and coal and establishing telegraph networks and railway lines to transport cotton for export. The Bombay Chamber of Commerce had been established in 1836 and banks like Hong Kong and Shanghai Bank and Standard Chartered Bank opened branches in Bombay. The stage was being set for large-scale industrialization in the latter half of the century.

Probably because he was a resident of Ahmedabad, Dalpatram anticipated that the first to heed his call to adopt modern industry would be the city's wealthy Vaniyas. However, the earliest positive response came from the Parsis of Bombay. In retrospect, it seems natural that the Parsis made the first moves towards industrialization. Since the late seventeenth century, they had close business and political links with the British. By the early eighteenth century, the British began to develop Bombay as their main port on the western coast and they encouraged Parsi traders, weavers and other craftspeople to move to Bombay. Soon Parsis began to dominate trade and commerce in Bombay. In 1836 seven Britishers and three Parsis together established the Bombay Chamber of Commerce, which played a decisive role in shaping British policy related to trade, commerce and industrialization.

By the first half of the nineteenth century, the Parsis were in a powerful economic position. Almost all the trade between Europe and India transacted through Bombay involved Parsis who were brokers or shipping agents and controlled storage and auction of commodities. They dominated the trade to the Far East, particularly the opium trade to China through which they gathered a vast fortune. Parsis earned huge profits in the commission business and dominated finance, banking and insurance. They played a leading part in the foundation of all new banks in Bombay: the Government Bank of Bombay, Oriental Bank, Asiatic Banking Corporation and Central Bank of India. This closeness to the British and access to capital was combined with a first-hand exposure to Europe. Unlike the Jain and Vaishnav communities, Parsis had no socio-religious taboos regarding interaction with foreigners or journeys over sea. Foreign travel gave the Parsis exposure to the enormous changes that the Industrial Revolution was ushering in the world of manufacturing and business. The emancipation of the Parsi laity from the domination of the clergy in the eighteenth century had already given the Parsi trading classes social prestige and their visits to England accelerated the modernization process. The number of Parsis who studied or transacted business in England grew constantly, especially during the nineteenth century.[2]

Being artisans originally, Parsis were receptive to new machines and were quick to recognize their potential in business terms. They promptly adopted the steam engine and put it to varied use. In 1834 Ardeshir Wadia started experiments in Bombay to use steam engines to draw water for irrigation. Parsis were already involved in the construction business, which grew as the city of Bombay expanded. Mechanization entered this area when in 1843 Jeejeebhoy Dadabhoy imported a machine for sawing wooden planks for house construction. Parsis were master shipbuilders and from 1845 onwards steamships were introduced on the rivers of Surat district and other parts of Gujarat.[3] However, the main business of western India centred on cotton production, processing and textile manufacture and when mechanization entered this field industrialization expanded rapidly.

What really gave an impetus to industrialization in western India was the steady rise of textile imports. In 1820 textiles worth 3.5 lakh rupees were imported from the mills in Lancashire and by 1860 they had grown to 193 lakh rupees. Parsis were astute enough to realize that given the low cost of labour, access to cotton and a vast local market there was a possibility of making good profits if they set up their own textile mills. During these decades, industries making machinery to manufacture textiles and paper expanded greatly in Europe. Yet, to boost their own textile and paper industries, Germany, England, France and Belgium enacted legislation banning the export of machinery to other countries. But by the 1830s the manufacturing industries grew rapidly and many countries repealed their laws to allow machinery export. However, in Britain the Lancashire textile mill lobby was influential in Parliament till the 1840s and the Act prohibiting machinery exports was repealed only in 1843. Shortly thereafter in western India, there were moves to mechanize the cleaning and processing of cotton, followed by the setting up of spinning and weaving mills.

British travellers, traders, bureaucrats and scientists stationed in the cities of western India were the catalysts who brought information, ordered machinery from England, installed it and oversaw production, and introduced English business methods. In Surat, R. Carr Woods, a scientist, and H.G. Briggs, a writer, brought news of developments in Europe, and though the local merchants responded cautiously, they were interested enough to form a joint stock company in 1845 to produce paper with steam power. But before long, they began to lose confidence and thought that, since their strength lay in the textile business, it might be better if the company were to manufacture cloth instead and use the waste from the textile unit to produce paper. Briggs was asked to manage the project, and though inquiries were made with machinery manufacturers in England, the project petered out in a couple of years.

At around this time, one James Landon was appointed superintendent of cotton experiments in Bharuch. Other such research stations had been set up by the British in Kheda, Surat, Dhandhuka and Ahmedabad. Landon had experience of cotton growing and processing in America and was a bureaucrat and trader. In 1850 he set up the first steam engines to clean and press cotton and exported it to England, making good profits. Bombay followed, with the first steam presses being set up in 1853. In 1854 Landon set up the first cotton mill in Bharuch, the Broach Spinning and Weaving Mill. Strangely enough, the local cotton merchants, instead of imitating Landon, saw him as a threat and thwarted his efforts. A few months later the Parsi business magnate Cowasjee Davar set up the Bombay Spinning and Weaving Mill, the first indigenous textile mill in India where most of the shares were held by Parsis and Gujarati Hindus. The deed of agreement between Cowasjee and the shareholders was drawn up in Gujarati and business practice moved from the age of oral agreements based on merchants' honour and arbitrated by the Mahajan to a new era of written documents which could be produced in courts of law in case of disputes. When production began two years later, the first hanks of yarn were displayed in the Barrack Museum. By 1870 there were thirteen mills, of which nine belonged to Parsi businessmen.

Businessmen in Ahmedabad were closely watching developments in Surat, Bharuch and Bombay. Dalpatram, who was editor of *Buddhiprakash*, regularly published articles about business events and trends in India and the latest developments in Britain and America. The journal also introduced the Gujarati reading public to new technologies such as electricity, telegraph, steamboats and new agricultural techniques. *Buddhiprakash* reported news of Landon's steam-powered spinning wheels and urged others to follow in his footsteps.

Though Ahmedabad had a strong business tradition and a strong artisan base of craftsmen allied to textile manufacture—spinners, weavers, blockmakers and printers—the long years of political uncertainty had disrupted business and discouraged entrepreneurship. British rule brought order and stability, and business revived gradually, bringing in its wake a new socio-economic order. Machine-made English yarn had entered the markets of Ahmedabad in the 1820s and was woven into cloth by Kanbi, Khatri and Muslim families from neighbouring rural areas. Though originally from the agricultural castes, they migrated to Ahmedabad and became weavers. Some Kanbis became wealthy and diversified into trading and moneylending.[4] Vaishnav Vaniyas, who had a relatively inferior position in the city's commercial life, increasingly dominated the textile trade and by the mid nineteenth century the Chautano Sheth or head of the cloth traders' Mahajan was a member of this caste. The Jains continued to dominate the sharaf or bankers' Mahajan and its head was the Nagarsheth. The Nagarsheth, who was traditionally considered the leader of the city, had to now start consulting the Chautano Sheth in important matters affecting the city.[5]

Indigenous innovations in textile manufacture began in this period and there were attempts to increase the output of traditional spinning wheels. At the same time British government officers held frequent demonstrations of steam-operated saw gins to convince the local population of the advantages of mechanization. Thus, persuaded by C. Daley, superintendent of cotton experiments at Dhandhuka, Tribhuvan Sheth set up the first steam-operated saw gin in Ahmedabad in the 1850s. Encouraged by the profits generated by the machine, a large number of cotton merchants in Gujarat and Saurashtra started inquiring about its cost and operation. Mechanization of cotton processing in Ahmedabad was accompanied by efforts to improve transport and communication networks to facilitate cotton exports. Telegraph lines linking Ahmedabad to Bombay were installed in the 1850s; roads and ports in cotton-producing areas were improved. George Fulljames, commandant of the Gujarat Irregular Horse, began efforts to construct a tramway connecting the town and port of Dholera to transport cotton for export. A tramway company was set up at Dholera in 1850 and the merchants of Ahmedabad bought most of its shares.[6]

Though the businessmen of Ahmedabad responded enthusiastically to these new technologies, the next move towards actually setting up a cotton textile mill was made neither by the traditional trading classes nor by the 'artisans-turned-traders' groups but by a Nagar Brahmin bureaucrat, Ranchhodlal Chhotalal. Ranchhodlal

started his career in 1842 as a government clerk and rapidly rose to become Assistant Superintendent to the Political Agent of Rewa Kantha (area between the rivers Mahi and Narmada in central Gujarat). The Nagars had taken to modern education, which apart from putting them in senior positions in the British administration made them familiar with developments in modern production processes. As mentioned before, unlike other Brahmin communities, Nagars were businessmen

Ranchhodlal Chhotalal

too and some of them were prominent and wealthy moneylenders. Ranchhodlal himself did not have business experience; he was interested in new technology and his spirit of entrepreneurship and dogged persistence made him the father of the textile industry in Ahmedabad.

In 1843 all legal obstacles to importing textile machinery had been removed by the British Parliament, and by 1847 Ranchhodlal was already exploring the possibilities of setting up a mill. He studied the documents that Fulljames had procured for the Surat merchants when they had set up a company to produce cloth and paper. At the time Ranchhodlal was posted in Baroda and he approached the traditional banking firms there but they were reluctant to take the plunge. He then formed a company and asked Fulljames to send him fresh estimates and tried, unsuccessfully, to raise money from the merchants of Ahmedabad. Then he contacted Landon in Bharuch to confirm the soundness of his venture and then approached Gaurishankar Oza, the diwan of Bhavnagar. Oza too was a Nagar Brahmin who had started his career as a trader and later entered government service. Oza persuaded the banking firms of Baroda to invest in Ranchhodlal's project and a fresh venture was initiated with Landon in charge of procuring machinery. The project however did not take off, though Landon continued on his own and set up the first spinning mill in Bharuch. Soon Ranchhodlal lost his government job on charges of corruption. He took up a job with a moneylender's firm and, with their support, again made efforts to set up a cotton-ginning mill, another project which was stillborn. By this time three mills had been established in Bombay and their success increased the confidence of the Ahmedabad merchants who now gave him their backing and Ranchhodlal floated the Ahmedabad Spinning and Weaving Company in 1858. Meanwhile, Dadabhai Naoroji had moved to England as a partner in Cama and Company, the first Indian trading firm in England. Ranchhodlal was acquainted with Dadabhai and orders for the machinery for this latest project were placed through him. Ranchhodlal's luck ran out once again as the main engineer for the project died and the ship carrying the machinery sank. Orders were placed once again through Dadabhai, the ship landed successfully at Cambay, the machinery was transported to Ahmedabad in bullock carts and the first textile mill was established in Ahmedabad in 1861.[7]

This detailed description is certainly a tribute to Ranchhodlal's tenacity; it also gives a glimpse of the emerging linkages between Gujaratis, local and overseas, the continuing role of traditional networks and their intersection with British partnerships. However, the expansion of the textile industry along these lines was interrupted for a few years as merchants' resources were diverted to the 'Share Mania'.

THE 'SHARE MANIA'

Trading in shares started in Bombay in the 1830s when there were about a dozen share brokers who gathered every evening under a banyan tree near Horniman Circle and conducted their business. The main transactions involved trade in the loan securities of the East India Company. Trade in bank shares started after the establishment of the Bombay Commercial Bank, Chartered Mercantile Bank, Agra Bank and others. Bombay was always a centre of cotton trade and there was brisk trade in the shares of cotton presses. Then came the telegraph systems and railways, which stimulated trading, and by the 1860s there were about sixty share brokers operating in the 'Share Bazaar'. They were formally organized in 1875 as The Native Share and Stockbrokers Association on Dalal Street with 318 members and a fee of one rupee.[8] This association grew to become the Bombay Stock Exchange, the financial nerve centre of India, which is still dominated by Gujarati share brokers.

The Civil War in America in 1861 was a turning point in the cotton textile business of western India. America was the main supplier of cotton to England and when the war interrupted cotton supplies to the Lancashire mills the demand for western Indian cotton soared. Cotton from the fields of Gujarat and Maharashtra poured into Bombay for export. So intense was the demand and so high was the price offered that traders tried to maximize their profits with no thought to the quality of the cotton exported, even ripping open mattresses and pillows and selling the stuffing. It is estimated that in the five years of the war Bombay gained 70–75 million pounds. The boom resulted in the flotation of a rash of new companies in Bombay: cotton presses, banks, shipping companies, loan companies and land reclamation schemes. Between 1863 and 1865, 115 new companies were floated and the public rushed to buy shares in these new ventures in the hope of making quick fortunes. It was a time that was later referred to as 'Share Mania'.

The Share Bazaar opened early in the morning and at sunset was not yet closed. An over-flowing throng crowded the premises and only the presence of a large number of local constabulary enabled order to be preserved. Share prices shot up, and the invitation to unscrupulous practices could not have been more whole-hearted. The market was frequently rigged, and increases in prices were often brought about by manipulation.[9]

In the eye of this storm was Premchand Raichand, a Surti Jain who was considered 'Napoleon of the Share Bazaar'. It is necessary to describe the rise and fall of this financial wizard in some detail as it points to a new kind of Gujarati entrepreneur who was coming to occupy the mercantile centre stage along with the early pioneers of industrialization. This entrepreneur was quick to grasp the new business order

Premchand Raichand

and was able to exploit the new regime of laws, and the loopholes within them, to maximize his profits. The construction of Premchand's image, during his lifetime and later, throws light on his personality as well as the approval he received from the Gujarati middle class, as revealed in this account written a century after the event by an admiring Surti:

In 1858, Premchand Raichand's fortune was estimated at Rs 80–90,000. In 1860, along with other share brokers, he artificially inflated the share prices of the Commercial and Mercantile Bank and made a fortune. Soon he was well known amongst the English and prominent traders came to seek his advice. By now his fortune ran into lakhs of rupees. In 1862 he became closely associated with Messrs. Richie Stuart Company and one of its partners,

Michael Scott, who was a member of the governor's council, became a close friend.

In addition to trading in shares, Premchand Raichand entered the cotton and opium trade and made an even bigger fortune during the American Civil War. He had wealth, he was enterprising and he was well connected. This made him more ambitious. He appointed numerous agents in the rural areas, purchased cotton through them and exported it. By now he had fame and fortune but he was still not satisfied. He started speculating in shares and for this he began to set up several new companies and banks. With Michael Scott, Cowasji Jehangir, Readymoney and other Englishmen, he floated the Bombay Joint Stock Bank which later came to be known as the Asiatic Bank, though people referred to it as 'Premchand bank' . . . About this time the Rice Bank and Bank of India were established and he indulged in large-scale speculation in the shares of these banks.

Following this, he acquired the government's permission for a land reclamation project near Colaba and Walkeshwar. For this he set up the Bombay Reclamation Company and made profits from this company's shares. Inspired by his success, others set up companies and Premchand made money through them too. It is noteworthy that Premchand had not affixed his signature on the documents of any of these companies and they were registered in the names of others. Thus he insured himself against future calamities.

Premchand was at the apogee of his career in 1864. He lived in splendour, the banks held him in awe and advanced money to anyone he named. He was the King of the Share Bazaar. The rise and fall of share prices was controlled by him. When he sold or bought a particular share, others followed suit. Even if he just visited a bank, people would assume that its share price would rise and competed with each other to acquire those shares . . .

Now his fortune ran into crores of rupees. When he

arrived at the Share Bazaar brokers would rush to walk on either side of him, holding umbrellas over his head and treating him like a king.

In 1865, he started futures trading and once again, made money hand over fist. He maintained a lavish lifestyle and donated generously to the universities of Bombay and Calcutta. He donated money for education, for hospitals, for schools in Surat, Bharuch and Ahmedabad and for religious activities . . .

In 1866, the share market crashed and with it began Premchand's decline. The banks from whom he had borrowed money started calling in their loans . . . Creditors were cautious in view of his prestige, but soon their numbers began to swell as did their demands for their money. Premchand's English friends tried to reason with the creditors to buy time and bail him out but they were unsuccessful. Finally he filed for bankruptcy, in 1866. His debt was about two crore rupees but he declared his assets to be worth a mere ten lakh. The prevailing laws were such that there were no legal grounds to hold Premchand accountable. It is said that, if he wanted to, he could easily have made good his debts, but he had steadily diverted his funds elsewhere. His wealthy father traded independently and it is said that his money too was actually Premchand's. Despite being declared bankrupt, Premchand cheerfully moved about in society and continued his business as before.[10]

Ahmedabad too was affected by the Share Mania. Between 1862 and 1865 twenty-eight new companies were floated. The Jain and Vaishnav Vaniyas of the city including the Nagarsheth Premabhai, who was closely associated with Premchand Raichand, took to speculation. Many government employees, teachers and intellectuals of the time left their jobs to try their luck at making a quick fortune. Bhogilal Pranvallabhdas resigned as headmaster of the government English High School to take up a position at the Central Bank of Western India at seven times his former salary. The poet Dalpatram resigned his job at the Gujarat Vernacular Society to take up a commercial job, where he speculated in shares and went broke. The educationist and social reformer Mahipatram Rupram also tried his hand at speculation as did the historian Maganlal Vakhatchand, who joined a bank as manager.

The Premchand Raichand saga also exposed the close association the traders nurtured with the colonial administration in much the same way as merchants had done with the Chaulukya kings, Gujarat Sultans, Mughals and the Portuguese. Some of Premchand's partners in business were senior members of the government, who profited from the drama, and in the aftermath they were the ones who pleaded with Premchand's creditors. The event also revealed the growing linkages between this class of traders and the Gujarati middle class, including professionals, who were drawn like moths to the prospect of quick riches, and the successful traders made fortunes at their expense. All the while he was making fortunes at the expense of others, Premchand donated generously towards higher education, instituted scholarships in his name and made contributions to religious charities. Punctilious religious piety coexisted serenely with ruthless business practice, and continues to draw praise a hundred years later:

> There is no option but to acknowledge that this Surti, who intoxicated by speculation, ruined not only himself but countless others too, was indeed a courageous entrepreneur.[11]

It is impossible to find a single account of Premchand Raichand in Gujarati in which he is portrayed in a negative light. This Napoleon of the Share Bazaar had many subsequent avatars in the twentieth century, almost every time as a Gujarati trader, stretching the financial system and the laws of the time in partnership with members of the administration, playing on the greed of a Gujarati middle class and, inexplicably, admired as a great hero.

EXPANSION OF TEXTILE INDUSTRY

By the 1870s the financial markets recovered from the excitement of the preceding years. After the Opium War in China, the profitable opium trade declined and new legislations to protect peasants from moneylenders made these two avenues of investment less lucrative. Many financiers diverted capital into the textile industry and some of the profits made during the American Civil War years were also invested in new industrial ventures. The number of mills in both Bombay and Ahmedabad grew. Ranchhodlal's mill showed profits right from the outset and his success inspired his friend Bechardas Lashkari to start the second mill in 1867. This marked the beginning of a new era in the economy of Ahmedabad as the new generation of older business families broke with tradition and began to invest in modern industry. Though the Jains and Vaishnavs financed Ranchhodlal, they were cautious and did not themselves set up any mills till the late 1870s.

Rise of Textile Industry in Ahmedabad: 1861–1946[12]

Year	Number of mills	Average number of workers employed daily
1861	1	63
1879	4	2013
1891	9	7451
1900	27	15,943
1914	49	32,789
1922	56	52,571
1939	77	77,859
1946	74	76,357

One of the distinctive features of the cotton textile industry in western India was its indigenous financial base. It was completely financed by Indian capital. After the initial phase the Bombay mills were financed by shareholders and banks though in Ahmedabad the mills' main source of finance was the small investor who formed the backbone of the cotton industry in the town. Up to the First World War, the public in Ahmedabad felt it was more secure to deposit their money with one of the Ahmedabadi bankers or mill owners than with a 'modern' bank. Ahmedabad's main newspaper, *Prajabandu*, wrote in 1909 that the depositors of Ahmedabad stood surety for more than 50 per cent of capital. While the starting capital for all the early mill ventures was raised by the families and relatives of the founders, members of the modern professions such as lawyers, teachers and doctors also started investing their money as depositors in textile mills. Thus, from the early days of industrialization, the middle classes invested their money in textile mills and other industries and the fortunes and ideologies of these groups became closely linked.

Significantly, Muslims did not play much of a role in this new era except for founding two cotton spinning mills in Surat in 1861 and 1874. In Ahmedabad the first Muslim-owned mill was established in 1912 by the Taiyabali family whose original business was in textile chemicals. Earlier, in 1905, Fateh Muhammad Munshi had set up a match factory and the Taiyabalis followed with their match factory in 1909. In Bombay the Khojas, who were primarily a trading community, entered the textile industry, notably the Currimbhoy family, which had ten mills by 1925. Interestingly, a glance at the composition of the board of directors gives an indication of intercommunity relationships when it came to big business. It appears that all mill owners preferred directors from their own communities, with the exception of the Muslims, who preferred Parsis. In Ahmedabad the ownership of mills was dominated by Hindus, with the other communities playing a very minor role. Among the Hindus, the Vaishnav Vaniyas owned a majority of the mills. Each new mill was inaugurated by Ranchhodlal and when the Millowners' Association was formed in 1891, he became its first president and remained in the position till his death in 1898.

IMPACT OF INDUSTRIALIZATION

We have seen that the period of industrialization saw the setting up of modern financial institutions such as banks, chambers of commerce, companies and the share market. The old Mahajan system continued, though the traditional authority was altered by new legislations such as the Factory Acts (1881 and 1891), which regulated conditions and hours of work, the Indian Companies Act (1866), which provided 'the first complete code for the formation, regulation and winding up of companies',[13] and the Contract Act (1872), which regulated terms and conditions of associations for trade and manufacturing. The Indian Societies Act (1860) required all groups to be registered as associations and regulated their affairs. Interestingly, the Native Share and Stockbrokers Association was registered as a 'voluntary and not-for-profit association' under this Act.[14]

Emergence of the working class

The introduction of modern industry was to change the social geography of Ahmedabad. The first few mills were established within the walled city though very soon new enterprises were set up outside the old town boundary, converting the villages lying to the east of Ahmedabad into an industrial area. Workers were recruited from these villages and the neighbouring rural areas of the district and, later, in the early twentieth century they came from outside the state. Mill workers first lived in areas like Raikhad and Jamalpur within the walled city and later in barrack-like chawls around the mills in villages like Saraspur, Rakhial, Asarwa and Gomtipur on the outskirts of the city.[15] By the first decade of the twentieth century, the limits of Ahmedabad municipality were extended to include all these industrial villages.

Workers were recruited by mukadams or 'jobbers' who were also called 'masters'. Jobbers were often textile workers themselves, and they recruited and trained men of their own caste or jamaat from their villages. As agents of the management, jobbers were responsible for ensuring the quality of production. The authority to recruit, train and supervise workers made jobbers very powerful, and abuse of authority was not uncommon. Workers retaliated to instances of harsh punishments by jobbers by swift work stoppages until the supervisor or manager promised to redress the situation. Close personal relationships were built up between the jobbers and workers, and workers would change mills in order to follow a particular jobber. The relationship was also a kind of bondage as a worker could not leave his job and return to his village if he had received an advance payment from his jobber.[16] This system of recruiting labour, built on traditional caste networks, persists to this day and continues almost unchanged in Gujarat's salt pans and brick kilns and when labour is hired to harvest cash crops such as sugarcane.

Men usually came to work in the mills without their families and several men lived together in one-room chawls. The wives visited their husbands by turn and the visiting woman would do the housework for the men. The large male migration into Ahmedabad is reflected in the decreasing proportion of females from 1010 per 1000 males in 1881 to 937 in 1891, to 919 in 1901, 848 in 1911 and 765 in 1921.[17] This downward trend reversed thereafter as families also moved to join the menfolk. Links with the original village remained strong and often one or two brothers would be mill workers while the other worked on their land at home (if the family already had land). Cash incomes from the mills would be invested in farmland or houses in the village and in the city. By the mid twentieth century, with rising real estate prices, many mill workers' families became part of a better-off middle class.

Mill workers were a heterogeneous group, though there was a pattern in the tasks which workers from different communities were assigned. For instance, all the workers in the spinning department were Dalit, mostly of the Vankar or weaver's caste. There were no Vankars in the weaving department, which consisted mainly of Patidars of the lower peasant castes, Muslims whose traditional occupation had been handloom weaving, 'bhaiyyas' from Uttar Pradesh and Padmashalis from Andhra. The frame department was dominated by Vaghris.[18]

Their chawls were also different, though Muslim and Dalit chawls were in close proximity, often contiguous and the two groups shared a common mill subculture. Caste hierarchies were reflected in the mill premises; workers of other castes would rarely work alongside Dalits in the spinning department and Dalits had separate water pots and separate places to sit and eat their food.

Women too worked in the mills and during the early decades of the twentieth century they constituted a substantial section of the workforce. In 1911 they formed 18.6 per cent of the workforce, growing to 20 per cent in the following decade. From the beginning they were confined mainly to the spinning, winding and reeling departments. This was (probably) because at that time it was Dalit women who worked outside the house and they were employed alongside their menfolk. Vaghri women too worked and they were restricted to the frame department along with their men. Women from the Muslim, Patidar and non-Gujarati communities did not traditionally work outside the home. A woman's first introduction to mill work was usually through her mother. Young girls accompanied their mothers, often to look after younger siblings, and later joined their mother's department. This method of recruiting through the mother was such an accepted part of mill life that women affixed their mother's name to their own, rather than their father's or husband's. This system was changed around 1955, after which women had to write their husband's name. Women whose mothers were not mill workers learnt the trade if they married into a mill worker's family, working alongside their husbands or mothers-in-law.[19] After the mid 1930s, the percentage of women in the workforce fell steadily as mills were increasingly mechanized and managements preferred to retrench women rather than men.

Working conditions in the mills were harsh in the early years when men, women and children worked for thirteen hours and twenty minutes a day; a half-hour break was allowed at midday and four holidays a month—usually on Sundays—but on these days they had to clean the machinery. The Ahmedabad mills paid a lower wage than the mills in Bombay, where the labour force had many avenues for work and had to be attracted to the mills with higher wages. Nevertheless, mill work paid better and in 1888 the average wage of mill workers in Ahmedabad was seven to ten rupees a month, as against five rupees for common labourers. They were paid by the piece (this piece-rate system persists to this day in salt pans and brick kilns of Gujarat). The long working hours and the unsanitary conditions prompted social reformers to campaign for an improvement in working conditions. The most tireless of these was the Parsi Sorabjee Bengallee of Bombay, who was connected with the industry as the agent of several leading manufacturers of textile machinery. He collected detailed information of the working conditions of mill hands, particularly women and children employed in the mills, and prepared a draft bill of reforms.[20] The Lancashire lobby too campaigned for new factory regulations, though their concern was that the Indian mills had an 'unfair' advantage through the low rates they paid for long hours of work. The first Factory Commission, constituted in 1875, gathered information about the situation in Bharuch, Surat, Ahmedabad and Bombay. The first Factory Act came into force in 1881 and applied to all manufacturing concerns where power-driven machinery was used and where 100 or more workers were employed. The term 'child' was defined for the first time as a person below the age of twelve and employment of children below the age of eight was prohibited. In 1891 the scope of the act was extended and applied to all factories employing at least fifty persons; the age of employment of children was raised to nine and their working hours were not to exceed seven. Women were to work at the same hours as children up to a maximum of eleven hours.[21]

The Factory Acts did little more than regulating working hours and working conditions in the industry. A few members of the Bombay Millowners Association proposed a schedule of minimum wages in the early 1890s but the mill owner community did not support the move. Mill owners were also known to introduce sudden wage cuts to decrease production costs in the face of competition from mills in China and Japan. Some which could not withstand the competition closed down temporarily and resumed production when markets were conducive. To protest against wage cuts, workers struck work in Bombay in 1892 and 1893, though they were unable to bring about any change in the situation. Employers were also known to announce arbitrary change in payment schedules or work hours, and workers responded with spontaneous strikes. In 1895 textile workers of thirteen mills in Ahmedabad went on an angry rampage when the mill owners decided to shift from a weekly to fortnightly payment system. The workers wanted to return to the earlier system and when the mill owners led by Ranchhodlal held firm, the workers burnt his house down. In spite of these protests, the new system continued and the strike was defeated.

While a working class had come into existence, the workers lacked a forum to voice their discontent. The traditional institution of the artisans' Panch, structured as it was along occupational caste lines, could not adapt itself to the needs of this new, multi-caste, multi-community workforce which brought many different occupational skills together under one roof. Workers' organizations could not be formed because the policies of the British administration were concerned with maintaining law and order and did not tolerate organizational activities that could disturb production. Any worker caught attempting to organize fellow workers faced harsh punishment, not only from the management but also from the police and judicial authorities. The mill owners, however, had organized themselves into Mahajan-like associations in Bombay in 1875 and in Ahmedabad in 1891, but it was only in the early twentieth century that workers' organizations were formed in these two cities.

Impact on caste restrictions

The leading industrialists also played a key role in their caste and religious organizations and initiated reforms to not only expose their communities to modern ideas and institutions but also to support business expansion. For example, within the Nagar community, it was Ranchhodlal who was instrumental in removing restrictions on overseas travel. Among the Jains, the monks and commercial leaders had a symbiotic relationship: the rich Jains gave large donations to religious organizations and the monks, who wandered in Gujarat and outside, highlighted the worldly achievements of the donors. In the late nineteenth century, these donors included textile mill owners whose worldly achievements were highlighted in the religious literature of the time. Around 1895 they started an association called the Shravak Sangh to unite Jains and spread education in the Jain community. In 1898 the association criticized the excommunication of one Jugaldas who had gone to England to study for the Bar. The young leaders of the Shravak Sangh argued that Jains were essentially a business community and, in view of the growing competition from others in trade and commerce, expelling a person for breaking caste restrictions on travelling abroad would harm the community's interests. In 1902 the Swetambar sect within the Jains formed the Jain Swetambar Conference and though it had an all-India character it was dominated by the mill owners and businessmen of Ahmedabad. Issues such as female education, child marriage, vocational and technical education were discussed at the annual conferences of this organization. Thus the emerging industrial elite consciously transformed traditional institutions to suit the community's business interests.

The Vaishnav Vaniyas followed in the footsteps of the Jains and set up the Gujarat Vaishya Sabha in 1903. This forum was dominated by the Vaishnav mill owners of Ahmedabad and along with increasing education levels in the community it addressed the issue of caste restrictions on foreign travel. Only a decade earlier, the most illustrious of their caste members, Mohandas Gandhi, had been forced to perform extensive rituals to avoid excommunication for travelling to England. The sabha brought pressure on the religious leaders of the Vaishnavs and in 1905, on the intervention of two leading mill owners, a resolution was passed withdrawing the traditional social sanctions against those who had crossed the seas. With this, social impediments to business expansion were removed in the two major business groups of Gujarat.[22]

Impact of new means of transport and communication

The first railway line was established in Gujarat in 1864 and the network expanded in the following years in both the British territories and the princely states. Towns along the railway lines prospered and expanded and the fortunes of well-established old towns which were not on the main railway lines declined. The following account is by a native of the prosperous town of Visnagar in north Gujarat:

> It would not be an exaggeration to say that when it came to trade, Visnagar was the most prominent town of Baroda state. The opium trade was flourishing, as was the business of the vessel makers . . . The dyers' trade was also flourishing and red dyed cloth from here was in demand all over the country. Visnagar's bankers were held in esteem and they dominated the money changing business.
>
> In the midst of this prosperity, in Samvat 1935 [1879] the railway line between Ahmedabad and Palanpur was established and thus began the decline of Visnagar. The ongoing trade with the big neighbouring towns declined and the Patan area linked itself to Unjha station, thereby increasing the trade at Unjha. In Samvat 1943 [1887], railway line were laid between Mehsana and Randala, Visnagar, Vadnagar and extended to Kheralu in Samvat 1944 [1888]; in Samvat 1965 [1909] it was extended until Taranga Hill. This definitely facilitated travel to surrounding areas but the established businesses of Visnagar were destroyed. Nobody had need to maintain contact, why would someone in Vadnagar or Randala keep in touch with Visnagar? The banker's transactions were also diverted.

The Baroda State Gazetteer Volume 2 commented:

Visnagar had in pre-railway days great influence as a centre of trade, and it was also of importance, before 1902, as the Judicial headquarters of Kadi district. It has now sunk into comparative insignificance.

. . .

A greater part of Visnagar's decline was also because of the British ban on opium trade, which flourished in the town . . . After foreign dyes entered the market, the printers turned away from indigenous dyes and in one stroke the dyer's business was destroyed. By Samvat 1956 [1900], the situation of the vessel makers also became fragile.

. . .

Due to the decline, the prominent bankers have migrated to Mumbai, Ahmedabad, Karachi, Poona and so on. Many live here but do most of their business in Mumbai.

The Baroda State Gazetteer Volume 1 commented:

Practically all the money-lending of the Kadi District is done by traders. Of such capitalists Visnagar formerly possessed some twenty or twenty-five, of whom about one-half possessed over two lakhs of capital but during the last twenty years, both their number and capital have declined owing to the opening of the Rajputana-Malva Railway.[23]

Navsari, the town of south Gujarat from where most of the prominent Parsis originated, was also transformed by new means of transport and communication:

When there were no trains in Navsari, people used bullock carts to go towards Mumbai. These carts did the job of the railways. It took 8 to 10 days to reach Mumbai. Most people who wanted to go to Surat simply walked, others took carts. The rich had covered carts. In those days, going to Mumbai was as dangerous as going from Hindustan to Africa because there was great fear of robbers and dacoits along the way . . . Because of this, people who went to Mumbai to earn their living scarcely returned before eight or ten years. If a person went to Mumbai to work, his family would weep as if he was never to return and the spectacle of his cart passing through the mohalla was as fearsome as a funeral procession. The weeping would start the night before, when the cart would come to the house in preparation for the journey and continue till the man left the next day. A stranger would think there had been a death in the family. The womenfolk would accompany the cart till the end of the mohalla, the menfolk would go uptil the market and friends would see the cart off at nearby Gandevi . . . Till Samvat 1800, many went to Mumbai by boat from Surat port. This ferry service was run by Parsis.

In this situation, going to Delhi was considered a courageous achievement. Going to Delhi was like visiting another planet. Inspite of this many leaders and dasturs of Navsari went to Delhi and even to China, Singapore and other distant places, though a majority never returned. These risks and hazards began to be removed only in 1857. On the one side a mutiny was taking place in Hindustan and on the other, in Navsari, the railway line was being laid. In 1864, the train service between Mumbai and Navsari commenced. The wonderstruck people remarked, 'A blink of the eye and one is in Surat!' We had heard about flying sandals in fairy tales but this was happening before our very eyes. With the railways came the rise in prices. In one pan [of the weighing scales] was joy, in the other, sorrow. As a result of the railways, business picked up . . .

Along with the railways, telegraph lines came to Navsari. That is, in 1857 itself, the task of laying telegraph lines too commenced. Before telegraph lines, couriers carried messages. It took them 3–4 days to reach Mumbai. Now, with telegraph services available at the post office and railway station, the convenience is doubled. Though, people tremble when a telegram arrives because it is always associated with news of death![24]

URBANIZATION

The expansion of modern industry and railway networks changed the social landscape of Gujarat. By 1911 Ahmedabad had fifty-two mills, and textile mills were established in many parts of Gujarat by the early decades of the twentieth century. These industries began to draw labour from the surrounding rural areas and set in motion a process of rapid and widespread urbanization first in British-controlled Gujarat and later in the princely states of Baroda and Saurashtra.

Growth of Textile Mills in Gujarat (except Ahmedabad)[25]

	1911	1920	1930
British Territory			
Bharuch	3	3	3
Surat	4	3	10
Nadiad	2	2	2
Viramgam	2	2	2
Baroda State			
Vadodara	3	3	4
Siddhpur	-	1	2
Kalol	-	-	3
Petlad	-	-	2
Navsari	-	-	1
Kadi	-	-	1
Bilimora	-	-	1
Vadhwan	1	1	1
Princely States			
Bhavnagar	1	1	1
Rajkot	-	1	1
Mahuva	-	1	1
Khambat	1	1	1

Towns Classified by Population 1872–1911[26]

Towns	Population				
	1872	1881	1891	1901	1911
Class I (100,000 and over)					
Bombay	644,405	773,196	821,764	776,006	979,445
Ahmedabad & Cantonment	119,672	127,621	148,412	185,889	216,777
Karachi & Cantonment	56,753	73,560	105,199	116,663	151,903
Surat & Cantonment	107,855	109,844	109,229	119,306	114,868
Class II (50,000–100,000)					
Baroda & Cantonment	116,274	106,512	116,420	103,790	99,345
Bhavnagar	35,871	47,792	57,653	56,442	60,694
Class III (20,000–50,000)					
Bhuj & Cantonment	25,020	22,308	25,421	26,362	21,579
Broach	36,932	37,281	40,168	42,896	43,403
Cambay	33,709	36,007	31,390	31,780	28,098
Dhoraji	15,562	16,121	20,406	24,815	24,116
Godhra	10,635	13,342	14,691	20,915	22,144
Jamnagar	34,744	39,668	48,530	53,844	44,887
Mandvi	35,988	35,980	38,155	24,683	24,235
Nadiad	24,551	28,304	29,048	31,435	27,145
Patan	31,523	32,712	32,646	31,402	28,339
Porbandar	14,563	14,570	18,805	24,620	24,821
Rajkot	11,979	15,139	21,564	27,159	26,412
Viramgam	19,661	18,990	23,209	18,952	20,769

Along with the railways, new sea routes and steam ships had their own impact. The opening of the Suez Canal in 1869 led to the rise of Karachi, as it became the port nearest to London. Till the late eighteenth century, Karachi was little more than a fishing village and its rise to prominence as an important port in the north Arabian Sea started after it was annexed to the

British Empire in 1843. Its hinterland stretched northwards and main exports consisted of opium from Malwa, wheat, indigo and madder. Imports included English silk, broadcloth, Bengal and China raw silk, dates, ivory, copper and slaves. Slaves came from Muscat and consisted of Abyssinians. After the establishment of British rule, cotton exports increased and reached its height during the American Civil War, when the demand for Indian cotton rose. In the 1850s and 1860s the British made efforts to improve the port by deepening the harbour and creating facilities for accommodating larger ships.[27] From the 1870s onwards, many traders from Saurashtra moved to Karachi (one of them was Jinnah's father) in search of greater opportunities. Many Gujarati trading houses had branches in Karachi and Bombay, thus maintaining a strategic presence in the two important ports of Bombay Presidency. This westward and southward migration intensified at the turn of the century when western India was ravaged by long years of famine.

Emigration from Kathiawad: 1911[28]

Total Emigrants: 171,582 or 6 per cent of total population born in Saurashtra

Emigrants to the Major Cities of Western India

City	Number of Emigrants	Percentage of Total Emigrants from Saurashtra
Bombay	58,775	34
Karachi	14,728	9
Ahmedabad	8,335	5
Surat	3,394	2
Total of 4 cities	85,232	50

THE FIRST SWADESHI MOVEMENT

Even while the business communities and intellectuals welcomed modern industry and technical know-how, resistance to British economic policies began within a couple of decades of the establishment of their rule. At first this resistance was expressed through the means most familiar to mercantile communities: hartal. We have already seen the hartal organized by the merchants of Surat against the increase in salt tax in 1844. A similar hartal was called in 1848 against the government's decision to introduce 'Bengali' weights and measures, which was ultimately withdrawn.

In 1849, through his writings in the Marathi newspaper *Prabhaker*, Gopal Hari Deshmukh, a native of Poona, gave the first call to adopt the Swadeshi attitude: using Indian products in the place of imported ones.[29] As member of the judicial service, Deshmukh was transferred to Ahmedabad in the 1870s as a judge of the small cause court. He became secretary of the Gujarat Vernacular Society and was instrumental in articulating the concept of Swadeshi in Gujarat. Over the next few years, Swadeshi ideas were promoted among the Gujarati reading public by journals such as *Swadeshvatsal* and in 1875 Hargovindas Kantawala wrote *Deshi Karigarine Uttejan* (Promotion of Indigenous Crafts) in which he addressed the urgent need for economic self-reliance. Kantawala was a teacher at Rajkot (where he started the Swadeshi Hitvardhak Samaj) and he went on to become director of education in Baroda state. In his book, Kantawala presented a picture of the prosperity of ancient India and contrasted it with the poverty of the time, tracing its cause to the widespread use of foreign goods by people in every aspect of their life.[30]

In this first phase of Swadeshi its proponents did not reject foreign industry or prescribe the boycott of foreign goods as the only solution. Reviewing Kantawala's book, Navalram, a leading educationist of Gujarat, proposed a practical plan of action:

There are only two ways to refresh local crafts. First and most important is that we should master European industry and introduce them into our country. The second is that as far as possible, we should not buy foreign goods. We are not in a position to fully implement both these options . . . Not one of us is in a position to completely avoid using foreign goods because for articles like needle and thread to weapons of war, we find ourselves dependant on others. We have fallen so far behind in both knowledge and skills that it is futile to expect that we will be able to reach the pinnacle straightaway. So we have to pursue both options simultaneously. We should introduce as much machinery as possible and use foreign goods as little as possible.[31]

These ideas were being discussed not just in intellectual circles. In 'Shalapatra', a series of periodicals Navalram published for schoolteachers in Gujarat, he discussed current debates, including Kantawala's book. Thus the public at large was being pollinated with new ideas. Yet, the movement was not left at the level of ideas. The January 1876 issue of *Buddhiprakash* announced the formation of the Swadeshi Udyam Vardhak Mandli (Organization for the Promotion of Indigenous Industry) at Ahmedabad by Ranchhodlal Chhotalal, Hargovindas Kantawala, Gopal Hari Deshmukh and Ambalal Sakarlal Desai.[32] Meetings were held every Thursday at the Himabhai Institute to discuss Swadeshi ideas which soon spread to other cities. Public meetings were convened in Surat, Bharuch and Rajkot and organizations were formed to encourage local crafts. With the efforts of the Mandli, shops for selling India-made goods were opened in cities such as Ahmedabad, Surat, Bharuch, Nadiad as well as Rajkot, Bhavnagar and Baroda, thus bringing together urban centres in the British territories and in the princely states for the first time on a single issue. Newspapers such as *Deshi Mitra* and *Gujarat Mitra* of Surat ran regular editorials in support of Swadeshi and local authors wrote prolifically on the subject in following years, notably in *Swadeshi Hit Bodhak*, *Swadeshi Hit Darshak* and *Swadeshi Sukhvardhak*.[33]

In 1889 the Gujarat Vernacular Society published Bhavanishankar Joshi's prize-winning essay '*Pardeshi Maal Aapna Deshman Taiyar Karva Sha Upaay Yojava?*' (What measures are necessary to be taken for the introduction of foreign industries into India?). A glance at the contents page of the book, combined with the fact that it was adjudged the best essay that year, indicates the seriousness and detail with which the subject was being looked at the time:

- Part 1 described the ancient crafts of India, lack of education and exposure to foreign lands among craftspeople, the constraints posed by religion, the daily drain of wealth, the lack of the spirit of invention and the lack of a single language and script in the country.
- Part 2 documented twenty-four categories of products which were being imported from abroad at that time, from cotton cloth to ceramic vessels, paper, medicines, perfumes and tools and machines.
- Part 3 explored the possibility of making all these imported items within the country and analysed whether the country had the required raw materials and machines, requisite skills and enough labour, and looked at matters of quality control, pricing and division of labour.
- Part 4 enumerated the conditions necessary for the successful production of such goods within the country: the need for relevant education and technical education; the duties of ordinary people, including suggestions for farmers and craftspeople; the importance of reading newspapers, listening to lectures and discussion; boycott of foreign goods; encouragement of new inventions; creation of village-level organizations to encourage entrepreneurship and bringing them together at city-level meetings.
- Part 5 detailed the duties of intellectuals: popularizing the ideas through speeches and writings in popular media, conducting experiments, translating technical manuals into the vernacular, establishing well-funded and influential platforms to further the cause and holding exhibitions.

- Part 6 described the dharma of the wealthy: creating organizations of wealthy people, taking steps to reform and increase productivity, supporting exploration for minerals, setting up large industries, getting experienced professionals from abroad, sending employees abroad for training, participating in larger forums, investing a tenth of the profits in research and development.

- Part 7 focussed on the responsibilities of the government: supporting organizations working for the uplift of indigenous industries, paying for training workers in new skills, investing in technical education, granting titles and patents to inventors, imposing levies on imported goods.

- Part 8 enumerated the qualities that the people of 'Bharatkhand' should acquire to meet the challenges: capacity for hard work, shrewdness, competitiveness, assertion, enthusiasm, self-reliance, determination, courage, concern for fellowmen, enterprise, questioning attitude, physical fitness and attentiveness.[34]

Around the time the essay was published, there was a spate of local initiatives in technical education, with Baroda leading the way.[35] The Kala Bhavan was set up in 1890 in Baroda under the stewardship of Tribhuvandas Gajjar, a chemistry graduate from Elphinstone College. Kala Bhavan's focus was twofold. One was to create a trained technical cadre which would manage existing industries and support the introduction of new industries, and the other was to serve as a route for the uplift of artisans and weaker sections displaced from their traditional occupations by new technology. Though a majority of the students were from Baroda, students came from all over Bombay Presidency and other princely states. By 1909 Kala Bhavan was offering licentiates in six subjects—mechanical technology, dyeing and chemical technology, weaving technology, architecture and civil engineering, commercial technology and art. A school of pedagogy was also established but closed later.

Significantly, the medium of instruction was Gujarati and Gajjar founded the *Sayaji Gyan Manjusha* series of scientific books translated from English into Gujarati. This led to the coining of scientific terms in Gujarati. By 1892 they had books on physics and chemistry and two years later on agriculture, heat, arithmetic, mechanics and steam power. The workshop at Kala Bhavan fabricated furniture and other products for the government departments of the Baroda state. Later lathes, drilling machines, looms and other textile machinery were manufactured for the local mills and factories. As the textile industry expanded, Gajjar realized the importance of research in synthetic organic chemistry. Alizarin had replaced indigo and by the 1890s India was importing alizarin worth thirty-one lakh rupees a year and dyeing and tanning materials worth seventy-three lakh rupees (1896-97). Teachers from German universities and experts from the German chemical industry joined the department of chemical technology at Kala Bhavan and by 1911 Kala Bhavan was turning out dye chemists for textile industries springing up all over India.[36]

Though the textile industry was the main focus of industrialization efforts, the British as well as the Gujaratis began to look at the building blocks of industrialization: sources of energy and mineral ores. In fact, Fulljames was a geologist who had discovered iron ore and coal in various parts of Gujarat. Ranchhodlal too realized the importance of these resources and in 1884 he formed the Gujarat Coal and Iron Company to develop coal and iron-ore deposits in Gujarat. The directors and shareholders included leading mill owners and industrialists of Ahmedabad but the scheme had to be abandoned because the government would not grant them mining rights.

Many of the leaders of the Swadeshi movement became entrepreneurs themselves. Ambalal Sakarlal had retired from the judicial service in 1899 and later bought a mill in 1902. With great foresight he bought a coal mine in 1905 to provide fuel for his mill. He bought two other mills later. Lalshankar Umiyashankar bought a spinning company and Kantawala set up a mill in Baroda. In 1906 T.K. Gajjar, along with two of his students, B.D. Amin and Kotibhaskar, started Alembic Chemical

Works, the first chemical industry in Gujarat. The foundation was laid for the future course of industrial development in Gujarat. In Bombay, the pioneer of the steel industry was J.N. Tata, who invested in large-scale geological research in various parts of India to help decide on the best location for a steel plant. Despite opposition from the British, the plant started production in Jamshedpur in 1912 with financial and technical collaboration f.om the Americans. Realizing the importance of steady sources of power for industry, Tata set up a hydel power project in 1914 in the Western Ghats to supply electricity to Bombay.

In the post-1857 period, we find two models of entrepreneurship developing in Gujarat: one represented by Ranchhodlal Chhotalal and the other by Premchand Raichand. The emerging middle class which forged intimate links with both the models validated them. Whether they were teachers or lawyers or government servants, these new professionals under colonial rule considered the establishment of new industries, banks and companies by indigenous entrepreneurs an expression of Swadeshi sentiment. In the process, along with Western science and technology, the entire Western knowledge system acquired legitimacy. Members of this group also secured senior administrative posts such as diwan and naib diwan, judges and educationists in the princely states and carried their world views there.

On matters related to social systems and religious traditions, this new elite and middle class opted for reform from within and this took the form of reforms within caste organizations and religious sects or traditions. A new tendency to go beyond subcastes and forge larger alliances at the caste or sect level becomes evident in the last decade of the century. For example, the formation of the Vaishya Sabha with the aim of uniting all Vaishya castes and the Shravak Sangh to unite all Jain sects were significant developments in the social sphere. Through such larger caste or sect associations the mobile middle class was able to implement a self-serving reform agenda and also tried to transcend restrictions imposed by subcastes or subsects which came in the way of urban life.

The expansion of railways and communication networks resulted in the greater unification of Gujarat: a Gujarat transcending the traditional limits of cultural zones like Saurashtra and Kutch and also traditional *panthak* or tracts like Halar and Sorath in Saurashtra and Charotar or Kanam in central Gujarat. All the same, caste hierarchies remained intact despite this process of unification. The social discrimination of untouchable communities and the so-called backward communities not only continued but was reinforced. The upper castes created a furore over the issue of 'untouchable' passengers sitting with them in the same railway carriage and, in some princely states like Junagadh, a separate coach known as 'dhed na dabba' (coach for untouchables) was attached to trains. The intimate alliance forged between the elite and the emerging middle class was essentially a Hindu Brahmin–Vaniya order which established its hegemony and communities like Kolis, Dalits, Adivasis and poor Muslims hardly received any attention in public discourse. The Patidars were waiting in the wings to be included into this order, though their assimilation with the Brahmins and Vaniyas had to wait another couple of decades.

With the first phase of industrialization, urbanization and rise of the middle class, a new self-confident section emerged in Gujarat. The Swadeshi movement sowed the seeds of nationalism and it was followed by the formation of the Indian National Congress in 1885. This was the first organizational effort by this new section of society towards sustained nationalist activity though most members continued to be 'loyal subjects of the British empire'. At this critical juncture, the leaders of the Swadeshi movement, the new tribe of lawyers, teachers and journalists, some captains of industry as well as maharajas like Sayajirao of Baroda, became catalysts for the beginning of the nationalist era in western India and we shall see more of them in the following chapter.

6

The Call for Swaraj

The nineteenth century ended in a series of crises. In 1896 ships from the Far East brought bubonic plague to Bombay and it soon spread northwards into Gujarat, all the way up to Mehsana. In 1900 a devastating famine spread across western India, followed by epidemics of cholera and influenza. Millions lost their lives in these years and virtually no family was untouched by disease or disaster. Even the Imperial Gazette of the Raj acknowledged that the century closed 'in gloom and depression'.[1]

Bubonic plague came with rats on grain ships from Hong Kong and the disease spread rapidly in the congested and overcrowded mill workers' chawls of Bombay. About 20,000 people died within the first three months and for a long time after this there were about 300 deaths every day. Panic gripped the city and there was a mass exodus of mill workers, traders and agents who fled to their villages. Thousands thronged the railway platforms and special trains supplemented normal services. The situation was aggravated by the inept handling of the crisis by the government. Armed with powers under the Epidemic Disease Act, officials forcibly entered houses to look for infected persons, destroyed infected property and demolished dwellings suspected of harbouring infection. Forced inoculation and insensitive physical examination, particularly of women, for symptoms of infection (which involved examination of neck, armpit and groin) by male, white doctors and forcible hospitalization in common wards without thought to caste sensibilities angered the people. This led to a riot in Bombay, where plague hospitals were attacked and set on fire.

In Pune the plague commissioner was assassinated.[2]

Amidst this, mill production was reduced to half the normal output and mill owners raised wages and offered bonuses to entice workers. The plague was most intense between 1898 and 1908 during which time it claimed sixty lakh lives. It lingered on till 1930. As it abated mill owners reneged on their promised bonuses, leading to friction between the management and workers. In Ahmedabad it was this conflict around plague bonuses that led to the first mill workers' strike, which culminated in the establishment of their organization, the Textile Labour Association or Majoor Mahajan.

THE GREAT *CHHAPANIYO* FAMINE

Just as people were coming to grips with the plague, an intense famine swept across western India. The *Chhapaniyo* (fifty-six), so-called because it occurred in the year 1956 of the Vikram Era (AD 1900), penetrated deep into the consciousness and memory of an entire generation of Gujaratis. It became a landmark event in relation to which ordinary people measured their ages and placed other momentous events in their memory: the popular reckoning was 'so many years after Chhapaniyo'. It wiped out over a fifth of the population around the turn of the century; it made destitute parents sell off their children so that they may survive in the better-off households. It emaciated the entire generation of hardy peasantry and wiped out a great many heads of cattle, affecting the farming of the future as it led to a shortage of farm animals and milch animals.

It began with a failure of rainfall in 1899, which was a mere 7.3 inches against a normal annual rainfall of 33.02 inches. This region was no stranger to periodic failure of rainfall but modern developments in industry, transport and trade wrought a radical change in the implications of a bad monsoon. Famine ceased to be a natural ecological calamity leading to a shortage of food; it was transformed into a socio-economic problem: the soaring food prices and a lack of purchasing power rendered food beyond the reach of poorer sections of society, resulting in starvation and large-scale death.

This new kind of famine became apparent from the 1860s onwards. Increasing exports of British cotton cloth and the growth of the textile industry displaced rural weavers and they turned to agriculture. The changing modes of living and pattern of consumption, brought about by increased exposure to the outside world through improved transport and communication, led to the gradual replacement of locally made products by cheap machine-made substitutes. Increasing numbers of village artisans were reduced to the status of wage labourers. When agriculture failed there was no work for this growing workforce. Local moneylenders were the main source of credit and they acquired control over agricultural land and crops, particularly of the small farmers. This led to food riots in the Deccan in 1875 when the indebted peasantry rose in revolt against the moneylender.

Since the country was accustomed to fluctuations in food production due to climatic uncertainties, the rural population had developed the practice of storing foodgrains to offset lean years. But after 1860 the trade in foodgrains increased with the expansion of the railways and farmers began to sell most of their produce to take advantage of the high prices offered. As a result they no longer maintained large reserves of food stocks. Encouraged by rising exports of cotton, indigo, opium, etc., they switched to cash crops; this too affected food surpluses. This short supply of food drove up the prices in years of rainfall failure, as it did during the Chhapaniyo. Yet, British policy ensured that export of grains continued despite the food crisis.

Like the plague, the famine too was handled callously by the British government. Unwilling to admit that a famine had occurred, as that would mean enforcing the relief works prescribed by the Famine Code, the administration opened the first relief camps only in late 1899. Hundreds of thousands of hungry people started making their way to these camps. With lack of farm work and depleting reserves of grains, the numbers in the camps rose to a few million by May 1900 and continued to rise till July that year. Twenty-five per cent of Gujarat's population was on relief during the worst months of the crisis.

As the distress spread the government became obsessed with economizing its resources and resorted to lowering wages for relief work by adopting fictitious prices. It also reduced the 'full wage' from 40 ounces of grain (as recommended by the Famine Commission of 1898) to 30 ounces. To add to the tragedy, most workers, who could not give the 'minimum' output of work, received only 15 to 18 ounces. And the net result was that diggers earned wages that were on an average lower than a subsistence wage. This callous policy followed to conserve resources resulted in excessive mortality. The Famine Commission estimated the 'excess' of mortality over the normal death rate in the year 1900 as 7,45,376 in the Bombay province, the highest in the western region. A visiting journalist of the time, William Digby, estimated that the loss of life was actually over double the official statistics and said local estimates were even higher. The Chhapaniyo decimated the cattle population too and a large number of landholding cultivators who had invested their wealth in cattle were ruined. An estimated twenty lakh heads of cattle died in Bombay Presidency and even after the rains returned farmers found it difficult to resume agricultural operations.

The government's attitude to suspension and remission of revenue demand during the famine added to the misery of the farmers. The British had raised tax rates to meet the increased expenditure incurred by imperial wars in Burma and Afghanistan. The principal sources of revenue at the time were land tax, excise, salt tax, stamps and opium. Increasing expenditure meant that the government became more exacting in its collection of taxes, refusing remissions and suspension of land revenue even in times of famine. Instead, the colonial government adopted even more coercive measures to collect revenue. This included auctioning off the property of peasants, including houses and cattle and even the land which had not produced anything. Ironically, even these strict measures left 32 per cent of the revenue uncollected. While it did not succeed in realizing the full revenue, it certainly succeeded in creating intense feeling of resentment, hatred and confrontation among the hitherto peaceful peasantry of Gujarat.[3]

Surprisingly this devastating event found no echo in contemporary mainstream Gujarati literature and our only sources are British government reports. There are hardly any accounts of the famine in the autobiographies and memoirs of intellectuals who lived through that time and the few glimpses we get of what the people experienced is through folksongs. The first novel about the famine was written thirty years later and the most poignant description was published fifty years later in the memoirs of Bhailalbhai Patel,[4] as he described his childhood memories:

> At first, people took the grass and leaves from their farms, sold it in the cities and bought grain with the money. Then they started cutting trees. Innumerable trees were wiped out but the pit in their stomachs could not be filled. Then, in the middle of winter, they began to sell their quilts and mattresses, querns and mortar-pestles, brass and bronze vessels and jewellery. When there was nothing left in the house to sell, they sold the beams and roof and finally door and doorway.
>
> . . .
>
> When there was nothing left, the farmers moved towards the cities. Farm labourers were in a similar situation. There was no work. Labourers were willing to work for a whole day for a mere three paise. Masons were available for 4 annas and carpenters for 6 annas but there was no one to give them work. There was no work except begging.
>
> Prostitutes came and bought young and even small girls. For a pittance of one or two rupees, parents would give away their daughters. In some places charitable people had opened community kitchens. In some places, khichadi was cooked and every beggar would get a bowlful. Beggars would gather on one side and as they received their bowlful they were pushed to another side so that they could not return to take more food. Even that bowl of khichadi could not be given to everyone. The number of

beggars also increased and there were major skirmishes during khichadi distribution. In every house, after every meal, leftovers were collected and even the water in which the rice had been boiled was saved. This water and leftovers were distributed to beggars in their bowls. This bowl was the beggar's only possession . . . At nightfall they would sleep wherever they happened to be, clutching the bowl to their chest as they slept.

. . .

As summer set in, we would see three or four corpses every day on the way to school. Every day the bhangis [the lowest caste in the Hindu social hierarchy which is responsible for the disposal of dead bodies] would drag the bodies away and dump them in a dried-up well. They did not cover the bodies with mud, as a result of which the stench lingered for two or three years. It was difficult to pass by that way. The village had a municipality but it did not occur to anyone to cover the corpses with mud. People would come and go by that road, pinching their nostrils to keep out the smell.

. . .

The cities of Gujarat had money during the Chhapaniya. The textile mills had started about half a century earlier and they were now well established. There were many wealthy people in the cities but it not occur to any of them to step in to save people dying from hunger. There were religious godmen in Gujarat, who had become rich with the contributions of farmers and poor people. Yet chhapan bhog was being offered at the Vaishnav havelis and the acharyas continued to enjoy their luxury.

Lakhs of rupees lay in the coffers of the Swaminarayan temples. A good sum was collected at the temple of Shri Ranchhodrai at Dakor. The wealth in the Jain temples multiplied as interest gathered upon interest generated by the fortune there. Yet not one dharmaguru had the good sense to keep alive the starving people by generating some work for them.

. . .
It is very unfortunate that even though they were faced
with such a great famine, the well-to-do lovers of the
Hindu religion, who profess to believe in vasudhaiva
kutumbakam, did not think of extending a helping hand
. . . Only foreign priests believing in a foreign religion felt
compassion for the suffering multitude. They begged for
funds in Europe and America and used the money to
rescue lakhs of people from the jaws of death without a
thought to their status or caste. A majority of the Gujarati
Christians today are those who survived due to the mercy
of these foreign 'paadris'.[5]

Wealthy citizens and Gujaratis in South Africa, including
Gandhi, collected money to help the affected people. Yet these
efforts were meagre in the face of the scale of the disaster. In
comparison, Christian missionaries of many denominations ran
comprehensive relief programmes which included food-for-
work projects, selling grain at pre-famine prices and distribution
of free cooked food, clothing and medicines. They started
orphanages in different parts of Gujarat and it is estimated
that about 16,000 orphans, mostly of the lower castes, were
given shelter. A history of the church in Gujarat acknowledges
that conversions did indeed take place, mainly among the lower
castes, which turned to the religion of their saviours.[6] The
largest number of conversions took place in central Gujarat
and these converts are derisively referred to as *Chhapaniya*
Christians. One can get an idea of the scale when one considers
that before 1899 there were around 500 Christians in Kheda
district; by 1901 there were 25,000, which represented
4 per cent of the population. In fact, after 1900 Kheda district
had the highest rural population of Christians in Bombay
Presidency.[7]

This expansion in Christian conversions brought the Arya
Samaj back to Gujarat. Set up in Bombay in 1875 by Dayananda
Saraswati, a Brahmin from Saurashtra, the Arya Samaj was
not able to put down roots in Gujarat at the time it was created.

Many intellectuals such as Mahipatram, Narmad, Ranchhodlal and others attended the early meetings of the Arya Samaj, though the group never received the popular response it got in the north. Dayananda's vitriolic attack against the Vallabhacharya and Swaminarayan sects could have contributed to this lukewarm response. However, the prospect of large-scale conversions to Christianity in central Gujarat brought the Arya Samajis there. The most active group was in Nadiad, where an orphanage was established in 1908 to save destitute Hindu orphans from the clutches of the missionaries. Many young men of central Gujarat were drawn to Arya Samaj activities at this time and what began as famine relief went on to become a source of nationalist ideas, as shall be described later.

*

The unpleasant experiences during the plague and famine brought about a change in the political mood in western India. Till then, for half a century, the tone was deferential, without in any way challenging British rule. Political articulation in western India began in Bombay when the Bombay Association was established in 1852 by former students of the Elphinstone College as a forum to bring social and political matters to the notice of the British government. In addition to college graduates, the association also had leading 'shethias', businessmen, such as Sir Jamsetjee Jeejeebhai (the first Baronet) and David Sassoon, who saw it as a useful instrument for furthering their economic interests. Within the first year of its existence, however, the association split when many of the shethias resigned in protest against what they thought were the too dangerous activities of the intellectuals in the group who were preparing an investigation into the inadequacies of British rule. The shethias felt that such a critical attitude would hamper the cordial relationship they had nurtured with the centres of power and have an adverse impact on their business interests. By 1862 the association was disbanded. The Bombay Association was revived in 1867 by Naoroji Furdoonji and he tried to build bridges with the shethias, particularly Jamsetjee Jeejeebhai. Once again Jamsetjee Jeejeebhai resigned, this time in protest against the 'radical' politics of the secretaries Pherozeshah Mehta, Dinshaw Wacha and K.T. Telang.

In the 1870s the friction between the intellectuals and shethias intensified as the former, fresh from their education in England, advocated the introduction of elected councils in place of the nominated councils, which the shethias dominated. In 1872 a law was passed which resulted in a compromise: half the town councillors would be elected by taxpayers, a quarter by the justices of peace and another quarter appointed by the governor. Another law in the 1880s increased the number of seats and broadened the voter base to include people with specific educational qualifications. By the end of the nineteenth century, there were municipalities in twenty-one towns and cities of British Gujarat and they were introduced to parliamentary practices, election mechanisms and political power.

Civic affairs, which had until then been dominated by the traditional elite, were now managed by municipal committees. The traditional elite did indeed try to extend their influence on the municipal committees, but the introduction of elected representation opened positions of authority to new groups, such as industrialists and professionals like lawyers, doctors and teachers. In Bombay Pherozeshah Mehta dominated municipal politics; in Ahmedabad it was Ranchhodlal. While in the mid nineteenth century a majority of the motions in the municipal commission of Ahmedabad were moved by the collector and Nagarsheth Premabhai, in later years it was Ranchhodlal and Bechardas Lashkari. In 1896 Hopkins observed:

> Not very long ago . . . the Nagar-Sheth of Ahmedabad was still a very influential person, but he has already lost much of his power, which has been taken by a leading manufacturer, a man who does not belong to any guild, but by public gifts and wealth, he has won in the business world a position of commanding influence, — a fact indicative of the rapid passing away of the old order.[8]

As we have seen earlier, ideas of economic self-reliance began to spread among the people by the 1870s. In 1876 Dadabhai Naoroji published his essay 'The Poverty of India' and the Pune intellectuals, such as M.G. Ranade, G.K. Gokhale and G.V. Joshi, also contributed to what became a deepening criticism of British economic policies. Their understanding of the political economy of the country was incisive enough for them to realize that the recurring famines in the Deccan during the 1860s and 1870s were not so much natural disasters as a reflection of conscious policies implemented by the rulers. Soon the protests became more vocal. In 1878 a licence tax was levied to cover expenses incurred by the British government to provide famine relief. The Nagarsheth of Surat and others published an appeal in the newspapers, calling for a public protest against the tax and this time the agitation was not restricted to Surat alone. Large protest meetings were held in Bombay, Ahmedabad and Poona as well. A month later there was a call for a hartal in Surat and the shops remained closed for five days. Though the district magistrate and the traders' group engaged in negotiations, the talks broke down. The law and order situation deteriorated. Riots took place and in the firing that ensued some people died and others sustained injuries and many were arrested. Pherozeshah Mehta defended the accused and he became so much an integral part of Surat that the city was referred to as 'Pherozeshah's backyard'.

Despite such vocal protests, when the Gujarat Sabha was formed in Ahmedabad in 1884 to represent 'the wants of the people' to the government, it adopted a moderate tone and the majority of its members were lawyers whose main activity was writing petitions related to municipal matters to the government. A year later the Indian National Congress was established and here too, to begin with, there was no open challenge to British rule. Delegates from Gujarat had been exposed to the petition and memorandum-writing variety of urban political activity in the people's associations and the Gujarat Sabha. At the first session in 1885, there were three delegates from Ahmedabad. Two of them were lawyers, one of whom was also a municipal commissioner (member). Of the six delegates from Surat, one was a merchant and four were lawyers of whom two were also municipal commissioners. The one delegate from Viramgam was a municipal commissioner. At the second Congress session in 1886 at Calcutta, where Dadabhai presided, delegates came from the Bombay Presidency Association, Gujarat Sabha at Ahmedabad, Praja Hitvardhak Sabha of Surat, Bharuch, Viramgam and Nadiad, and the editor of the newspaper *Gujarati* from Surat covered the event.[9] Many other Gujaratis presided over the annual sessions in the first two decades of the establishment of the Congress: Badruddin Tyabji (1887), Pherozeshah Mehta (1890), Dadabhai Naoroji (for the second time in 1893), Rahimtulla M. Sayani (1896) and Dinshaw Wacha (1901). The mill owners of Bombay and Ahmedabad, though they supported the Congress directly or indirectly and publicly associated with Swadeshi organizations, deliberately adopted a pro-British stance in order to secure and further their economic interests. One of the notable exceptions was J.N. Tata, who in 1887 christened his newest textile unit Swadeshi Mill. His anti-British tenor made him the only prominent Parsi of his time who was not knighted.

In 1892, in keeping with the respectful Congress tone, Dadabhai Naoroji contested elections to the British Parliament, hoping to influence British policy in India. Since the 1850s Dadabhai had divided his time between England and India, engaged in business and forming the East India Association to raise awareness among the British public about the state of affairs in India. Students from western India who went to study in England carried letters of introduction to him. M.K. Gandhi too carried one such letter and though he never approached Dadabhai, he attended meetings of the association and became acquainted with the issues of the time. Dadabhai's election campaign (one of his campaign assistants was M.A. Jinnah, who was in England to qualify for the Bar) was successful and in 1892 he became the first Indian to be elected to the British Parliament.[10]

These were the developments of the last fifty years of the nineteenth century. However, at the dawn of the twentieth century, four intertwined and increasingly forceful streams of nationalistic thought began to emerge in western India:

1. The second Swadeshi movement
2. Rise of 'radicals' within the Congress
3. The assertion of Sayajirao Gaekwad
4. Revolutionary nationalism

THE SECOND SWADESHI MOVEMENT

As we have seen in the preceding chapter, by the turn of the century, the first Swadeshi movement in Gujarat had created indigenous institutions for technical education, popular literature on Swadeshi themes in the vernacular and stores for the sale of Swadeshi products. By 1901 even Dadabhai abandoned his customary mellow tone to refer to this growing economic nationalism which he anticipated would expand into political nationalism:

About 1880, Dr Birdwood has brought to the notice of the English public certain songs now being spread among the people of Western India, against the destruction of Indian industry and arts. We may laugh at this as a futile attempt to shut out English machine-made cheaper goods against hand-made dearer ones. But little do we think what this movement is likely to grow into, and what new phases it may take in time. The songs are at present directed against English wares, but they are also a natural and effective preparation against other English things when the time comes, if the English in their blindness allow such times to come. The songs are full of loyalty, and I have not the remotest doubt in the sincerity of that loyalty. But if the present downward course of India continues, if the mass of the people at last begin to despair for any amelioration, and if educated youths without the wisdom and experience of the world, become their leaders, it will be but a very, very short step from loyalty to disloyalty, to turn the course of indignation from English wares to English rule. The songs will remain the same; one word of curse for the rule will supply the spark.[11]

Ahmedabad Congress
In 1902 Gujarat hosted the eighteenth session of the Indian National Congress at Ahmedabad. The chairman of the reception committee was Ambalal Sakarlal Desai and his welcome address reflected concern for the economic situation of the time, while echoing Dadabhai's warning:

> Guzerat was an industrial and commercial region, and the two terrible famines through which it had just passed has aroused it to seek the reason of such horrors; nearly 25 lakhs had died out of a population of less than a crore. They saw one reason in the huge amount of wealth drained out of the country. Many of their people emigrated, and they found that their inferior political position hampered their trade, and that it was therefore necessary to agitate politically. They had many cotton mills, forced to pay the unjust excise duty and they felt that commercial pursuits without political action were suicidal. Agriculturalists suffered under inelastic revenue conditions and all asked: 'Why are we so poor?'[12]

The Ahmedabad Congress was significant in that Gujarati women attended Congress sessions for the first time. These were the two sisters Vidyaben Nilkanth and Sharadaben Mehta, who together sang 'Bande Mataram' before the assembled public. Alongside the Congress session was an industrial conference with exhibitions of Swadeshi products and this was inaugurated by Sayajirao Gaekwad, the maharaja of Baroda state. As we have seen, the Swadeshi movement took root in many princely states through the establishment of Swadeshi mandlis which campaigned for the revival and popularization of local crafts and industries.

Thus, when the countrywide Swadeshi movement began in 1905 in protest against the partition of Bengal, the positive response in Gujarat was in fact the continuation of a quarter-century-old movement for economic self-reliance. Yet there was a new note of political nationalism. Ambalal Sakarlal and others formed the Swadeshi Mitra Mandal in Ahmedabad, composed nationalistic songs and brought out a booklet of patriotic songs called *Swadesh Kirtan*.

Cartoon from *Hindi Punch*, 1907

This organization also celebrated birth anniversaries of prominent political leaders to raise public awareness and also brought out a monthly called *Udbodhan*. To make up for the lack of patriotic songs in Gujarati, Dr Chandulal Desai composed several songs and these were printed in new editions of *Swadesh Kirtan*. Ambalal Sakarlal provided the leadership for all these activities, organized exhibitions of Swadeshi products and established a chain of *bhandars* or stores to sell Swadeshi products. After 1905, inspired by revolutionary activities in Bengal, the first *vyayamshala* or gymnasium was established in Baroda by Chhotubhai Purani and subsequently many such vyayamshalas were established. Besides providing physical training, they functioned as youth clubs and study circles to prepare young people for national service.

This second phase of the Swadeshi sentiment, which was characterized by a boycott of foreign cloth, was enthusiastically supported by the mill owners, and the textile industry expanded considerably. A year before the movement, Ahmedabad had only thirty mills, with 5.09 lakh spindles and 6571 looms, but by 1908, when the movement began to die down, there were forty-seven mills, with 8.5 lakh spindles and 12,807 looms, and a doubling of the workforce.[13] As we have seen earlier, many of the leaders of the Swadeshi movement in Ahmedabad and Baroda became entrepreneurs in the textile sector and this second phase saw the establishment of other industries.

In 1908 Sayajirao established the Bank of Baroda, which took over the work of the state treasury. Soon new branches were opened in places as far away as Bombay. At the opening ceremony of the bank Sayajirao outlined his version of the Swadeshi sentiment and the importance of mastering Western science and methods:

> The obvious moral is, that India, after the noble example of Japan, must set herself diligently to the mastery of Western science and Western methods in all that concerns finance and industries . . . No reactionary sentiment of mere respect for the past will save India from the unrelenting pressure of foreign competition; no amount of emotional patriotism will drag us out of the slough of economic dependence. We must set our faces as a nation grimly and patiently to master modern methods and the implements that have mastered us.[14]

RISE OF 'RADICALS' WITHIN THE CONGRESS

In 1906 Dadabhai Naoroji was elected president of the Congress session at Calcutta and in his presidential address he gave his historic call for Swaraj:

> We do not ask any favours. We want only justice. Instead of going into any further divisions or details of our rights

as British citizens, the whole matter can be compromised in one word—'Self-Government' or Swaraj like that of the United Kingdom or the Colonies.

. . .

So, for India also, there can be no national greatness, strength and hope except by the right political principles of self-government.[15]

Though the Grand Old Man was becoming increasingly assertive, he still envisaged self-government within the British Empire. But there was a growing group of younger members within the Congress who wanted to put up a stiffer resistance to British rule. The friction between the 'moderate' and 'extremist' groups within the Congress began to surface and played itself out in the following session at Surat in 1907.

Among the many resolutions passed at the Calcutta Congress were four strongly worded resolutions regarding the demand for self-government, boycott of British institutions, expansion of the Swadeshi movement and revamping education on national lines and under national control. It was also resolved that the next session would be held at Nagpur. Anticipating that the growing influence within the Congress of the 'extremist' wing consisting of Tilak, Aurobindo Ghosh, Ajit Singh (father of Bhagat Singh) and others would be further strengthened as Nagpur was Tilak's home turf, the 'moderate' group of Pherozeshah, Gokhale, Dinshaw Wacha and others manoeuvred to shift the venue to Surat. Gujarat had its share of followers of the 'extremist' group—K.M. Munshi, Nrusinh Vibhakar and others—but the 'moderates', including Ambalal Sakarlal and Tribhuvandas Malvi, were in greater number. Recognizing the politics at play and realizing that the four resolutions were not cleared by the subjects committee, Tilak rose to interrupt the proceedings. Uproar followed and amid scenes of violence the Congress split into two factions. The 'extremist' members of the Congress from Gujarat went on to play an active role in the Home Rule movement about a decade later.

THE ASSERTION OF SAYAJIRAO GAEKWAD

Apart from support to the promotion of Swadeshi industries, the princes of Gujarat were, on the whole, subservient to the British and grovelled before the Residents, who were the local representatives of the government in their kingdoms. The only exception was Sayajirao Gaekwad (1863–1939) of Baroda state. In 1881 Sayajirao assumed full powers as monarch of Baroda, a Class I state which occupied an area almost equal to that of British Gujarat. The developments in Baroda state after his ascension marked the beginning of a new phase as Sayajirao consistently resisted all British attempts to control his state. He launched a radical set of reforms to uplift and strengthen his people and thus expose the hollowness of British claims of the superiority of their rule. He overhauled the administration of the state, shifting magisterial responsibilities from revenue officers to a separate class of judges and reducing the royal retinue from hundreds to a handful. Sayajirao also embarked on a social reform programme whereby he enacted legislation in 1902 to allow Hindu widows to remarry. In 1904 he passed the Infant Marriage Prevention Act and Local Self-Government Act, which aimed to devolve greater power to his subjects.

But the programme that was to have far-reaching consequences was his effort to make primary education compulsory and free. Sayajirao believed that 'education must be spread not merely among princes and wealthy people but among the peasants and the poor'. As a pilot project he started schools in 1893 in Amreli mahal, the most backward area in his kingdom, and boys and girls, regardless of caste and status, were required to attend. The project turned out to be a success and in 1906 Baroda became the first territory in India—British or native—to provide free and compulsory schooling for all citizens: girls between the ages of seven and ten and boys between the ages of seven and twelve. Sayajirao employed Arya Samaji teachers to teach 'untouchable' children, as upper-caste Gujaratis were reluctant to teach children from these communities. This one initiative created a revolution among

Cartoon from *Hindi Punch*, 1911

the 'untouchable' communities and generations to come benefited from it. In 1907 Sayajirao opened two hostels for 'untouchable' students and set up scholarships for them to study in India and abroad. One of the students who received this scholarship was the young B.R. Ambedkar, who studied at Elphinstone College and went on to study at Columbia University. Sayajirao launched a library movement and by 1912 there were nine town libraries, 265 village libraries and sixty reading rooms throughout the state.

Sayajirao travelled widely in Europe, America and Asia and sought inspiration and assistance from a variety of sources. Expertise for his education programme and library movement came from America and for scientific initiatives from Germany. Many German professors came to set up departments at Kala

Bhavan and teach there. Sayajirao also travelled to China and Japan to observe their efforts to cope with developments in the West.

Sayajirao actively resisted attempts by the British to restrict the freedoms and powers of the princely rulers; he ignored Lord Curzon's directives on taking approval from the government before foreign travel and refused to follow the protocol expected of him at the Durbar ceremony to mark King Edward's coronation as Emperor of India. He encouraged officers from his state to participate in Congress sessions and, in recognition of the progressive steps taken by his administration, Congress leaders too began to welcome him, inviting him to inaugurate the Industrial Exhibition organized alongside the Ahmedabad session in 1902 and deliver the inaugural address at the National Social Conference held alongside the Bombay session in 1904. He attended the 1906 Calcutta session along with R.C. Dutt, his diwan.

REVOLUTIONARY NATIONALISM

While radical politics was heating up, there was a group of Gujaratis who were active abroad in the cause of self-rule for India: Shyamji Krishna Varma, Bhikaiji Cama and Sardarsinh Rana. Little is known about this triumvirate and the complex web of their interrelations with each other and prominent activists and intellectuals of their time.

Shyamji Krishna Varma (1857–1930) was a Kutchi who gained fame as a talented Sanskrit scholar, attracting the attention of people as diverse as the Sanskrit scholar and lexicographer Monier-Williams and Dayananda Saraswati. Monier-Williams invited Shyamji to study at Oxford and he became the first Indian to receive an MA there. However, before leaving for Oxford, he became closely associated with Dayananda. It was around the time Dayananda had published *Satyarth Prakash*, where he set out his concept of Arya nationalism. The association between the two continued, and Dayananda eventually named Shyamji in his will as one of the trustees. After his MA, Shyamji studied for the Bar and came back to India to practise law. With the help of Gopal Hari Deshmukh, the Swadeshi activist who was also closely associated with Arya Samaj, Shyamji became diwan of Ratlam state. Later Shyamji also served as diwan at the courts of Udaipur and Junagadh. While at Junagadh he came into conflict with a British bureaucrat and, in disgust, he decided to leave India in 1897 and fight for India's self-rule from England. During his appointments as diwan, Shyamji invested in three cotton presses and from these derived a steady income, which later helped him fund his nationalist work.

In London Shyamji set up India House, which became a centre for nationalist activities. He then instituted five travelling fellowships in the name of the English philosopher Herbert Spencer to help Indian graduates finish their education in England and prepare for an independent profession. A sixth fellowship, dedicated to Swami Dayananda Saraswati, was open to a graduate of Panjab University. The only condition he set was that on their return to India these students would not accept any form of employment with the British. He then instituted scholarships in memory of Edmund Burke and G.V. Joshi to enable young Indian journalists, authors and other professionals to visit Europe and Shyamji became mentor to a generation of young Indian 'revolutionaries'. Interestingly, the first two Dayananda Fellowships were awarded to Muslim scholars. In January 1905 Shyamji started an English monthly, the *Indian Sociologist*. In the first issue he declared his political faith quoting Herbert Spencer: 'Resistance to aggression is not simply justifiable but imperative. Non-resistance hurts both altruism and egoism.' In the following month, inspired by the Irish struggle, he founded the Indian Home Rule Society in London and advocated a policy of passive resistance for the purpose of removing foreign rule. Increasingly under scrutiny for his support to revolutionary activity against British interests, Shyamji moved to Paris in 1907, where he outlined his Principle of Dissociation, calling on Indians to not invest money in securities of the British government, to boycott all civil and military service in the British government, to boycott government schools and colleges and asking Indian solicitors and barristers to shun British courts in civil cases.[16] He translated *La Marseillaise*, the song of the French Revolution, into Sanskrit, Hindi, Gujarati, Bengali, Marathi and Urdu, believing the song to be 'the outpouring of the heart of a nation, clamouring for freedom'. The French too began to find his presence uncomfortable, which forced Shyamji to move to Geneva, from where he continued his activities till his death in 1930.

In Paris was another Gujarati freedom fighter, Bhikaiji Cama (1861–1936). She was born into a wealthy Parsi family and was married to Rustom Cama, a lawyer who was active in Congress politics. When the plague broke out in Bombay, Bhikaiji cared for the sick and brought relief to the afflicted during the famine. Relief work affected her health and she was advised to go to England to recuperate. While in London she was Dadabhai's secretary. She became acquainted with Shyamji Krishna Varma and for some time managed India House. While Shyamji did not overtly recommend violence, Bhikaiji increasingly leaned towards armed resistance to the British. In a speech at India House in 1908 she said:

> Some of you say that as a woman I should object to violence. Well Sirs, I had that feeling at one time. Three years ago it was repugnant to me even to talk of violence . . . But owing to the heartlessness, the hypocrisy, the rascality of liberals, that feeling is gone. Why should we deplore the use of violence when our enemies drive us to it?[17]

After the arrival of V.D. Savarkar in London, Bhikaiji was associated with his group Abhinav Bharat. She also took part in women's movements and used a meeting of the International Council of Women in 1906 to plead for justice in India. In 1907 Bhikaiji attended the International Socialist Congress at Stuttgart. Here she unfurled the first Indian national flag and gave an impassioned speech persuading the Congress to support the cause of Indian independence. The flag she unfurled had three broad stripes: the top band was green, the sacred colour of the Muslims; the next was saffron or golden, the sacred colour of both the Buddhists and the Sikhs; and the lowest stripe was the Hindu red. There was a line of eight blooming lotuses on the green stripe, emblematic of the eight provinces of India; the words 'Bande Mataram' were embroidered in Sanskrit on the golden band; and on the bottom stripe towards the staff was the crescent of Islam, and near the outer edge, the sun. The flag represented the diverse groups in the country's population.[18] A month after the Socialist Congress, at the suggestion of Bhikaiji, some Indian women living in Paris got together to offer a lectureship of the value of 1000 rupees. The lectureship was open to Indian women only, the recipient would deliver not less than five lectures in support of Home Rule or Swaraj in India and the lecture would be delivered free of charge in Hindi or some Indian vernacular or in English in principal towns of India.[19]

In 1909 Bhikaiji's group started the nationalist monthly *Bande Mataram* and the first issue described the stages through which independence could be won. The first was the education of the people, then war, followed by reconstruction. She believed that these were the stages through which every national movement must pass. She was also convinced that not only must Indians of all religions come together but that a national language was necessary. She believed that Hindi should be the language of independent India. In 1913 the Home Department referred to her as 'The recognised leader of the revolutionary movement and was said to be regarded by the people as a reincarnation of the goddess Kali'. She was allowed by the government to return to India only in 1935 and she died soon after.[20]

The third member of the triumvirate was Sardarsinh Rana (1870–1957), who was closely associated with both Bhikaiji Cama and Shyamji Krishna Varma. Rana was a prince in the kingdom of Limdi in Saurashtra and one of the claimants to the throne. Rana studied law in England and later moved to

Paris, where he became a French citizen and was associated with a Gujarati firm of pearl merchants. After Shyamji's announcement of travelling scholarships for Indian graduates, he instituted three travelling fellowships to enable them 'to visit self-governing countries and to appreciate the blessings of political freedom'. He proposed that two of the fellowships be named after Rajput and Maratha heroes—Rana Pratap and Shivaji—and the third after 'some distinguished Mahomedan ruler'. On Shyamji's suggestion the third fellowship was named after Akbar. Significantly, the first Shivaji fellowship was awarded to V.D. Savarkar. In Paris Rana helped young Indian revolutionaries find lodgings, often at his own expense. He managed the finances of Savarkar's Abhinav Bharat group and invested their funds from time to time. He also managed the finances of India House and the personal funds of Bhikaiji and Shyamji. It is said that he even acted as the intermediary between Indians and the Russian revolutionaries and was involved in the smuggling of weapons to India. Because of his nationalist activities, his estates were eventually seized by the Bombay government. He returned to India after Independence but was disillusioned with the state of political affairs. He died in Veraval in 1957, a disappointed and broken man.[21]

*

Revolutionary politics or the *Bomb yug* (bomb era) flourished for a while in Gujarat too. In 1892 Aurobindo Ghosh arrived in Baroda as a professor at Baroda College and later became private secretary to Sayajirao. His brother Barindra Ghosh also came to Gujarat and established the Ganganath Bharatiya Sarva Vidyalaya, a school for preparing youth for militant activity, where training in the use of arms was part of the curriculum. Kakasaheb Kalelkar and Mamasaheb Phadke, who later became prominent in the public life of Gujarat, were both teachers here. Originally set up on the banks of the Narmada in 1907, this school was moved to Baroda in 1909 but was closed a couple of years later.

The most important militant group in Gujarat was formed by Mohanlal Pandya, Punjabhai Bhatt and Narsinhbhai Patel, all from central Gujarat. Mohanlal studied in Bombay university and, along with Narsinhbhai, worked in the Baroda government. Punjabhai was a lawyer. Narsinhbhai learnt Bengali so that he could translate nationalist literature into Gujarati. The three men received training from Barindra and, though no proof was ever gathered, they are widely suspected to be behind the attempted assassination of Lord and Lady Minto in 1909 at Ahmedabad. Mohanlal and Narsinhbhai later became Gandhi's followers, unlike Punjabhai, who continued his career as a lawyer.

Thus, the younger generation of Gujaratis was drawn to nationalistic activities of various hues in the early twentieth century. Their energy and idealism were encapsulated in probably the earliest visualization of 'Hind Devi' conceived by two activists of the Paisa Fund at Ahmedabad, Kripashankar and Professor Barve, at

Hind Devi

the height of the Swadeshi movement. In their visualization (where Hind Devi took the shape of the map of the country), Mother Hind's long tresses were draped over the Himalayas, one hand, holding a trishul, reached towards Sind and the other stretched out towards Bengal. Below this image were the words *'janani janmabhoomishch swargaadapi gariyasi'* (Mother and Motherland are more glorious than Heaven). The image was drawn by the Ahmedabadi artist Maganlal Sharma. It was printed at the Ravi Varma Press and thousands of copies were distributed at every village square and crossroad in Gujarat and all over the country. Subsequently different artists made their own variations: some depicted Mother Hind as Jagadamba astride a lion and circulated the image widely in order to enthuse people to join the struggle against British rule.[22]

At about the same time, another young Dalit artist, Makanji Kuber Makwana, gave the call for a different kind of assertion. In 1908 he wrote 'Mayavat Rajput Prakash' and argued that Dhed or Vankars (weaver caste, considered untouchable in Gujarat) were originally Rajputs and so began a movement for raising the social status of the caste. Under his stewardship a Panch Sudharak Committee was formed in 1907-08 to frame the rules for the Mahyavanshi caste and later he helped various caste councils of Vankars in various parts of Gujarat and in South Africa and United Kingdom to frame their rules and regulations. Makanji brought different Vankar groups together to anchor a movement for claiming Kshatriya status, which continued even after his death in 1924 and eventually resulted in the withdrawal by the British government of the pejorative term 'Dhed' and its replacement by Mahyavanshi for his community.[23]

Thus before Gandhi arrived on the scene, public life in Gujarat was humming with social and political activity. The situation was summed up by Dr Sumant Mehta, who was physician to Sayajirao Gaekwad and later participated in the freedom struggle:

> People who think that there was no life in Gujarat before the arrival of Gandhi are making a mistake. It is absolutely true that Gandhiji created a new climate. There were workers, there was commitment, there was a fighting spirit. With great perseverance, he united these forces, organised them, trained them, tested them and gradually developed them—this was the significance of his leadership.[24]

7

Gujarat, Gujaratis and Gandhi

Gujarat has no leaders: not the kind of leaders found in Bengal, Maharashtra, Punjab and other provinces. In Mumbai, Ahmedabad or princely states intelligent Gujaratis are working for their country's good in their own ways. Yet, there is a dearth of leaders who can lead Gujarat. We lack leaders who can so energize us that, like Bengalis and others in the south, Gujaratis too can show their mettle—within Gujarat and in other parts of the world. We need a guide who can instill such self-confidence among Gujaratis that they feel that they too are participants in the shaping of India's present and future and in resolving the enormous questions related to this task; that they have the requisite capabilities, intelligence, commitment, assertiveness and enthusiasm . . .

Why is such a leader-thinker not born in this province, the province which has given a commander to the Indians fighting a battle against the white in Africa?[1]

The 'commander' was, of course, Gandhi and the author Ranjitram Mehta[2] was not to know that in a few years Gandhi would return and Gujarat and Gujaratis would scarcely be the same again.

In 1909, at the time this passage was written, Gandhi had already crystallized the ideology which was to guide his life's work. He had completed *Hind Swaraj*, established Phoenix Settlement which was to be the prototype for all his subsequent ashrams, fashioned the weapon of Satyagraha with its commitment to the twin ideals of truth and non-violence, and

RESERVED FOR
WHITES ONLY
ગોરાઓ ખાટે રાખેલ

"NIGGERS NOT ALLOWED!

Policeman Boer—Get out from here, sir! This is no
place for you !   Mr. Gandhi (Bar-at-law) No-o-o-o-o !
P. B.—Then I'll make you ! And you'll have to go and
break stones—— or break your head with them !

[Mr. Gandhi, the leader of the Indians in the Transvaal, has
been sentenced to two months' rigorous imprisonment for not
leaving the Transvaal and is forced to break stones on the
public road.]

" નીગરોએ અંદર દાખલ થવું નહી ! "

પોલીસમેન બોઅર-ભાઇ બહાર મિ, અહીંથી ચાલ્યો જા ! અહીં ૬ `ઇ
 તાર` છ્છુ` રહેવાનું ક્ષમ નથી!
    મી૦ ગાંધી-(બારીસ્તર) નહાંઇઇંઇં ઇ નહી ખાનેા !
    પેા૦ બોાઅ—નહીં!ત્યાનો તો ખ્ળ છ્ તુ ને ધક્ષ મારીને અળુઇથી કઢાવઇ !
અને તુ ને પથરા ભાંગવા પડશ, ઇ——પથરા ભાગ તાર`ાટ્ઠુ ફોડઇ ચ શઇ !

Cartoon from *Hindi Punch*, 1908

conducted what turned out to be trial runs of the civil disobedience strategies he was to use later. He had begun his experiments in education centred on the primacy of the mother tongue and was convinced that nothing could be achieved without Hindu–Muslim unity. But before one looks at Gandhi's return and how he shaped Gujarat, it is important to see how Gujarat had shaped Gandhi.

Much has been written about the Western influences on Gandhi's thought: his interest in Christianity as well as the impact of Tolstoy, Ruskin, Thoreau and Western critics of industrialization. His exploration of Indian sources is also well known: his focus on the Gita, Upanishads, Mahabharata and Ramayana and rejection of unquestioning obedience to shastras. Less known are the influences that can be traced to his Gujarati roots.

Gandhi was born in Porbandar (in the princely state of the same name), an ancient port town with a long mercantile tradition and a flourishing trade with ports of the Persian Gulf, Arabia and the eastern coast of Africa. Gandhi belonged to the Modh Vaniya caste of traders and merchants and brought the Vaniya traits of shrewdness and strategic compromise to many aspects of his political career. Unusually, the Gandhi family was open to a range of religious and spiritual beliefs. The *kul devata* of the Modh Vaniya caste is Ram and it was one of Gandhi's ancestors who founded the Ram temple in Porbandar. Yet, the family followed Pushtimargi Vaishnavism, a devout and orthodox sect with Krishna bhakti at its centre. At the same time, Gandhi's grandfather Uttamchand was also attracted to Ramanandi Vaishnavism, which rejected differences of caste and creed and whose followers included Kabir and Tulsidas. Gandhi's father, Karamchand, who had inaugurated the permanent recital of the Tulsi Ramayana at the family Ram temple, was also open to other religions. Jain monks, Muslims and Zoroastrians visited his home and there were frequent discussions on religious matters.

Gandhi was exposed to a completely different but very significant religious denomination through his mother, Putaliba, who belonged to the Pranami sampraday. Like other Vaishnav Hindu sects of Gujarat, the Pranami sampraday too has Krishna bhakti at its core. At the same time, it is the only one which has synthesized Hinduism and Islam, focuses on Hindu–Muslim unity and lays equal emphasis on Ram and Rahim. There was a Pranami temple near their house and Gandhi recalled that 'there were no idols or images in it; and on the walls there was writing that looked very much like texts from the Koran. The dress that the priest wore was unlike what Hindu priests in temples generally wear and their way of praying also resembled somewhat that of the Muslims.'[3]

The Pranami sect was founded in the early seventeenth century by Prannath, a Lohana (a trading caste originally from Sind) from the neighbouring princely state of Jamnagar. Prannath, a contemporary of Aurangzeb, travelled widely in the subcontinent and even visited Mecca. His religious philosophy brought together elements of mystical Islam and the bhakti tradition and as part of his teachings he forbade his disciples from using intoxicating drugs, tobacco, wine, meat and unlawful visits to women. Abstinence from the last three was the vow that Putaliba made Gandhi take before he sailed for England in 1888, at the age of nineteen.

Gandhi was twenty-four years old when he reached South Africa. At the time there were over one lakh Indians there, the bulk of whom were either *girmitiya* (indentured labourers, corruption of the word 'agreement') or those who had completed their period of indenture and had become hawkers or petty traders. Most of them belonged to Madras or Bengal Presidency, and spoke Tamil and Hindi. The remaining, about a tenth of the total, were rich traders and merchants who were mainly Muslims from Bombay Presidency: Khojas, Memons[4] and Bohras from in and around Bombay, south Gujarat and Kathiawad. A few were the Gujarati-speaking Parsis. Most of Gandhi's clients belonged to this South African Indian elite and, to begin with, his world there was a mini mercantile Gujarat. In fact, his first case there was resolved with Gandhi brokering a typical Vaniya compromise between his client, Dada Abdullah, and his relative Tyeb Sheth. While working on this case, Gandhi began acquainting himself with the situation of Indians in South Africa and concluded that civil and political rights of the community could be secured and protected only if all Indians came together. 'In the face of the calamity [a Bill introduced in the Natal Legislative Assembly to disenfranchise Indians] that had overtaken the community, all distinctions such as high and low, small and great, master and servant, Hindus, Musalmans, Parsis, Christians, Gujaratis, Madrasis, Sindhis, etc., were forgotten.'[5] Uniting Indians across caste, class, religious and regional differences was not mere strategy. It was backed by conviction developed from his personal spiritual search which continued while his legal practice blossomed. He had closely read the Bible and an English translation of the Koran, and his correspondence with the Jain mystic Srimad Rajchandra, which had begun during his days in England, continued.

Thus, along with the Vaniya ethos and the Pranami centrality of Hindu–Muslim unity, the third powerful influence of Gujarati origin was of Jainism. On Rajchandra's suggestion, Gandhi read the Jain texts *Panchikaran*, *Maniratnamala*, *Mumukshu*

Prakaran of Yogavasishtha and Haribhadrasuri's *Shaddarshana Samuchchaya*. The last text expounds the Jain doctrine of *syadvad* or *anekantavad*, that is, the 'manyness of reality' which became one of the foundations of Gandhi's spiritual thought.

> It has been my experience that I am always true from my point of view, and am often wrong from the point of view of my honest critics. I know we are both right from our respective points of view. And this knowledge saves me from attributing motives to my opponents or critics . . . I very much like this doctrine of the manyness of reality. It is this doctrine that has taught me to judge a Mussalman from his own standpoint and a Christian from his. Formerly I used to resent the ignorance of my opponents. Today I can love them because I am gifted with the eye to see myself as others see me and *vice versa*. I want to take the whole world in the embrace of my love. My *anekantavada* is the result of the twin doctrine of *Satya* and *Ahimsa*.[6]

In 1897 Gandhi returned to South Africa with Kasturba and their two children and this led to Gandhi's experiments with education and pedagogy; the most significant of these was the primacy he accorded to the mother tongue. With single-minded insistence he began speaking and writing Gujarati for every audience conversant with the language. In 1903 he started the first of his journals, *Indian Opinion*. Every issue had articles in Hindi, Gujarati and Tamil—the principal mother tongues of Indians in South Africa—and English for those not familiar with these languages. Great effort was made to get printing types of these scripts and to train people to typeset and proof-read these languages. Most of Gandhi's writing in *Indian Opinion* was in Gujarati, as was the bulk of his correspondence. He wrote to all Gujaratis in the language: relatives and friends, whether Hindu, Muslim or Parsi. Similarly, his principal books, *Hind Swaraj, Satyagraha in South Africa* and *An Autobiography or The Story of My Experiments with Truth*, were also originally written in Gujarati.

As part of his professional work in Africa, Gandhi was required to make extensive translations into English, as details of business transactions were usually maintained in Gujarati. As his public work expanded he increasingly translated from English, rendering into Gujarati ideas and concepts which appealed to him and which he wanted to put before his people. The first major translation was of Ruskin's *Unto This Last* in 1904, which he entitled *Sarvodaya* (Uplift of All), revealing his exceptional talent as a neologist or 'coiner of words'. An open competition announced in the pages of *Indian Opinion* at the end of 1907 said:

> We have been using some English terms just as they are, since we cannot find exact Gujarati equivalents for them . . . The following are the terms in question: Passive Resistance; Passive Resister; Cartoon; Civil Disobedience. There are some other words too, but we shall think of them some other time. It should be noted that we do not want translations of these English terms, but terms with equivalent connotations. There will be no objection if the words are derived from Sanskrit or Urdu.[7]

In looking for renderings for these terms in Gujarati (and later in other Indian languages), Gandhi was looking for a way to communicate these ideas to Indians, using the Indian cultural idiom, rooting the struggle in the Indian ethos. As a result of the competition, he coined the word *satyagraha* (firmness in truth) for 'passive resistance'; one who offers satyagraha was a *satyagrahi*. Words were conceived to describe new concepts— often his synthesis of ideas from East and West—and this resulted in innovations that barely resembled the original influences or became a lens through which familiar ideas could be seen in a completely new way. In so doing, the new words lifted the ideas to a different plane from the original English. Later 'civil disobedience' was rendered as *savinay kanoon bhang* where 'civil' was rendered not in the sense of 'civic' or 'citizen' but in the sense of 'respectful' or 'compassionate' and inclusive of the idea of non-violence. *Sarvodaya, satyagraha, savinay kanoon bhang* and *harijan* have become so much a part of the vocabulary in all Indian languages that it is sometimes difficult to remember that they were Gandhi's innovations.

During the act of translation, Gandhi was acutely sensitive to the connotations of words as the concept or idea moved from one language to another. In the early days he personally translated his Gujarati writings, particularly *Hind Swaraj*, and his attention to the nuances of various words in English and Gujarati can be seen in the correspondence with his associates in Phoenix who were typesetting the English translation which Gandhi sent from Johannesburg. By the time it came to the translation of his autobiography, he was increasingly preoccupied with his innumerable programmes and he left the translation to Mahadev Desai, and many scholars have commented on the differing semantics between the original Gujarati and the English version.

The sensitivity to the 'root' of words, seen in his competition announcement, continued to vex Gandhi as he tried to ensure that the new words did not carry Sanskrit (and therefore synonymous with 'Hindu') connotations. Writing to his nephew Maganlal in 1909 on the name 'Phoenix' for his experiment in communal living, he said, 'And even when a name is given, we shall have to find a common word over which the question of Hindu or Mussalman will not arise. The word *math* or *ashram* has a particularly Hindu connotation and therefore may not be used.'[8] On the eve of the Non-cooperation Movement in 1919, before an audience of North Indian Muslims, he was groping for a word to describe his new programme. 'I could not hit upon a suitable Hindi or Urdu word for the new idea, and that put me out somewhat.'[9]

Coming back to *Unto This Last*, in 1904, within a couple of months of reading this book, Gandhi bought land and set up a farm at Phoenix, a small town near Durban. It became the prototype for all his later ashrams and the site for his experiments in community living, self-reliance, health, nutrition and education. He began a boarding school open to Indians of any caste or community where:

For three hours in the morning, the boys perform some kind of manual labour, preferably agricultural, of the simplest type. They do their own washing, and are taught to be self-reliant in everything. There is, too, attached to the school a sandal making class, as also a sewing class . . . Non-smoking, non-drinking and vegetarianism are obligatory on the farm. Mental training is given for three and a half hours at least, consisting of the vernaculars of the respective scholars, English, Arithmetic, and so much history and geography as may arise from the lessons in English or in the vernacular. The medium of instruction is chiefly the vernaculars, which are Gujarati, Hindi and Tamil . . . One hour in the evening is devoted to giving the scholars some idea of their respective religions, and, to that end, lessons are read from the Mahomedan, Hindu and Zoroastrian scripture . . . All the boys attend throughout the hour when the respective readings are given. An attempt is made to inculcate in them the spirit that they are first Indians and everything else after that, and that, while they must remain absolutely true to their own faiths, they should regard with equal respect those of their fellow-pupils.[10]

Gandhi's first satyagraha was on the issue of the anti-Asiatic legislation in the Transvaal. The movement began in 1902 with petitions to the government to withdraw the proposals. Over the next twelve years, it progressed to mass meetings of Indians in South Africa, lobbying with Members of Parliament in Britain, a general strike in Transvaal and a dramatic burning of registration certificates, the documents which entitled them to stay in South Africa. The satyagraha was halted after an agreement with General Smuts.

It was during this period that Gandhi wrote *Hind Swaraj*, where he first articulated his life-mission: moral regeneration of Indians and political emancipation of India. It spelt out his main ideas about Indian and Western civilization; a searing indictment of modernity through his analysis of modern machinery, modern professions and modern education; the nature of Swaraj, personal and political, and the ways to achieve it. He wrote it in just ten days, on the ship journey back from a disappointing lobbying trip to England. The whole manuscript was written by hand on the ship's notepaper with hardly any corrections or rewriting.

Satyagraha was revived again when Indian marriages were derecognized, and unrest intensified among Indian miners in South Africa. Gandhi responded with his second dramatic event,

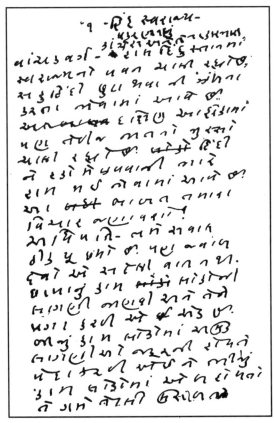

First page of *Hind Swaraj* in Gandhi's handwriting

a protest march from Newcastle to Volkrust with 2221 associates. The event ended with another round of negotiations and assurances from General Smuts that legislations infringing on the rights of Asians would be reviewed.[11] It was then that Gandhi decided that his work in South Africa was over and that it was time to return to India.

In July 1914 Gandhi left South Africa for India and he was given farewells at receptions organized by Indians and Europeans at most of the big cities and towns. Separate farewell meetings were organized by indentured labourers in several towns, and addresses and purses were presented on behalf of the Europeans, British Indian Association, Chinese Association, Tamil Benefit Society, Transvaal Indian Women's Association and by the Gujarati, Mohammedan and Parsi communities. Significantly, he was given a reception by the Dhed, or untouchable, community at Durban. At a function organized by the Gujarati Sabha, Gandhi said he was about to leave a *bhog-bhumi* (land of enjoyment) for a *karma-bhumi* (land of duty).

Gandhi had been away from India for twenty-one years, though people back home were well aware of his exploits. On two brief visits in 1896 and 1901 he had met senior political leaders and had kept in touch with them through letters and by regularly sending them copies of *Indian Opinion*. *Hind Swaraj* had gone into two editions in Gujarati and its English translation was also in circulation. So, on landing in Bombay in 1915, forty-five-year-old Gandhi, in his native Kathiawadi dress, received a hero's welcome. A public reception was hosted by Pherozeshah Mehta, where he was hailed as the 'great Gandhi'. The Bombay National Union arranged a meeting, which was attended by Bal Gangadhar Tilak. But it was at the garden party organized in his honour by the Gurjar Sabha that one can see the response of the Gujarati elite. The welcome was conducted in English and presided over by M.A Jinnah (also a Kathiawadi), and K.M. Munshi[12] hailed him as 'the greatest son of modern Gujarat'. When it was his turn to respond, Gandhi 'spoke in Gujarati, thanked Jinnah for presiding over the function saying that while he was in South Africa and anything was said about Gujaratis, it was understood to mean the Hindu community only and Parsis and Mahomedans were not thought of. He was therefore glad to find a Mahomedan a member of the Gurjar Sabha and the chairman of that function.'[13] Thus, within four days of arriving in India, Gandhi began making an impact—through his dress and speech as well as by emphasizing an overarching Gujarati unity cutting across religious differences.

Gandhi spent his first year in India as an observer and student, acknowledging what Gokhale had pointed out: that having been out of India for so long, he had no business to form any conclusions about matters essentially Indian. He therefore travelled around the country to acquaint himself with the ground realities and to speak about his experiences. There were public receptions everywhere he went and in Rajkot, Ahmedabad, Calcutta, Rangoon and Madras, the crowds unhitched the horse on his carriage and pulled it themselves. Members of the Modh Vaniya caste, which had excommunicated him for going to England, honoured him in many cities and Gujaratis living in different parts of the country threw parties for him. He was welcomed by Annie Besant in Madras and also honoured by the Muslim League and the Indian South Africa League there. Significantly, in most cities he spoke to student groups and in many cities members of the 'depressed classes' welcomed him.

As he travelled, Gandhi was faced with the decision of where to settle down and what kind of work to engage in. His initial plans to associate with the Servants of India Society in Pune fell through after Gokhale's death within a few weeks of his return. Other friends suggested Hardwar Vaidyanathdham and Rajkot. His final decision revealed him to be a pragmatic Gujarati:

> I had a predilection for Ahmedabad. Being a Gujarati I thought I should be able to render the greatest service to the country through the Gujarati language. And then, as Ahmedabad was an ancient centre for handloom weaving,

it was likely to be the most favourable field for the revival of the cottage industry of hand-spinning. There was also the hope that, the city being the capital of Gujarat, monetary help from its wealthy citizens would be more available here than elsewhere.[14]

Unstated, but equally important, was the fact that Ahmedabad was in British territory (unlike Rajkot, which was a princely state) and struggle against the British could not be effectively launched from non-British territory. Thus, within five months of arriving in India, Gandhi established an ashram, the first of the many institutions he experimented with in South Africa, fine-tuned in Gujarat and then replicated all over India. Student ashrams or hostels already existed in towns where students from the surrounding villages came to stay while they studied in high schools and colleges. Ashrams as communes were introduced by Gandhi and in a decade after the establishment of Satyagraha Ashram, many more were started all over Gujarat and became centres for Gandhian activity. Later, ashrams were established in other parts of the country too.

The name of the ashram was selected to convey Gandhi's agenda for his life's work:

> Our creed was devotion to truth, and our business was the search for and insistence on truth. I wanted to acquaint India with the method I had tried in South Africa, and I desired to test in India the extent to which its application might be possible. So my companions and I selected the name 'Satyagraha Ashram', as conveying both our goal and our method of service.[15]

Every resident of the ashram was required to take *ekadash vrat* or eleven vows and this collection of vows reveals how Gandhi innovated by synthesizing traditional beliefs with his own convictions. The Hindu shastras prescribe *yama–niyama* or abstentions–observances. The chief yama are *ahimsa* (non-violence), *satya* (truth), *asteya* (non-stealing), *brahmacharya* (chastity) and *aparigraha* (non-possession). The main niyama are *shaucha* (bodily purity), *santosha* (contentment), *tapa* (forbearance), *swadhyaya* (study of scriptures) and *ishwarpranidhana* (resignation to the will of God). Gandhi adopted the five yama, added a sixth, *aswaad* (control of the palate, which he may have derived from Jain vows), and these became the first six Ashram Vows, which remained unchanged and non-negotiable. The niyama were replaced by vows of his own conception as the ones essential for preparing Indians for the service of the country. These changed with the changing circumstances. Thus in 1915 subsidiary observances included vows of Swadeshi, fearlessness, removal of untouchability, *jaatmehnat* (manual work), commitment to the mother tongue, weaving and, interestingly, politics.[16] By 1926, 'in view of the many changes and ups and downs that the Ashram had undergone', the last three vows were replaced by *sahishnuta* (tolerance) in response to the growing conflict between Hindus and Muslims. In 1930, in a series of lectures on Ashram Vows, Gandhi, ever conscious of the lightest shades of meanings of words, replaced sahishnuta with one of his own creation, *sarvadharma sambhaava*:

> Equality of Religions. This is the new name we have given to the Ashram observance which we know as 'Tolerance'. '*Sahishnuta*' is a translation of the English word 'Tolerance'. I did not like that word, but could not think of a better one. Kakasaheb, too, did not like that word. He suggested 'Respect for all religions'. I did not like that phrase either. Tolerance may imply a gratuitous assumption of the inferiority of other faiths to one's own and respect suggests a sense of patronizing whereas ahimsa teaches us to entertain the same respect for the religious faiths of others as we accord to our own, thus admitting the imperfection of the latter.[17]

Earlier, in South Africa, Gandhi had been reluctant to use the word 'ashram' to describe the commune in Phoenix. Yet, we find no reference to this in his writings at the time when names for the new settlement were being considered. Nor is there any reflection in his autobiography regarding why he finally chose to add the suffix 'ashram' even though he elaborates on this period in his life in some detail. So we are left to speculate on the issue and for this we find several clues in the events of the time. In mid 1915, Gandhi circulated draft copies of the ashram constitution to a large number of friends in Gujarat and outside. There was a great uproar from upper-caste Gujaratis, particularly the merchant community, over the vow against untouchability and, not to alienate potential funders, he compromised by including a paragraph on his faith in the *varnashram*.[18] He probably felt that the appellation 'ashram' would mollify the upper-caste Hindus and keep the peace. Later that year crisis loomed again when Gandhi invited Dudhabhai, the first untouchable, to join the ashram. The merchants withdrew all financial assistance and the ashram was on the verge of shutting down. This time Gandhi stood firm and was prepared to shift to the untouchable colony in town but this move was averted by a timely contribution by an unnamed merchant (later revealed to be the mill owner Ambalal Sarabhai).

Gandhi simultaneously turned his attention to the existing forums for political and social action in Gujarat and proceeded to inject them with his viewpoint and then to assume leadership over them. Social, political and cultural activism was strong in the cities and small towns of Gujarat. Gujaratis were active in the Congress and even presided over the annual sessions. The most prominent political organization of Gujaratis in Bombay was the Gurjar Sabha and most of its members were professionals, mainly lawyers. Many national social organizations were also active in Gujarat. Gokhale's Servants of India Society had branches in many cities of Gujarat and prominent among its members were Amritlal Thakkar (also known as Thakkar Bapa) and Indulal Yagnik,[19] who started and edited the journal *Navajivan* from Bombay. In 1915-16 both Annie Besant and Tilak started their Home Rule Leagues, which worked in cooperation with each other, and established a wide network in the cities and towns in Gujarat's British territories and the surrounding rural areas. Several Gujaratis in Bombay were active in the Home Rule League and prominent among them were Shankerlal Banker, Jamunadas Dwarkadas and Umar Sobani, who together started *Young India*.

In Ahmedabad political activities were conducted under the aegis of the Gujarat Sabha, which was a forum of moderates. The Gokhale Society in Ahmedabad established the 'Ahmedabad Parliament' and functioned like a study circle where political issues were discussed and debated. Youth groups like the Swadeshi Mitra Mandal were also active. Prominent among the social organizations was the Samasta Paisa Fund, another youth organization which collected funds to run night schools in the industrial areas of Ahmedabad. Here mill workers learnt Gujarati and English, and read newspapers and books through which they acquainted themselves with the political questions of the time. To raise awareness among the educated classes the Fund ran the Dadabhai Naoroji Library. The library movement started by Motibhai Amin in the early 1900s also contributed to awareness building in central Gujarat. The situation was summed up by Dr Hariprasad Desai, a surgeon who had persuaded Gandhi to settle in Ahmedabad and later became the city's mayor: 'Thus, before Mahatma Gandhiji made this town [Ahmedabad] his home, public life here was well ploughed, enriched with manure, and trained and mature farmers cultivated the land to the best of their ability.'[20]

Gandhi drew people from these organizations into his fold. By 1918 Kakasaheb Kalelkar and Mamasaheb Phadke (who were teaching at the Ganganath Bharatiya Sarva Vidyalaya), Indulal Yagnik and Amritlal Thakkar, Mohanlal Pandya and Narsinhbhai Patel (of Minto assassination attempt fame), Vinoba Bhave, the ascetic Swami Anand, the philosopher Kishorelal Mashruwala (the first registrar of Gujarat Vidyapith and who, along with Vinoba, was nominated by Gandhi to be his successor at Sevagram Ashram at Wardha), Narhari Parikh (the executor of Gandhi's will), Mahadev Desai and Vallabhbhai Patel all were associated with Gandhi in one way or another. In

1919 he took over both *Young India* and *Navajivan*, moved them to Ahmedabad and also started a printing press.

At the same time, Gandhi began assuming leadership over these different organizations. He applied for a life membership of the Gujarat Vernacular Society in 1916. In 1917 he was invited to become president of the second Gujarat Educational Conference and later that year, president of the first Gujarat Political Conference. The following year he became president of the Gujarat Sabha as well as Gujarat Stree Kelavani Mandal (Gujarat Women's Education Association), which focussed on promoting women's education in Gujarat. What is significant is not only that did Gandhi begin to dominate public organizations but that he began to integrate political and social reform activities which were, till then, separate and unconnected. So in 1917, when he was invited to be president of the first Gujarat Political Conference at Godhra, he suggested holding the first Gujarat Social Conference on the following day and proposed a woman, Shardaben Mehta, as president. Later he also sought to connect the towns and rural areas through his satyagraha campaigns, ashrams and schools.

It was at the Political Conference at Godhra that Gandhi chided Tilak for coming late and delaying Swaraj, and also persuaded Jinnah to speak Gujarati in public (probably for the first and only time!). It was here that Gandhi put to an end the contemporary practice of commencing the passing of resolutions with a declaration of loyalty to the Crown, which marked another turning point for activists of the time. The Social Conference took place the next day and on the last day Gandhi organized the historic Untouchables Conference at the *bhangi vaas* (Bhangi colony) of Godhra town, which had been swept clean and festooned with flags: 'And for the first time in Gujarat wealthy merchants, lawyers, traders and other elite mingled with dheds and bhangis on one platform . . . It was a mighty gathering impossible for even the Gods to achieve and not seen by anyone in Hindustan for centuries or rather thousands of years.'[21] Thus, the fight against untouchability was put on the social agenda of Gujarat.

At the time that Gandhi was setting up the first of his institutions, the Satyagraha Ashram, he also began working towards creating a national school:

> For many years past, several friends and I have felt that our present education is not national and that in consequence people do not get from it the benefit they ought to. Our children languish as a result of this education. They become incapable of any great achievement and the knowledge they acquire does not spread among the masses—not even in their families. Nor do the young people have any aim in mind in taking this modern education except to get a job and make money.[22]

Efforts to develop an alternative education system had begun in the princely states such as Bhavnagar where Nanalal Bhatt had established the Dakshinamurty Vidyarthi Bhavan. Sayajirao had made primary education compulsory for all children, even fining teachers and parents if children were not in school. At Phoenix Gandhi's engagement with education was prompted by the fact that in South Africa's racist environment there were no schools for Indian children and he eventually developed a philosophy of education which emphasized manual work as much as book learning, using the vernaculars as the medium of instruction and religious instruction covering all the world religions. Systemizing and expanding on this, he decided to start a national school on the ashram campus, the objective being:

1. To adopt a new method of education
2. To pay special attention to character building, the aim being that ten per cent of the pupils at any rate get trained for national service
3. To raise the status of the Gujarati language
4. To work for the spread of the national language, Hindi
5. To open schools of the new pattern in every place, and make this school a model for them, and for the Government as well, to copy. The aim is to have

      teachers trained in this school who will go to the villages
      and run schools there.
    6. To get the new pattern adopted by the Government.[23]

The school was co-educational, the medium of instruction
Gujarati, with an emphasis on music, art, indigenous games
and cultural training in the form of handicrafts. Thus, the
national school began as an experiment in alternative education
and a rejection of modern education and from this evolved the
Gandhian education programme, Nai Talim. It was only after
Gandhi gave the call for non-cooperation that the Gujarat
Vidyapith and Mahavidyalaya were set up.

The Vidyapith was conceived of as a university, with national
schools and colleges affiliated to it. The Mahavidyalaya was
one of the colleges where Gandhi gathered eminent teachers:
A.T. Gidwani left Ramjas College in Delhi to become principal;
religious studies were conducted by Vinoba Bhave; Gujarati
was taught by Ramnarayan Pathak and Narhari Parikh;
Sanskrit by Rasiklal Parikh; economics by Kakasaheb Kalelkar;
and Pali, Magadhi and ancient history of Gujarat by Muni
Jinvijayji. The Vidyapith was set up in 1920 and over the next
few years 30,000 students studied in 137 affiliated national
schools and two colleges. These included thirteen high schools,
fifteen middle schools and fifteen special schools for
untouchables where 300 boys and girls studied. However, the
number of girls studying in these institutes was never more
than 500.

One of the significant achievements of the Vidyapith was its
contribution to the Gujarati language. From the lowest grade
to college, all education was conducted in Gujarati, with
Gujarati as a compulsory subject. Students from outside the
state also had to learn the language though a lighter syllabus
was devised for them. By 1928 all question papers were set in
Gujarati or Hindi. To make such education possible, the
Vidyapith created Gujarati textbooks in various subjects, from
the primary level upwards. By 1922 sixty textbooks were ready
and in 1929 there were 161. Another important contribution

Gandhi as Sahitya Parishad president, 1936

was the compilation of the first authoritative Gujarati dictionary with standardized spellings in 1929.

Also affiliated to the Vidyapith was Puratatva Mandir, a centre for research initiated by Gandhi. It considerably enriched studies in philosophy, Indology, history and Prakrit. Under the leadership of Muni Jinvijayji and Rasiklal Parikh, critical editions of Jain and Buddhist religious texts were published. The centre's research was published in its quarterly *Puratatva*. The scholars Dharmanand Kosambi and Pandit Sukhlalji were also associated with this centre. In 1936 Gandhi became president of the Gujarati Sahitya Parishad and, in his presidential address, he called upon the literary community to leave their ivory towers and write for the most ordinary farmer. In the literary history of Gujarati, the period between 1920 and Independence came to be referred to as 'Gandhi Yug' (Gandhian Era).

As the ashram and Vidyapith were taking shape, Gandhi initiated several satyagrahas. The institutions and the movements had a symbiotic relationship: the ashram and Vidyapith, along with their residents and students, became the base and organizational structure through which the movements were conducted and through the movements Gandhi drew diverse individuals and groups into his fold. The first tentative steps were taken in 1917 on the question of the exploitation of the indigo planters in Champaran, where Gandhi conducted an inquiry, presented a report to the government and negotiated a settlement. Most of the satyagrahas which followed took place in Gujarat—Viramgam, Ahmedabad, Kheda, Bardoli, Borsad, Dandi—on a variety of issues, using a range of strategies, refining the ones he had used before and innovating new ones.

The first of the satyagrahas in Gujarat took place in Ahmedabad in 1918 when Gandhi intervened in a dispute between textile mill owners and mill workers. At the time the Ahmedabad mills employed about 50,000 people, living and working in very poor conditions. During the First World War, the mill owners had made enormous profits and now wanted to cut the workers' plague bonus which had been offered as an incentive to panic-stricken workers to stay in the city and not flee to their villages to avoid the disease. Gandhi advised the workers to go on strike and, in response, the owners declared a lockout. Huge mass meetings were held every evening on the bed of the dry Sabarmati river. Thousands of workers paraded the streets of the city peacefully with banners proclaiming *Ek Tek* (Keep the Pledge). The impasse continued for three weeks, after which the movement began to weaken as the workers lost hope and were on the verge of starvation. They accused Gandhi of living in comfort and travelling in cars while they became weak with hunger. Stung by the attacks on his integrity, Gandhi went on a fast.

Gandhi's siding with the workers brought him into sharp conflict with the mill owners, whose charity supported the ashram. The mill owners had withdrawn all financial help when Gandhi admitted an untouchable family into the ashram. This time they tried a different approach. They asked an elderly mill owner to be their spokesperson and initiate a dialogue. 'Mahatmaji,' began the old man respectfully, 'Even bullock carts stray from their narrow ruts [a Gujarati saying implying that there is a way around every obstacle]. You are a Vaniya and so are we. . . [implying that this shared identity should enable them to strike a deal and end the deadlock].' Gandhi lost his temper: 'I do not want to become that kind of Vaniya. I do not want to enjoy riches at the expense of the mill workers' sweat.' Reacting with presence of mind, Vallabhbhai Patel intervened and tried to guide the conversation towards a settlement. Both sides agreed to the appointment of a neutral arbitrator and a satisfactory compromise was reached, whereby the workers got a bonus of 27.5 per cent, which was halfway between the offer of the mill owners [20 per cent] and the workers' demand [35 per cent].'[24] This satyagraha led to the formation of the Gandhian trade union Majoor Mahajan, which dominated labour politics for decades, even after Independence.

No sooner had the mill workers' concerns been resolved than Gandhi became involved with the problems faced by the peasants of Kheda. Their crops had failed due to excessive rainfall and they were in no position to pay taxes. When the situation was brought to Gandhi's notice, he ordered a survey of the 600 affected villages. For the first time, ashram workers and youngsters attached with various youth and political organizations in the area were brought together to conduct the survey. Indulal Yagnik recalled in his autobiography that though many youths had toured the villages during their involvement with the Home Rule agitation this was the first time that they studied the village economy in detail. Gandhi asked them to complete the assessment of the crop yield within fifteen days and imposed strict discipline on the youngsters. The group of thirty was not allowed to hire vehicles or ask for transportation from the villagers but had to travel on foot from place to place and food consisted of a ration of peanuts and roasted gram.[25]

Convinced that farmers in the area were genuinely affected, Gandhi requested the authorities to suspend land revenue for that season. And when letters and meetings brought no response, he initiated a no-tax campaign and big and small farmers rallied under his leadership. Soon the authorities began to threaten the peasants and attach their movable property. This went on for three months, the tension increased and after a while the

Gandhi in Kheda, 1929

weaker peasants started paying up. Realizing that the people had reached the end of their tether, Gandhi was looking for 'some graceful way to terminating the struggle'[26] when the collector finally suspended taxes.

Gandhi later analysed the significance of the event both for the rural peasants and for the urban educated:

> The Kheda Satyagraha marks the beginning of an awakening among the peasants of Gujarat, the beginning of their true political education.
>
> Dr. Besant's brilliant Home Rule agitation had certainly touched the peasants, but it was the Kheda campaign that compelled the educated public workers to establish contact with the actual life of the peasants. They learnt to identify themselves with the latter. They found their proper sphere of work, their capacity for sacrifice increased. That Vallabhbhai found himself during this campaign was by itself no small achievement. [27]

This was the beginning of Vallabhbhai Patel's (1875–1950) lifelong relationship with Gandhi. Although Patel had heard of Gandhi and his effort to establish an ashram in Ahmedabad, he had scarcely paid any attention. Being a successful lawyer, he was more interested in his game of bridge at the Gujarat Club and ignored Gandhi when he had visited this club of lawyers. It was only after the Champaran Satyagraha, in the summer of 1917, that this son of a farmer was attracted to Gandhi and started collaborating with him. During the Kheda Satyagraha, he offered his full-time services and at the end of the struggle Gandhi spoke about his discovery of Patel in the following words:

Gandhi with Sardar Patel, 1944

A leader's skill is judged by the competence in selecting his assistants for the execution of his plans. Many people were prepared to follow my advice, but I could not make up my mind as to who should be my deputy commander. I then thought of Vallabhbhai. I must admit that when I met Vallabhbhai first, I could not help wondering who this stiff-looking person was, and whether he would be able to do what I wanted. But the more I came to know him, the more I realised that I must secure his help. Vallabhbhai too has come to the conclusion that although he has flourishing legal practice today and is doing very important work in the municipality, he must become a whole time public worker and serve his country. So he has taken the plunge. If it were not for his assistance, I must admit that this campaign would not have been carried through so successfully.[28]

About a year after resolving the Kheda issue came the satyagraha against the Rowlatt Act, which aimed at curtailing revolutionary activity against the British by giving extraordinary powers to law enforcement authorities. As a sign of protest, Gandhi called for a nationwide hartal on 6 April 1919. Once again Gandhi was innovating by reinterpreting tradition. As we have seen earlier hartal as a technique of protest was not new and in the pre-British period too the merchants of Gujarat adopted this technique to express their dissatisfaction against oppressive acts of the state. Gandhi refined this weapon and put it into the hands of common Indians to give voice to their resentment against British rulers. The sixth of April was set as the date for the commencement of satyagraha and on this day, in Bombay, Gandhi sold proscribed copies of *Hind Swaraj* and *Sarvodaya* and issued an unregistered newspaper, *Satyagrahi*. Apart from Bombay the other places where the books sold were Ahmedabad and a few other towns of Gujarat. Gandhi refused to obey an order banning him from entering Punjab, and he was arrested, sparking off spontaneous rioting in many places in Gujarat, including Ahmedabad, Viramgam, Nadiad, Uttarsanda and Anand.

Though Gandhi asked the people to keep peace, the situation soon went out of control. In Ahmedabad people armed themselves with bamboo sticks and went on a rampage, setting on fire the collector's office and the telegraph office and burning police stations. An English sergeant was caught in the mob's fury and killed. Mill workers struck work and added to the melee. Martial law was declared in Ahmedabad and angry crowds derailed a train carrying troops by sabotaging the railway tracks near Nadiad.[29]

The satyagraha was called off on 18 April and within three weeks Gandhi was drafting a memorandum to the viceroy regarding the Khilafat. What followed was the Non-cooperation Movement, which included boycott of government titles, government functions, government and government-controlled educational institutions, government law courts, service in Mesopotamia, legislatures and foreign cloth. The Non-cooperation Movement not only strengthened Gandhi's leadership in Gujarat but also represented the peak of the acceptance of his programme by large sections of Gujarati society. The most perceptible response came from the middle class as hundreds gave up government jobs, lawyers like Patel and Mavlankar (the first Speaker of the Lok Sabha) gave up their lucrative practice, the municipalities were boycotted and members of the legislative assembly from many cities resigned. Students left government schools and colleges and joined the many Rashtriya Shalas or national schools established at this time under the umbrella of the Gujarat Vidyapith. Older students boycotted government colleges and joined the Gujarat Mahavidyalaya.

National schools were started at the Anavil and Patidar Ashrams in Surat and these institutions became nerve centres for future Gandhian programmes. As the Non-cooperation Movement was the first satyagraha to be formally adopted by the Congress, there was a great expansion of the Congress party in Gujarat and what was once an elite organization spread to the rural areas. In thousands of villages, elected Congress committees sprang up and became the vehicle for Gandhian programmes. In fact, Gandhian institutions and the Congress structure became virtually indistinguishable. As the Khilafat issue was also part of the focus of the movement, sizeable numbers of Muslims from cities such as Surat, Bharuch and Ahmedabad as well as the surrounding villages participated.

There was a powerful resuscitation of Swadeshi with bonfires of foreign clothes and revival of charkha and takli spinning. Many small industries in decline were revived and Swadeshi stores and khadi bhandars were inaugurated. It gave hope to many that Gandhi's movement would give them employment and improve their lives. In the villages and towns *prabhat pheri* or morning processions were taken out to spread the message of the movement and *vanar sena* or children's organizations were established. Dinkar Mehta, a Gandhian-turned-socialist and later communist mayor of Ahmedabad, recalls: 'For the first time, we saw women participating in processions, in

Prabhat Pheris and singing songs for collecting funds and selling khaddar. We had never seen women coming out except when they went to temples.'[30]

Jyotsna Shukla, a poet from Surat, started editing a weekly paper at the time. Other women who became prominent in public life were Vidyaben Nilkanth, Shardaben Mehta and Anasuya Sarabhai. This was the time when popular nationalist songs were composed in Gujarati. A popular song was *Ratanbano garbo*, which described the burden of British rule through the eyes of a young girl, Ratanba, and was set in the form of the traditional Gujarati folk garba. Urdu songs were composed by the many Muslims drawn into the movement. Collections of rashtriya geet or nationalist songs were printed and sold in the thousands.

As part of the movement's constructive programme, social reform and educational activities were started in the tribal areas of Gujarat. The Vedchchi Ashram was set up in south Gujarat and it established residential schools for tribal boys and girls. Under the leadership of eminent Gandhians such as Jugatram Dave, an anti-alcohol campaign was started among the tribals and toddy palms were cut down in large numbers in Surat district. This mobilization of tribal communities was reflected in their strong participation in the Salt Satyagraha less than a decade later.

In 1928 the Bardoli Satyagraha took place under Patel's leadership without Gandhi's direct involvement. Vallabhbhai had independently led the Borsad Satyagraha in 1923, where he had mobilized peasants of villages around Karamsad and Borsad towns of Kheda district, the area where he had grown up. But it was during the Bardoli Satyagraha in Surat district that his leadership style blossomed and he was hailed as 'Sardar' of India. In 1927 the peasants of Bardoli taluka or block (with 137 villages, and a population of nearly 90,000) were alarmed when the British government imposed a 22 per cent increase in land revenue after a new revenue settlement. For the peasants, the stiff increase was not only excessive but also arbitrarily fixed despite their protest. A deputation of peasants of Bardoli along with two leaders of the Kheda and Borsad Satyagrahas,

Mohanlal Pandya and Ravishankar Maharaj, met Patel, who was then president of both the Gujarat Pradesh Congress Committee and the Ahmedabad Municipality. They presented a survey of sixty villages of Bardoli and, convinced by their data as well as the peasants' preparedness to face all dire consequences, Vallabhbhai approached Gandhi. Gandhi gave them the green signal with the blessing, 'Go forward and victory to Gujarat.' After four months of harsh struggle in the scorching summer, the peasants of Bardoli brought victory to Gujarat. The government was forced to appoint an inquiry committee and the revenue assessment of Bardoli and adjoining Choriyasi taluka was reduced by almost 75 per cent.

Through the struggle, Patel displayed the qualities of a general: meticulous planning, a shrewd strategy for taking on the adversary, skill for mobilizing people and winning their abiding loyalty while being a strict disciplinarian, and tenacity to sustain the struggle in the face of repression. Describing the intensity of the resistance and the strength of Patel's leadership, the *Times of India* observed:

> The leaders of the no-tax campaign have succeeded in producing such a complete paralysis of the machinery of Government in the Taluka that not a finger can be moved, not a person stirs out of his house without their knowledge and consent. Even the officers of Government themselves are practically dependent for supplies, conveyance, etc. upon the good will of Mr. Vallabhbhai Patel and his "volunteers" . . . The power of the social boycott, the wide net of Mr. Patel's followers and informers, the complete success that has hitherto attended the campaign and the utter helplessness of the Government has given to the people a vivid realization of their power [which will produce] . . . a crisis that the country has rarely experienced. [ellipses in the original][31]

In the wake of the Bardoli victory, Vallabhbhai was honoured at large meetings organized in almost all the major cities of

Gujarat. Patel's response on receiving a *manpatra* (address of honour) at Ahmedabad reveals the extent of Gandhi's mobilization in Gujarat as well the public perception of Patel's status as second-in-command to Gandhi:

> The citizens of Ahmedabad in giving me this address have described me as the chief disciple of Gandhiji. I only wish that I deserved the description; I know, however, that I am not worthy of it. I do not know how often I shall have to be reborn in order to achieve that distinction . . . If anyone else deserves to be honoured, it is my colleagues who showed astonishing discipline, and who had complete confidence in me. It was not I who trained such colleagues. If we have such men of whom the whole of Gujarat is so justly proud, the credit again goes to Gandhiji.[32]

The satyagrahas at Kheda, Borsad and Bardoli were all tax-resistance movements where peasants of mainly the Patidar community played a leading role and acquired prominence, first in the Congress and after Independence in the politics of Gujarat.

SALT SATYAGRAHA

It was in early 1930 that Gandhi started making plans for the most dramatic of his Indian satyagrahas, the last one conducted from his ashram in Ahmedabad. On 11 March, as he left on his march to Dandi to break the salt laws, he vowed that he would not return till Swaraj was won. The Salt Satyagraha was a carefully constructed event where all the sections of Gujarati society which had been mobilized through earlier satyagrahas, students educated in the national schools and colleges and others drawn into the Gandhian network through the ashrams and the constructive programme played their own part. The event was steeped in symbolism which was to be used and reused in later decades in different ways by different people.

In December 1929 the Congress met at Lahore and declared Purna Swaraj or complete independence as its goal and a couple of months later Gandhi was vested with the power to launch a

Dandi Yatra, 1930

movement at a time and on an issue of his choosing. Much to the bewilderment of his colleagues in the Congress, Gandhi decided to march to the seashore, manufacture salt and thereby break the salt laws. Tax on salt, he felt, affected all Indians and a movement around this would bring together disparate groups. So, on 2 March 1930, he sent Viceroy Irwin what is now well known as his 'Dear Friend' letter, describing his intention to embark on civil disobedience.

Gandhi's skilful use of symbols set the Salt Satyagraha apart from all his other satyagrahas. Gandhi gradually and painstakingly transformed salt from an everyday seasoning to a symbol of Swaraj by emphasizing its various dimensions: emotional (essential for the survival of all living things), economic (unjustly high tax on an article used by the poorest of the poor), political (an opportunity for joint action cutting across caste, class and religious differences) and cultural (symbol of loyalty and fidelity). Also, he exploited the fact that the march in Indian tradition is viewed as a kind of penance and in the Western world, associated with courage and righteousness.

The decision to march was a shrewd one as it gave Gandhi an opportunity to rouse the countryside and made the event a live drama sustained for a considerable period of time which would have not been possible if he had simply taken a train to the coast. The destination was also carefully chosen. Local leaders of Kheda suggested the coast of their district, but finally Dandi in Surat district was chosen. Apart from having a long seashore, Surat had a strong network of Congress committees at the village level (strengthened after the Bardoli Satyagraha), ashrams, national schools and khadi bhandars. Congress workers, ashram residents, students and constructive workers provided the infrastructure for speedy and reliable transmission of information, local arrangements for staying and food, and organized Gandhi's meetings in the villages on the way to Dandi. Surat district adjoined the princely Baroda state where the Gaekwad was sympathetic to the freedom movement. People avoiding arrest or looking for shelter during the movement could easily escape into Baroda territory. Also, the timing was decided such that Gandhi would march for about a month and reach Dandi on 6 April, the anniversary of the Rowlatt hartal. The following seven days (ending with 13 April, the day of the Jallianwala killings) had been celebrated as National Week since 1921.

The lawyer in Gandhi had noted that the penal sections of the salt laws were not severe and the law could be broken in many ways: manufacturing, possessing, selling, buying and exhorting to buy and sell were all breaches of the law. As long as the march was conducted peacefully, there were no provisions of law which prohibited it. The bulk of the research on salt, its history, the economics of its manufacture and so on was done by the students at Vidyapith, who also passed on the material for publication in *Navajivan*. Students also formed the *agrim tukdi*, pilot group, which went ahead to make arrangements in the villages on the way.

The members of the marching group were chosen to be a symbol of the united India that Gandhi visualized. The group of seventy-nine represented all the provinces of India, covered a wide age group and included Muslims, Christians and Hindus with representation from the lowest castes. By selecting Abbas Tyabji to replace him as leader in the event of his arrest and Sarojini Naidu as next in line for leadership, he symbolically conveyed his regard for Muslims and women. Though Gandhi had already become 'Mahatma' by the end of the Non-cooperation Movement, religious imagery began to be used extensively around this event. Local and international journalists likened the march to Moses leading his people in the Exodus, Jesus leading his followers to Jerusalem, Ram leaving Ayodhya and Buddha's *mahabhinishkraman* in search of enlightenment. The event was managed by Patel and when he was arrested shortly before the march two senior leaders of south Gujarat—Dayaljibhai Desai and Kalyanjibhai Mehta, founders of the Anavil and Patidar Ashrams respectively—organized the cadres, managed the tight schedule and kept up the tempo. As Gandhi passed through the villages in central and south Gujarat, he spoke about the meaning of Swaraj, the importance of the constructive programme, the removal of untouchability, Hindu–Muslim unity and the importance of greater women's participation. Gandhi reached Dandi on 5 April and broke the law the next day by gathering salt from the seashore. He set up camp at a nearby village and planned further campaigns, including a protest at the Dharasana salt depot. He was arrested in the first week of May and it was left to his lieutenants Abbas Tyabji and Sarojini Naidu to lead the Dharasana campaign, where the British responded with severe violence and mass arrests.

If the Non-cooperation Movement was an all-India event, the Salt Satyagraha was a world event. Day by day, the march was reported in newspapers around the world. Gandhi was nominated *Time* magazine's Man of the Year and was twice on its cover: at the start of the satyagraha and, again, about a year later. Many underground news-sheets were produced in Gujarat: *Congress Bulletin* and *Congress Patrika* from Bombay, *Dholera Satyagraha* from Dholera, *Tankha* from Barvala, *Rajdroh* from Dhandhuka, *Kranti* from Savarkundla and *Viramgam Satyagraha* from Viramgam. Dinkar Mehta and his team produced an investigative report on the atrocities at Dharasana entitled *Dharasanano Kalo Ker*. The event also inspired two epic poems in Gujarati. Manibhai Desai composed *1930no Mithano Ransangram* soon after the Dharasana raid as a panegyric to the martyrs and participants in the event. The next year Jaikrishna Surti described the march to Dandi in *Mahabhinishkraman*.

The most significant aspect of this satyagraha was the extensive participation of women and Adivasis. Gandhi had decided not to allow women to march with him, though he had appointed a woman as one of the leaders to take over the movement after his arrest. Women were involved in writing and producing underground newsletters, picketing foreign cloth shops, anti-alcohol campaigns and organizing village meetings along the route. Adivasis turned out in large numbers in Surat district, a reflection of the impact of the ashrams, national schools and the constructive programme. Many Adivasi men and women went to jail and their contribution to the freedom struggle is one of the most meagrely documented subjects. Despite all efforts, the participation of Muslims was not significant. Probably, Gandhi's quotes from the Koran failed to appeal and they could not identify with Gandhi's use of imagery from Hindu mythology in his speeches (such as describing independent India as Ramrajya, likening Dandi to Haridwar and presenting Sita and Draupadi as models of courage). Neither the credibility of the nationalist Gujarati Muslims such as Abbas Tyabji nor salt as an economic, non-religious issue could succeed in uniting the two communities.[33]

By this time, Gandhi's stature in Gujarati society was close to divine and Patel was regarded as his worthy deputy, as can be seen in a Sanskrit couplet composed by the celebrated Gujarati poet Narsinhrao Divetia. It was 1931 and Vallabhbhai was president-designate of the Congress session at Karachi. Gandhi and Vallabhbhai were on their way to Karachi from Bombay when Narsinhrao handed a couplet to Gandhi. In his composition he had rephrased a famous excerpt from the Bhagvad Gita to liken Gandhi to Krishna and Patel to Arjun:

Yatra Yogeshwaro Gandhi Vallabhbhashch
Dhurandharah
Tatra Shrirvijayo Bhutirdhruva Nitirmatirmam

Where Gandhi is the leader and Vallabh the bearer of
the yoke
There, victory will prevail I do firmly believe

Narsinhrao wrote in his diary that for two days he had pondered over what adjective would be appropriate to describe Patel. He first tried the adjective 'Karnadharak' or steersman and later changed it to 'Dhurandhara' or mighty one bearing a yoke.[34] Indeed, Vallabhbhai was both a steersman of Gujarat Congress from the early 1920s and a mighty leader of the Indian National Congress from the early 1930s. It was Patel's style of leadership that became a model for future generations in Gujarat.[35]

*

Women in Gujarat were greatly empowered by the Salt Satyagraha and leaders like Mridula Sarabhai, niece of Anasuya Sarabhai, were concerned that 'the women who had been energized and awakened' should not 'relapse into apathy and go back to be confined to their homes'. Gandhi wrote to her: 'Our women joined the salt *satyagraha*. They came out of their homes. It is now your duty to see that they should not be imprisoned within the four walls of their homes.'[36]

This led to the formation of Jyoti Sangh in Ahmedabad, the first autonomous women's organization in Gujarat. Gandhi laid the foundation stone of its first building and marked the beginning of a new phase where women, who had till then been at the receiving end of reform activities of enlightened male members of Gujarati society, came together to form and run their own organization and articulate their concerns. Jyoti Sangh focussed on education for women, vocational training, entrepreneurship, running libraries for women and organizing lectures for them by distinguished speakers. It published a weekly magazine, *Jyotiputri*, which carried articles on the status of women, oppressive traditions and the need for reform and so on. One wing of Jyoti Sangh focussed on rescuing women from domestic violence and social and physical harassment.

More women began to enter the public domain and this was reflected in the large participation of women in the Quit India Movement in 1942.[37] Later Mridula Sarabhai and her associate Kamalaben Patel worked to rescue and support women abducted during Partition.

However, the period following the Salt Satyagraha proved to be a turning point for the Gandhian movement in Gujarat. As promised, Gandhi never returned to live in Ahmedabad and instead set up a new ashram at Wardha. With this, the locus of the movement shifted outside Gujarat. The repression of the British intensified; they closed down the Satyagraha Ashram in 1933. The Vidyapith was closed down around the same time and its students dispersed. Even before its final closure, student numbers were steadily falling. With the adoption of a new Constitution in 1935 and the formation of the first interim government in 1937, many Gandhians who were prominent in Congress politics veered towards careers in office, and power politics came to occupy the centre stage for them.

Many of the issues dear to Gandhi were in disarray as Gujarati society resisted his efforts. In the face of bitter opposition from the elite of Ahmedabad, Gandhi had invited a Dalit family to live in the ashram and followed this gesture with a programme to remove untouchability from Hindu society. Just before dismantling the ashram in 1933, he renamed it Harijan Ashram and founded the Harijan Sevak Sangh. Yet despite all efforts, Parikshitlal Majmudar, an eminent Gandhian and Brahmin who dedicated his life to the removal of untouchability, regretfully wrote to Gandhi in 1937 that 'save one or two exceptions not a single temple or well has been thrown open for Harijans in Gujarat'.[38] Harijans also turned to Ambedkar as their leader and with the assertion of their identity under him, rejected the very word 'Harijan' and replaced it with 'Dalit' later.

Hindu–Muslim unity too seemed impossible, with the relationship between the two communities steadily worsening as the Muslims were increasingly drawn to another Gujarati, Jinnah. There were several communal riots in Bombay, Veraval and Ahmedabad with their echoes in other cities culminating in Partition. After Partition, many Muslim leaders of Gujarat left for Pakistan, leaving a void in the community, and relationships between Hindus and Muslims only deteriorated. The Adivasis continued to work within the Gandhian fold, though some were drawn to Indulal Yagnik's Kisan Sabha movement, which worked to prevent the exploitation of Adivasis by the peasant community and moneylenders. After Independence there was a growing feeling that while the Gandhians had made an immense contribution to education and social reform among Adivasis, they had stifled the development of leadership within the community.

As for Satyagraha, if the people of Gujarat showed Gandhi the might of this weapon, they also showed him its limitations. In 1939 Gandhi embarked on a satyagraha against the autocracy of the ruler of Rajkot. This ruler was the grandson of the king in whose court Gandhi's father had served as diwan. His father had held a reception in Gandhi's honour in 1915. However, this British-educated son was least responsive to Gandhi's urging that it was time to grant some measure of political power to people even in the princely states. Patel hammered out an agreement on a scheme of political reform but the ruler reneged on it. Then Gandhi went on a fast but it had no impact on the ruler or his advisers. Finally, the Chief Justice of India was called to comment on the legality of the agreement with the ruler and he ruled in Patel's favour. Gandhi called off his fast but the ruler continued to play fast and loose with the Congress and the citizens of the state. Gandhi was devastated by this blow to his most cherished ideals and beliefs and he never really found a way to overcome the limitation of using satyagraha before an unresponsive opponent.

Over time, four streams developed within the Gandhian movement. The first stream consisted of committed Gandhians who shared Gandhi's ideology and to a large extent his spiritual concerns and carried out the constructive programme in their own spheres, in their own ways. Prominent among these were Kishorelal Mashruwala, Ravishankar Maharaj and Jugatram

Dave. The second stream was a group of youngsters, mainly Vidyapith students, who had begun to be exposed to socialist writings. Having participated in the Bardoli and Salt Satyagrahas, they felt that leaders like Patel focussed overly on peasants' rights, ignoring issues related to bonded labour, debt slavery and problems of the really backward sections of the rural populations. This section consisting of Dinkar Mehta, Kamalashankar Pandya and Ishwarlal Desai formed the Congress Socialist Party in 1934 and seniors such as Dr Sumant Mehta supported them. Their communication lines with Gandhi always remained open with feelings of mutual regard, though Patel, the leaders within the Majoor Mahajan and, later, Morarji Desai remained hostile. The third stream consisted of people associated with the Congress network who were increasingly drawn to the Gandhian movement for the opportunities it gave them to enjoy power in the municipalities and legislatures particularly from the late 1930s onwards when the party captured these institutions after the elections. Many in this group had been students in the Vidyapith who were now a decade older and looking for a career in politics. A fourth stream was of what we could call Gandhi *bhakts*, who deified Gandhi, reduced his ideology to dogma and crushed the spirit of inquiry and critical reinterpretation of Gandhism. Within Gandhian circles they were referred to as *guru-ashrami*.[39] Many in this category occupied important positions in the ashrams and Vidyapith even after Independence. Not only did they control the resources of the ashrams and Gandhian educational institutions, but they also used their influence within the system to ensure that accounts of satyagrahas, ashram life and Vidyapith were written like odes to Gandhi, narrowing the space for a critical understanding of events and people associated with Gandhi.

These were not, of course, watertight groups but together they dominated the events in Gujarat till Independence and after.

8

'Hindu' and 'Muslim'

For an outsider, the distancing between Hindus and Muslims of Gujarat has become the leitmotif of the Gujarati social landscape of the twentieth century: two religious communities simply unable to get along and finding it impossible to resolve their differences through any means other than increasingly barbaric violence. As we have already seen, Gujarat had experienced an uneasy encounter with three groups who came from outside: 'Muslims', Portuguese and the Marathas. The local population established a working relationship with all three—in politics, trade and everyday life. The Portuguese phase was of course short-lived and the Maratha menace was replaced by 'benevolent' British rule. But the relationship with 'Muslims' became progressively strained. Embodying the poles of this situation of seemingly irreconcilable differences are two Gujaratis: Gandhi, the father of India, and Jinnah, the father of Pakistan, born within a few hundred miles of each other, with a common mother tongue but hardly speaking the same language. This chapter explores the contours of the changing relationship between the two communities and tries to delineate the forces which powered the course of events.

SOMNATH AS METAPHOR

In the last decade of the nineteenth century, a violent Hindu–Muslim conflict in Prabhas Patan, the holy city of Somnath, set off ripples which were felt in Bombay and London. In mid 1893 local Muslims carried a *tazia*[1] near the 'Dehotsarga' pipal tree for burial. This tree was worshipped by Hindus as the sacred place where Lord Krishna completed his earthly existence. To prevent conflict, local authorities had issued prohibitory orders but tazia processionists defied them. In the ensuing commotion, six sadhus, two Brahmins, a government doctor and his three Hindu staff members were killed. The Lakshminarayan temple adjoining the Dehotsarga was desecrated and burnt. A number of Muslims were also wounded in the melee.

Prabhas Patan was part of Junagadh state and, alarmed by the carnage, the nawab and his Hindu diwan rushed additional police forces and arrested several people. Nevertheless, the killing of Hindu sadhus and Brahmins created an uproar not only in Saurashtra but also in faraway Bombay. A series of protest meetings were organized by the various Mahajans and sects there and Hindu Gujarati merchants of Bombay carried out a virtual boycott of the Muslim community. Muslims countered this Hindu mobilization by rallying their community in Bombay, resulting in a large-scale, bloody communal riot. During the week-long riot, more than 500 people were injured and sixty-five were killed.

The observations of *The Times* of London show that the British media automatically viewed the events in Prabhas Patan and the response to it in Bombay in the context of Somnath's long history of destruction:

> It was to certain meetings and counter-meetings for an avowedly charitable object that the Bombay riots were directly due. Somnath, in the native state of Junagarh; has been the scene of outbursts of Muhammadan and Hindu fanaticism from the days of Mahmud, the Idol Smasher, in 1024 A.D. It is now a city of ruins and graves. On the west the plain is dotted with Muhammadan tombs; on the east with temples and shrines to the two great Hindu deities. Under its modern name of Prabhas Pattan it is still the scene of bloody religious tumults and this year the proceedings proved rather more murderous than usual. The Hindus in Bombay accordingly convened a public meeting to raise a relief fund for their suffering coreligionists in the native state of Junagarh; the Bombay

Muhammadans responded by a counter-meeting to send succour to wounded and afflicted followers of Islam. A rumour spread among the lower Hindus that the Muhammadans were going to hold a general slaughter of cows; a counter rumour spread among the lower Muhammadans that the Hindus were going to wreck all the Muhammadan butchers' shops. The excitement was allowed to gain head, mosques were desecrated, temples attacked and a fairly equal number of Hindu and Muhammadan rioters were killed in street fighting.[2]

Yet, the 1893 conflict was not related to the Somnath temple at all. The ancient Somnath temple was in ruins and the newer eighteenth-century temple built by Ahilyabai Holkar was located elsewhere in the walled city. At this new temple, the daily worship of Lord Shiva was performed by the local Brahmins and the daily music before the God was played by Muslim musicians, reflecting the shared culture which had evolved over the centuries. In fact, the friction this time was around a site which was sacred for the Vaishnav community. It is believed that Vallabhacharya, the founder of Pushtimarg, the most influential Vaishnav sect of Gujarat, visited Prabhas Patan and stayed at Dehotsarga. The place is recognized as the sixty-fifth 'baithak' of Vallabhacharya and, for the followers of his sect, this place has the sacredness of a great tirth. Not surprisingly, the rich Gujarati Vaishnav merchants of Bombay considered the violation of this sacred space a frontal attack on their power and prestige.

The Dehotsarga had gradually eclipsed the Somnath temple. The site of Dehotsarga had been violated earlier, in 1850, when Muslims wanted to rebuild the adjoining mosque. The Mahajan of the city made a representation to the Gaekwad of Baroda who in turn reported to Company sarkar. The governor of Bombay wrote to the Nawab of Junagadh, who prohibited the rebuilding of the mosque. The issue remained local and did not evoke wider expression or cause reverberations. In 1888 there was a similar conflict involving sacred places, a holy pipal tree on Dehotsarga and cow killing. This time the Nawab of Junagadh sent his Hindu diwan to settle the matter. Though the diwan tried to settle claims and counter-claims of both communities, the bitterness continued and flared into communal violence on Ramnavami day in 1890. The Hindu merchants of Bombay asked the governor to intervene. The newspapers of Bombay also took sides and the event was turned into a Hindu–Muslim issue contested in the public arena of Bombay.

Realizing the gravity of the situation, the Bombay government appointed a three-member commission headed by Colonel J.M. Hunter. The commission asked both the communities to nominate their *mukhatiyar* or representatives. While the Hindus nominated a group of seven representatives comprising Brahmins and Vaniyas, the Muslims nominated a group of four comprising two Saiyyads and two Memon traders. The Hunter Commission submitted its report after three years and during the inquiry the notion of two antagonistic blocs, Hindu and Muslim, was reinforced over and over again. No sooner had the din of the Hunter Commission subsided than Prabhas Patan was again engulfed by violence precipitated by the tazia procession.

The Nawab of Junagadh immediately appointed a tribunal. This attracted wide attention not only because of the nature of the incident but also because it was headed by the eminent national leader Pherozeshah Mehta. The tribunal found eighteen Muslims guilty and they were sentenced to imprisonment ranging from one to five years. But the bitterness and mutual mistrust deepened, and the two communities, intimately connected to each other in day-to-day economic activities, tried to arrive at a compromise. By 1896 leaders of Prabhas Patan reached an understanding: the Muslim community agreed to abandon forever the mosque adjoining the Dehotsarga pipal tree and the Hindus reciprocated by promising that no music would be played near the mosque. As a goodwill gesture, it was also decided that all the imprisoned Muslims would be released. The Nawab of Junagadh accepted the compromise and thus the fire of communal conflict at Prabhas Patan was extinguished.

Despite the rapprochement, the chain of events at Prabhas Patan left a deep mark on the newspaper-reading Hindu middle class of Gujarat. Earlier a few arms-bearing Muslim groups like Arabs and Pathans were perceived as killers but now the entire Muslim community was looked upon as slayers of sadhus, Brahmins and cows. As the site of Dehotsarga was at the centre of the conflict, the powerful and dominant Vaishnav mercantile section of Gujarat was perturbed. The sacredness of Prabhas Patan became pre-eminent in their perception and all Muslims were turned into present-day rakshasas.

The decade before the riot in Bombay saw a series of communal riots throughout North India.[3] This wave of religious riots attracted the attention of the British government at the highest level. As MP, Dadabhai Naoroji raised the issue in the British Parliament, asking for a report on the Hindu–Muslim riots during the previous five years with details about how each riot was organized, how it was dealt with and how many persons were killed and wounded. Other parliamentarians also asked similar questions. In response, the government of India submitted a report emphasizing its neutrality in religious matters and gave the following reasons for the spurt in Hindu–Muslim conflicts:

1. Improved means of transport and communication and interchange of news between different parts of the country, causing the publication of exaggerated reports and partisan statements.
2. Embittered feelings of the Muslims, who were becoming more and more conscious every day that the Hindus had outstripped them in the race of life and had obtained almost a monopoly of public employment and of success in legal and other professions.
3. Hindu religious revival. The development of Cow Protection Societies was given as one of the marked features of this movement which aimed at drawing tighter the bonds of Hindu religious discipline by inculcating among the Hindus respect for Brahmins and veneration for the cow.[4]

ROLE OF BRITISH POLICIES

British policies—the census, elections in local self-government, and separate electorates for Hindus and Muslims—too contributed to hardening communal identities. The introduction of the decennial census by the colonial rulers from the 1870s had already made the populace conscious of their religious and caste identities. Even though it was fraught with problems, British census officers persisted with their efforts to qualify Hinduism and Islam and define the religious boundaries between the two communities. In the process they succeeded in imposing a framework for classifying people, first on the minds of the enumerators and later on the educated middle class. For common Gujaratis, like their counterparts in the rest of the Indian subcontinent, caste and subcaste, sect and subsect identities were more tangible and real and were the categories they used for social classification rather than 'Hindu' and 'Muhammadan' religious categories imposed by the census. Moreover, there were sects such as 'Matiya' or 'Piranapanthi' and such groups as 'Shekhada' and 'Molesalam' in Gujarat that could not be placed in macro-religious categories of 'Hinduism' and 'Islam'. Even forty years after the census was introduced, the Bombay superintendent of census classified members of such sects and groups under 'Hindu Muhammadans'. The commissioner of census, E.A. Gait, said that though the persons in this category did not exceed 35,000 it 'has perhaps served a very useful purpose in drawing prominent attention to the extremely indefinite character of the boundary line between different religions in India'.[5]

The introduction of elections in institutions of local self-government also contributed to intensifying community and caste feelings. When Lord Ripon initiated reforms in 1883-84, municipalities and local boards in Gujarat experienced the process of elections for the first time. Even though only half the seats were open to election and voting rights were restricted to property owners, taxpayers and educated sections, the electoral system added a new dimension to social dynamics at the local level.

In 1895 Dahyabhai Zaveri, who founded the Deshi Natak Samaj and also established the first theatre in Ahmedabad, wrote and performed his play '*Municipal Election*', which astutely captured how the process of election generated social dilemmas and discord. At one point in the play Pirbhai, a Muslim voter who is indebted to a moneylender, expresses his predicament in the following words:

What can be done? It is really a difficult time! If I do not vote for the Musalman, the community will be annoyed. [And] if I do not vote for the Vaniya he will put me behind bars![6]

Dahyabhai also highlights the growing conflicts between the Shethias and the new English-educated elite; between the Parsi and the Hindu elite; and Muslim–Hindu tension on the eve of the municipal elections.

In addition to the introduction of the census (which engendered caste and religious identification) and elections (which generated conflicting allegiances and loyalties at the grassroots level), the Morley–Minto Reforms instituting separate electorates for Muslims gave religious identities a potent, political edge as religion acquired numerical value and religious symbols found a place in political mobilization. The colonial rulers believed that religion was the defining principle for Indian society and history. While presenting the constitutional reforms to the British Parliament in 1909, Morley affirmed, '[O]nly let us not forget that the differences between Mahommedanism and Hinduism is not a mere difference of articles of religious faith. It is a difference in life, in tradition, in history, in all the social things as well as articles of belief that constitute a community.'[7]

In 1909 the Morley–Minto Reforms introduced the 'communal principle' only for provincial legislative councils but the principle was later extended to municipalities. By 1923-24 separate Muslim and non-Muslim constituencies were instituted in all major cities of British Gujarat. Commenting on the impact of separate electorates in Surat city, the historian Douglas E. Haynes writes:

> With the first municipal campaign under the new election law, the idiom of community concerns assumed new preeminence in the city. On the streets of the city, candidates began to champion the causes of their own communities with increased aggressiveness, knowing that such rhetoric won votes in electorates that coincided with religious groupings. Once in office, Muslim councillors repeatedly appealed to the principle of minority rights, raised fear of discrimination, and evoked the backwardness of their community in calling for greater allocations of political resources and power. Hindu councillors from the Congress Party, on the other hand, tended to represent their own opinions as expressing the sentiments of an undifferentiated public or people, but they actually only spoke for Hindus since they were setting themselves against the Muslims' claims to justice.[8]

EVOLUTION OF ARYAN IDENTITY

Parallel to these developments in the political sphere was a slow churning in the sociocultural sphere. In the last quarter of the century the emerging middle class of Gujarat, drawn from Brahmin–Vaniya castes, was increasingly attracted more to an 'Aryan' identity rather than a 'Hindu' identity. Through his writings in the 1860s and 1870s, Narmad had already popularized the notions of 'Arya', 'Aryajan' (Aryan people) and Aryadharm (Aryan religion). In *Rajyarang*, his history of the world's civilizations, he wrote extensively about ancient Indian kings, using the Puranas as his source and developed the notion of Aryajan. In his monumental Gujarati lexicon, *Narmakosh*, he listed the following meanings to define 'Arya': *highborn, noble,* followed by *best, established* and, lastly, *Brahmin, Kshatriyas and Vaishyas who came first and settled in India.*[9] Not surprisingly, upper-caste, educated Gujaratis responded enthusiastically to this construct of Aryajan.

Around 1875 Narmad played host to Dayananda Saraswati, who had come to Gujarat on a lecture tour. Dayananda's concept of a glorious 'Aryadharma' and 'Vedic religion' certainly reinforced Narmad's notion of 'Aryajan' though his crusade against image worship did not find much acceptance. Narmad's notion of 'Arya' became popular in the cities and towns of Gujarat by the mid 1880s. Young Brahmins and Vaniyas of the princely states of Saurashtra founded Arya Sabhas; in Junagadh and Prabhas Patan, Aryotkarsh Sabhas were established as early as 1880. Dayananda's Arya Samaj did not gather many followers and it was the formation of Arya Sabhas, along with the basic notion of 'Arya', that received wider endorsement in the princely states as the orthodox Sanatani section among upper castes also welcomed them.

Narmad also played a crucial role in the formation of the idea of 'Gujarat'. His famous poem *'Koni Koni Chhe Gujarat'* asked, 'To whom does Gujarat belong?' and replied, 'It belongs to those who speak Gujarati; to those who observe Aryadharma of all varieties; and also to those who are foreigners but nurtured by this land; and to those who follow other religions (*Paradharma*) but are well-wishers of Mother Gujarat and therefore our brothers.' Thus, the Gujarati language and land of Gujarat became the binding forces for all Gujaratis. This poem, along with his other famous composition *'Jai Jai Garvi Gujarat'*, which has come to be the anthem of Gujarat, was taught in schools during the closing decades of the nineteenth century and they became the foundations for a broad, inclusive Gujarati identity for the new generation. Yet, within the overarching category of Gujarati, there was the seed of distinction between 'Aryadharma' and 'Paradharma' or other religions.

Meanwhile, a contemporary and caste-fellow of Narmad's, Nandshankar Mehta, who was also for some time diwan of Kutch state, wrote the first Gujarati novel, *Karan Ghelo: The Last Rajput King of Gujarat*. Published in 1866, the novel revolves around the last king of the Chaulukya–Vaghela dynasty, who was defeated and later killed by the army of Alauddin

Khilji in the thirteenth century. Throughout the novel, which runs into more than 300 pages, Nandshankar uses the terms 'Muslim' army and 'Hindu' army and derogates the Muslims. Moreover, he equates the 'post-Rajput' period or the 'Muslim' period with the degradation and decline of Gujarat. The novel concludes with the following paragraph:

> Readers! Shed some tears over the dead body of Karan. Gujarat has been widowed after his death; it has passed into the hands of mlechha people of foreign countries; it has been oppressed by barbaric foreigners. Muhammad Begada and other Sultans of Ahmedabad have much degraded it. The Marathas plundered it extensively. The land was divided into small kingdoms. Thus, Gujarat was completely ruined.[10]

The novel became immensely popular in the newly educated section of society and, as the education department prescribed it in the curriculum of high schools, the idea and idiom of the novel informed more than one generation of Gujarat. This first novel played a crucial part in the construction of the image of Muslims as destroyers of Gujarat and of Hindus as a community that was devastated at their hands. A close examination of the literary production of the period shows that parallel to the emergence of Indian nationalism, inclusive Gujarati subnationalism along with the notions of Aryadharma as well as Hindu–Muslim dichotomy sprang up within the small but influential Hindu middle class.

EDUCATION AMONG MUSLIMS

The Muslim middle class was much smaller than its Hindu counterpart and was struggling hard to find its proper place. In big cities such as Bombay, Surat and Ahmedabad, trading communities of Bohras, Khojas and Memons were wealthy and well entrenched but the vast majority of Muslims were not inclined to pursue or promote English education. Realizing this, Badruddin Tyabji, a Sulaimani Bohra whose family originally came from Cambay, and other Muslims founded the Anjuman-i-Islam in 1876 'for the betterment and uplift of Mussalmans in every direction'. Badruddin Tyabji's father understood early that the future lay in modern education and members of this family became the first among the Muslim community in western India to enter modern professions. Badruddin rose to be acting chief justice of the Bombay High Court; he emerged as a national leader and became president of the Congress in 1887. Aware of the deplorable condition of Muslims and the cultural, economic and linguistic divisions between them in western India, he felt the need to unify Muslims under one umbrella. Writing to Nakhoda Mohammad Ali Rogay, the nominated member of the governor's council and president of Anjuman-i-Islam, he underlined the 'great aim' of his life:

> We must remember that we have to deal with a mass of ignorant, bigoted and fanatical population—that instead of finding all the points on which all Mussalmans agreed, they will magnify those on which we are unfortunately divided. Now the great aim of my life has been to cement those discordant elements into one compact mass whose watchword should be 'Islam' without any of the later difference.[11]

And the binding agent he found was the Urdu language. When Badruddin was fifteen years old his father decided to give up Gujarati and adopt Urdu as the language of the family. Throughout his life, Badruddin revered the language and remained a great champion of Urdu, always advocating it as the critical component of Muslim education. He believed that Urdu was essential for Muslim unification. Yet, the Urdu education he envisaged for the Muslim community was not one which drew them away from the mainstream but a system which would root Muslims in their culture and empower them to participate in public life and further their interests as a community. At the same time, he was vociferous in his opinion that the Congress was the only vehicle for advancing political issues, a point on which he differed with Sir Syed Ahmad Khan and Ameer Ali, both senior Muslim leaders of the nineteenth century. (Sir Syed Ahmed Khan was the founder of the Aligarh Muslim University and Ameer Ali was the head of the London branch of the Muslim League.) He attended Congress sessions as a representative of the Anjuman and campaigned relentlessly to make space within it for the participation of Muslims and bring to it their concerns as a community. Badruddin died a year before the formation of the Muslim League, when he was sixty-two. Given his stature within the Muslim community and his uncompromising liberal views, it is possible that had he lived the subsequent course of events could have been different.

Both in the educational activities started and developed by the Anjuman-i-Islam at Bombay and in the later efforts by other agencies in Gujarat, Urdu became synonymous with Muslim primary education. In Ahmedabad the Anjuman-i-Islam was established in 1884 and it started the first Urdu–Gujarati school with four students; in two years the school had 152 students. Significantly, while the Muslim elite took the initiative in Bombay, in Ahmedabad it was a collective effort by local Muslim leaders, Hindu educationists and British officers. The Baroda state also started Urdu schools in the capital city and other important towns in the same decade. In the princely state of Junagadh, Vazir Bahauddin established a separate school for Muslim students in the mid 1880s, which was inaugurated by the governor of Bombay. By the close of the century a number of Urdu schools for Muslim boys and girls were established, paving the way for the emergence of a section of educated Muslims in Gujarat. A separate school system and a separate language, Urdu, engendered a distinct identity among Muslims, transcending traditional sect and jamaat divisions.

The Anjuman-i-Islam of Ahmedabad convened an educational conference in 1894, a year after the communal riots in Prabhas Patan and Bombay. More than 500 delegates from twenty-one cities participated. Educationists and members of the Hindu and Parsi elite, and local British officers attended the conference. They adopted a four-point programme which emphasized the need for a greater effort for Muslim education; raising awareness in Muslim society for the promotion of girls' education; cultivation of fraternity among followers of all religions; and discontinuation of extravagant spending on social celebrations.[12] In his presidential address, Abdullah Maherali Dharamshi, a well-known Muslim leader of Bombay and a close associate of Badruddin Tyabji, underlined the need for communal amity. He emphasized that, more than the police or military, it was the educated Hindus and Muslims who could prevent the occurrence of riots. 'Simply because we did not actually participate in the fighting,' he said, 'let us not assume that we are guiltless. But for petty jealousies or rivalries, these riots could never break out.'[13]

Thus, participation in electoral politics and expanding modern education in the community were two ways by which the Muslim middle class tried to make space for themselves towards the end of the nineteenth century.

KHILAFAT AND HINDU–MUSLIM UNITY

Gandhi's arrival coincided with the widening division of the middle class into Hindu and Muslim, majority and minority. While in South Africa, he had constantly tried to bring the two communities together. Equally committed at the time to the cause of Hindu–Muslim unity was Muhammad Ali Jinnah, who, as we have seen, presided over Bombay's welcome to Gandhi in 1915. Jinnah grew up in Karachi and, after years of being an indifferent student at school, his father sent him to England as apprentice to a businessman- friend, hoping he

Jinnah and Gandhi, 1944

would eventually expand the family business. In England Jinnah was exposed to the politics of the day and interacted with Dadabhai Naoroji and joined his election campaign team. He drifted away from business and discovered that his interest lay in studying law. Just as Gandhi's career was unfolding in South Africa, Jinnah returned to Bombay and began practice in the Bombay High Court. While he was abroad, he had become highly westernized in dress and manner, imbued with the high idealism of British notions of justice, equality and fair play. As his practice flourished, he was drawn to politics, favouring the 'Constitutional' approach.

Jinnah participated in Congress activities and kept his distance from the Muslim League. He initially rejected the formula of separate electorates because he felt that such divisions would be against the national interest. However in 1910 he reluctantly participated in the elections and became one of the first Muslim members from Bombay to be elected to the Imperial Legislative Council. He finally agreed to join the Muslim League in 1913 on the condition that his 'loyalty to the Muslim League and in the Muslim interest would in no way and at no time imply even the shadow of disloyalty to the larger national cause to which his life was dedicated'.[14]

With his elegant style and youthful enthusiasm, he became popular among students who thronged to his passionate speeches as president of the Home Rule League in Bombay's Shantaram Chawl. He always emphasized that 'students should work for inter-communal unity without which we would not be able to shake off the British yoke and attain freedom for our country'.[15] So total was Jinnah's commitment to oneness and cooperation between the two communities that Sarojini Naidu described him as 'India's true ambassador of Hindu–Muslim unity'.[16]

In 1917-18, incidents of Hindu–Muslim conflicts took place in many parts of India. So when the Khilafat movement (to support the independence of the Ottoman Sultan as Khalifa of all Muslims and to ensure his suzerainty over Islamic holy places) was started in 1918 by Maulana Abdul Bari and the Ali brothers, Gandhi supported it wholeheartedly. He was convinced that a joint Hindu–Muslim struggle on the issue would lead to greater unity between the two communities, which was imperative for the larger struggle for Swaraj. In the next two years a powerful anti-British movement emerged, where Hindu–Muslim cooperation reached its peak. But it was also the beginning of the divergence between Gandhi and Jinnah. Jinnah was not religious nor did he then believe that religion should play a role in political mobilization.

Some of Gandhi's followers in Gujarat too were a little unhappy about linking the Khilafat movement with the struggle for Swaraj. Indulal Yagnik says in his autobiography, 'Religious life and political life revolve around two separate premises. The combination of the Khilafat Committee's demands and those of Gandhiji appeared odd to me.' He also quotes Vallabhbhai's scepticism about the programme: 'How can we fight for the Muslims of Arabia and Palestine, Syria and Iraq? It is only meaningful if we first achieve freedom and then fight for

WELCOME TO BOMBAY.
[The advent of the All-India Moslem League to Bombay next Christmas is hailed with delight by all right-thinking Moslems and by the whole Indian Press.]

ભલે પધારો મુંબઇ.

Cartoon from *Hindi Punch*, 1915, showing Jinnah escorting Muslim League

others.'[17] It was only after Gandhi linked the Jallianwala Bagh massacre with the Khilafat question that these followers of Gandhi joined the Non-cooperation Movement wholeheartedly. The fourth Gujarat Political Conference, organized in Ahmedabad by Sardar Patel and Indulal Yagnik in late 1920, endorsed the programme and started political mobilization throughout British Gujarat. During this phase Gandhi became a towering figure in public life; Jinnah found himself losing his prominent position in national politics and he quit the Congress in 1920.

The first stage of the Non-cooperation Movement was remarkably successful in Gujarat but by late 1921 signs of discord in the Hindu–Muslim alliance became visible. First, the Moplah rebellion from August to December (when Muslim cultivators of Malabar attacked their Hindu landlords and killed or converted many Hindu families) revived old Hindu–Muslim antagonisms. The rebellion was hotly debated at the Ahmedabad session of the Congress in December 1921, and Hakim Ajmal Khan, the acting president of the Congress, publicly regretted 'this deplorable incident'. But Hasrat Mohani, an eminent leader of the Khilafat movement, opposed a resolution condemning the Moplahs in the same session. Second, the communal riot in Bombay on the day the Prince of Wales arrived (17 November 1921) indirectly widened the rift between the two communities. Gandhi had called for a nationwide peaceful boycott of the official welcome, and Bombay observed a successful hartal. Yet, that evening a large number of Hindus and Muslims attacked Parsis, Christians and Anglo-Indians who were returning from the official programme. The rioting continued for four days and at many places even Parsi women and children were attacked. Gandhi took responsibility and went on a three-day fast. In his statement before going on the fast he admonished Muslims for being the main perpetrators of the violence, a charge most Muslim leaders and their followers considered one-sided and unjust.

Even though Gandhi emerged as the supreme leader in the Ahmedabad Congress session and the programme of civil disobedience got the stamp of approval, factional differences persisted. While Pandit Malaviya and his group favoured a round table conference and temporary suspension of civil disobedience, Hasrat Mohani and some other Muslim leaders insisted on the immediate declaration of Purna Swaraj, complete freedom, and the use of force if necessary. Gandhi wanted to start a civil disobedience movement from Bardoli in south Gujarat from 6 February 1922. However, the violence at Chauri Chaura village in Uttar Pradesh, where a mob set fire to the police station killing twenty-two policemen, disheartened him and he suspended the movement. Many leaders of the Congress resented this decision though very few of them expressed their views in public, but the leaders of the Khilafat Committee chose to openly criticize Gandhi. Gandhi was arrested in early March that year and, after a historic trial at Ahmedabad, he was sentenced to jail for six years. There was gloom all over as the dream of 'Swaraj in one year' promised by Gandhi was shattered. The Congress was divided in two camps and the alliance between Hindus and Muslims started weakening. In early 1924 the Turkish prime minister abolished the Khilafat altogether and the Khilafat movement in India ended.

The rise and fall of Khilafat and Non-cooperation movements generated forces which changed many equations in the socio-political life of India as well as of Gujarat. While Muslim and Hindu masses collectively participated in the nationalist struggle on such a scale for the first time, their separate political identities as Hindu and Muslim got reinforced. It was not just the language and idiom of the movement but the entire symbolism associated with mass mobilization that raised religio-political consciousness. In meetings at the village or town level, Hindu audiences would respond enthusiastically to the slogan of 'Bande Mataram' and Muslim participants would respond to the slogan of 'Allah ho Akbar'. Leaders of the movement addressed gatherings according to the social composition of the audience. Indulal Yagnik, who spoke at a number of meetings in various villages and towns of Gujarat in those days, describes how in Tankari, a Muslim-dominated village of

Bharuch district, the audience shouted, 'Aameen Aameen' when he delivered a lecture on the Khilafat. The next day in a nearby Hindu-dominated town, Jambusar, he spoke on non-cooperation and the importance of khadi, and the audience gave donations with great enthusiasm. Khilafat committees were formed in all British districts of Gujarat and they served to spread pan-Islamism by constantly reminding the Muslim populace of Khilafat as the holy symbol of Islam and the holy places of Islam in West Asia. Transcending their local social boundaries, Muslim communities, both Shia and Sunni, took part in the Non-cooperation Movement as a bloc. This gave them a sense of unity and purpose in the public arena.

Throughout the Non-cooperation Movement Muslim religious leaders remained prominent. The ulema endorsed the Khilafat demand and the programme of non-cooperation and civil disobedience. They saw defiance of government authority as a religious duty and in their sermons in the mosques they generally raised the cry of 'Islam in danger'. It is significant that along with the Khilafat Committee, the Jamiat al-ulema-e-Hind was formed in 1919. It endorsed the movement and the ulema became the driving force in the movement. Before the Non-cooperation Movement, the educated Muslim middle class played a leading role in the anti-British movement but between 1919 and 1924 it was the Muslim religious leaders who occupied the centre stage.

Congress leaders of Gujarat did not overtly use religious symbolism in grassroots mobilization programmes. While addressing Hindu audiences, they always began by reaffirming Hindu–Muslim unity but their discourses would inevitably focus on Hindu religious idioms with metaphors drawn from Ramayana, Mahabharata and Puranas. For instance, the Non-cooperation Movement was referred to as *dharmayuddh* and British rule described as *Ravan raj*. It is not surprising therefore that with such contradictory vocabulary, a sense of inclusiveness and exclusivity flourished simultaneously in both the communities.

SHUDDHI AND TABLIGH

With the suspension of the Non-cooperation Movement and the imprisonment of Gandhi, the Hindu–Muslim alliance collapsed by mid 1922. The emotion and energy raised by the movement in both the communities started finding new directions. The Moplah rebellion and forced conversion of Hindus in Malabar led to the reappearance of the Shuddhi movement under Swami Shraddhanand, a leader of the Arya Samaj. In early 1923 about 7000 Malkans, a Rajput caste that had converted to Islam but observed mixed religious practices, was 'purified' by Shraddhanand and brought back to the 'Hindu fold'. In July the Arya Samaj claimed to have purified another 30,000 Malkans. Predictably, the Muslim leaders of the central Khilafat Committee and Jamiat al-ulema reacted angrily and started a powerful campaign for conversion to counter the growing influence of the Shuddhi movement.

In this climate of mutual mistrust, fear and anxieties, the Hindu Mahasabha, which started in 1915 as the Hindu Sabha, became more active and in August 1923 organized a big conference at Banaras with Pandit Malaviya as president. They extended support to the Shuddhi campaign and resolved to work for *achhutoddhar* or uplift of untouchables. Alarmed, a number of Muslim religious leaders started a missionary movement known as Tabligh. After the Multan and Amritsar Hindu–Muslim riots in September 1922 and April 1923 respectively, Lala Lajpat Rai called upon Hindus to unite in self-defence under the umbrella organization Sangathan. Among Muslims, Dr Kitchlew, a leader from Punjab, set up the Jamiat-e-Tanzeem in late 1923.[18] Within no time the newspaper-reading public of India was discussing 'Shuddhi and Sangathan' versus 'Tabligh and Tanzeem' as counterveiling forces.

Gujarat did not remain untouched by the escalating Hindu–Muslim antagonism. Like many cities and towns in north and eastern India, Gujarat was affected by communal violence in the aftermath of the Moplah rebellion. While Gandhi was in jail, Siddhpur in north Gujarat and Wadhwan in Saurashtra (a Hindu pilgrim place and Jain religious centre respectively) were rocked by Hindu–Muslim riots. Mahadev Desai immediately visited Siddhpur and tried to establish a peace committee but returned unsuccessful; the violence continued for a few days. From 1927 onwards music near mosques and cow killing were the contentious issues that divided the two communities. The Ganesh Chaturthi festival and Shivaji Jayanti procession popularized by the Hindu Mahasabha ignited communal passions in Surat and Godhra in 1927-28. To celebrate the birthday of Shivaji, the Hindu Mahasabha organized a large procession on the streets of Surat, with hundreds of pictures of Shivaji and saffron flags. When the processionists ignored protests by Muslims and continued to play loud music and sing religious songs in front of two mosques, a bloody riot broke out. One Hindu and one Muslim youth were killed in police firing. After this several caste panchayats called for the economic boycott of Muslims. They imposed fines up to eleven rupees on caste members who either bought from Muslim shops or employed Muslims in any service. After a few months, the leaders of the Hindu Mahasabha decided to celebrate Ganesh Chaturthi on a grand scale. When local authorities refused to give permission, they called for a general strike and organized a protest meeting where over 10,000 Hindus assembled. The Mahasabha went ahead with the celebrations despite prohibitory orders and once again there were communal clashes. In the second round of rioting, six people were killed and about a hundred injured.

In Godhra too there was a clash at the Ganesh festival celebrations. In early 1930 there was a violent Hindu–Muslim conflict in Una town in Junagadh state and the next year Veraval was engulfed in communal violence when six prominent Hindus of the city were killed. Two other smaller towns of Junagadh state, Keshod and Vanthali, also witnessed such clashes.

It is perplexing how, parallel to the Bardoli Satyagraha and Dandi March, there was such a series of violent clashes between Hindus and Muslims in Gujarat. In Surat, just fifty kilometres from Bardoli, there were two rounds of rioting, one before the famous struggle and another immediately after it. Thus we see that by the mid 1920s Hindus and Muslims had begun to articulate their feelings and assert their rights and were competing and contesting with each other in Gujarat.

The Shuddhi movement, Hindu Mahasabha, Tabligh movement and the missionaries of the Aga Khan, all exacerbated the differences between Hindus and Muslims in Gujarat. From 1923 onwards the Shuddhi movement was revived by the Arya Kumar Sabha and the Shuddhi Sabha in Baroda. The reformist and orthodox forces of the Hindu community were brought together when the Hindu Mahasabha endorsed the Shuddhi movement at the national level. Jugalkishore Birla, an industrialist with a Sanatani background, called a meeting of Arya Samajis and Sanatanis in Bombay and the Gujarat Hindu Sabha was formed to unite all Hindus, including the untouchable communities. Between 1923 and 1924, the Sabha established nineteen schools for untouchables in the villages near Ankleshwar and Baroda and also carried forward missionary work among those Muslim communities who observed many Hindu religious practices and were considered mixed Hindu–Muslim groups.

Pandit Anandapriyaji, the founding secretary of Gujarat Hindu Sabha, seemed to articulate the sentiments of many Hindus when he said:

Many conspiracies were hatched in Gujarat to convert Hindus into non-Hindu folds. Hindus remained ignorant of these intrigues. Since several years Christians have established camps and have tried to convert Bhils [tribals] and untouchables. Meanwhile, the religious head of the Khojas, His Highness The Aga Khan also established missions. In village after village, 'nakalanga mandals' were established in untouchables' neighbourhoods and to draw them to the sect the Aga Khan was projected as the tenth incarnation of 'nakalanga'[tenth incarnation of Lord Vishnu]. Impoverished untouchables were snared by offers of money. Arrangements were made for their education, weaving schools, hostels and missionaries. Thus Christians

and Khojas worked day and night to transform the great
devotees of Ram and Krishna into Johns and Alis.[19]

In early 1924 Swami Shraddhanand toured Gujarat and
addressed several meetings in prominent cities and towns along
the Bombay–Ahmedabad railway line. The meetings attracted
large crowds and more Hindu Mahasabha centres were set up.
Some city-level Congress leaders of the Non-cooperation
Movement joined the Sabha. The president of the Surat Khilafat
Committee, Dr Manantrai Raiji, emerged as a powerful leader
of the Hindu community and called for a vigorous campaign
to reconvert Muslims. He started a Gujarati newspaper called
Hindu. It was Dr Raiji who had led the Hindu Mahasabha
processions during the Shivaji Jayanti and Ganesh festivals in
Surat, which turned into bloody riots. Another leader of the
Non-cooperation Movement in the city, Dr Mohannath Dikshit,
openly defended Hindus during these riots. In 1951 he became
president of the Jan Sangh. Similarly in Godhra, Vamanrao
Mukadam, a prominent leader of the Congress (who had
organized the Gujarat Political Conference of 1917 which
Gandhi, Jinnah and Tilak attended), led the Ganesh Chaturthi
procession in 1928, which provoked a violent conflict between
Hindus and Muslims.

Even as some Congress leaders joined or allied with Hindu
Mahasabha activities, a devoted circle of Gandhians remained
critical of the Shuddhi campaign and continued their efforts
towards Hindu–Muslim unity. Dayalji Desai, founder of Anavil
Ashram in Surat, and Jhinabhai Desai, president of Surat city
Congress (who later became known as the poet 'Snehrashmi'),
went all out to establish peace and harmony in their city. To
break the deadlock created by the economic boycott of Muslims,
Snehrashmi organized a weeklong khadi exhibition and invited
the famous Razaak Band of Muslim musicians to play at the
venue every day. Local senior Congress leaders cautioned him
to get Vallabhbhai Patel's permission before embarking on such
an adventurous programme. Snehrashmi describes the meeting
in his autobiography:

When I met Sardar, the first question he asked me was, 'Are you ready to face the displeasure of Hindus?' I replied, 'This programme is not in anyone's personal interest but for the nation and the Congress has never looked for anyone's approval in order to undertake programmes in the national interest.' He was convinced by my reply. He said, 'You are right but all of you are still very young. You are going to face stiff resistance. Do you think you have enough experience of the patience and diplomacy required to cope with this?'[20]

When Snehrashmi gave details of the programme, Patel was convinced and not only gave permission but also attended the inauguration. Because of Patel's presence and Razaak Band's popularity, the programme turned out to be successful and its main objective to break the economic boycott of Muslims was achieved.

For the Congress, 1930 was the year of the Dandi March when the whole of Gujarat was revitalized as it was chosen as the main theatre for the satyagraha. Similarly, for the Muslim League the year proved to be historic as Muhammad Iqbal spelled out the concept of a 'Muslim' state for the first time in his presidential speech at the League's annual meeting. From that year, the Congress–League relationship entered a new era of conflict and Gujarat also experienced the sound and fury of escalating antipathy. Over the next two decades, two kinds of responses to the question of Hindu–Muslim relations emerged and got consolidated. The first was the response of devoted Gandhians within the Congress who continued to emphasize Hindu–Muslim unity in word and deed. The second response was that of the majority of Congressmen, who were engaged in power politics, particularly after the 1935 Constitution and who focussed increasingly on their 'Hindu' constituency. Both at the municipal level and at the provincial level, these politicians showed greater interest in securing position and distributing patronage to ensure Hindu support. Although they continued to speak the language of Gandhi, they were scarcely proactive in promoting Hindu–Muslim unity. A section within this politically ambitious group nurtured a deep-rooted prejudice against Muslims and remained favourably inclined towards the Hindu Mahasabha position.

K.M. Munshi's portrayal of Gujarat's past in his historical novels also greatly influenced the urban middle class's attitude towards Hindu–Muslim relationships. In his trilogy—*Patanni Prabhuta* (The Glory of Patan), *Gujaratno Nath* (The Lord of Gujarat) and *Rajadhiraj* (King of Kings)—published between 1916 and 1925, he glorified the Rajput Chaulukya period and, as Nandshankar Mehta before him, identified the decline of Gujarat with the end of Hindu rule. These historical romances became very popular and caught the imagination of the younger generation. They continue to be in print to this day and sustain the glorification of a Hindu past.

MUSLIM LEAGUE IN GUJARAT

The Muslim League remained dormant in the early 1930s when it had no leader of national stature. In 1935 Jinnah returned after five years in England and he set about the task of revitalizing the party by adopting a clearly communal line. It is difficult to explain how the secular Jinnah got transformed as there are few contemporary accounts of him and his personal writings and reflections are as scanty as Gandhi's are voluminous. The closest glimpse we get of Jinnah are in the writings of M.C. Chagla, a lawyer and fellow Gujarati Muslim who was Jinnah's junior for six years. The two remained associates till Jinnah veered towards communal politics which culminated in his 'two-nation theory'. Chagla, who rose to be Chief Justice of Bombay High Court and later education minister, recalls Jinnah's baffling transformation in his autobiography:

> The evolution of Jinnah from a national to a communal leader remains an enigma . . . Why did Jinnah change? There could be many possible explanations for this . . . Jinnah's besetting fault was his excessive egoism . . . With the emergence of Gandhiji in Indian politics, Jinnah felt

that his importance would gradually diminish . . . After he was dropped from the Third Round Table Conference [in 1932], Jinnah became convinced that if he had to have a place under the sun, he would have to stand on a communal platform.[21]

Coming back to the 1930s, the results of the election in 1937 showed that despite the strong mobilization, even in seats reserved for Muslims, the League under the leadership of Jinnah could re-emerge as a political force only in Bombay and United Provinces. In the Bombay assembly, it won twenty of the thirty seats reserved for Muslims and not a single Congress Muslim leader won in this category. The Congress won eighty-seven seats and needed just one more to form the ministry. Jinnah offered to form a coalition ministry in Bombay but Patel insisted on the merger of the League with the Congress as a precondition. Inevitably, the talks broke down and with that the possibility for constructive dialogue between the two parties ended forever.

The Congress did eventually form the ministry in Bombay, prompting Jinnah to accuse the Congress of 'representing Hindu Raj'. Accusations and counter-accusations continued between leaders for the next two and a half years, percolating to the municipal level and deepening the communal divide within the urban population. The split was apparent in the debates and discussions between Congress and League members in Ahmedabad municipality. For instance, when the ruling Congress members wanted to name a new bridge on the river Sabarmati 'Sardar Bridge', League members opposed the move. Again, in 1940, when Congress members wanted to name another bridge after Gandhi, League members put up stiff resistance.[22] With their overwhelming majority in the municipality, Congress defeated all these moves but League members continued to oppose all the actions related to Congress history and ideology, whether it was khadi or celebration of Gandhi's birthday. Each action and counteraction reinforced bitterness and hostility between leaders of the two communities in the city.

Concurrent to the Congress–League political encounter, textile mill owners and workers were engaged in a bitter conflict in Ahmedabad. In 1937 mill owners cut the wages of weavers by 25 per cent. As the Majoor Mahajan was associated with the Congress, it maintained studied silence. The Lal Vavta Mill Kamdar Union, established by the communists, assumed leadership and about 50,000 weavers, mostly Muslim, went on a strike. Other mill workers also joined the strike the next day and it continued for three weeks. The Congress government of Bombay first imposed prohibitory orders banning all meetings and processions and then arrested several communist–socialist leaders and workers. When the combined force of Congress leaders and mill owners failed to break the strike, Gulzarilal Nanda, the prominent Majoor Mahajan leader who was in charge of the labour portfolio in the government, brokered a settlement reducing the wage cut to 7 per cent. Commenting on this textile strike and workers' political consciousness, Dinkar Mehta, one of the leaders of the striking workers and a pioneer of the Communist Party in Gujarat, wrote in his autobiography:

> Almost all the workers of the weaving sections participated in this strike and a sizeable number among them were Muslim. We realized through experience that although Muslim workers had respect and sympathy for Lal Vavta, their political consciousness had not broken out of the confines of the Muslim League. This ambivalent attitude persisted among Muslim workers for a long time.[23]

After the strike, some textile mills discharged a large number of Muslim workers and thousands lost their jobs. The Muslim League leadership condemned the action of mill owners and held the Congress ministry responsible. On the face of it, the Congress ministry protested against the dismissal of Muslim workers but neither the Congress leaders nor the Majoor Mahajan took steps to reinstate the workers. As a result a majority of the Muslim workers turned to the Muslim League as their only saviour.

The situation worsened in early 1940 when the Muslim League, passed the 'Pakistan' Resolution following Jinnah's presidential address in which he declared:

> [T]he Mussulmans are a nation by any definition with the need for a homeland, territory and state if we are to develop to the fullest our spiritual, cultural, economic, social and political life.[24]

The Muslim League's influence was mainly in the big cities of Gujarat such as Ahmedabad and Surat where it had already established a volunteer corps. In Ahmedabad members of the Khakhsar movement—mostly Muslim artisans and the lower middle class—underwent military training in uniform and they considered themselves the 'Army of Islam'. By early 1941 rumours were afloat in Ahmedabad that Sikh–Muslim clashes were round the corner as a Sikh had allegedly been killed by a Pathan moneylender. In April, the rumour was that Sikh contingents were coming from Punjab for a show of strength. It culminated in a bloody Hindu–Muslim riot in the entire walled city on 18 April, which continued for ten days. In this riot, eighty people were killed and about 400 injured. All the textile mills were closed for a week and about one lakh people left the city in panic.

During the first three days of the riot, Hindus were at the receiving end and could offer little resistance apart from closing the huge wooden gates of their pols or obstructing the rioters by barricades. By the second phase Hindus had organized themselves and attacked Muslim residential areas, though all in all Hindus suffered heavily and their loss of life and property was far more than that of Muslims. The local police force was ill prepared and remained ineffective under a Muslim police officer. This strengthened the Hindu belief that British rulers and Muslim League had jointly planned this riot.

Gandhi was distressed by the turn of events in Ahmedabad and the apathy of Congressmen who played a negligible role in maintaining peace in the city. Expressing his anguish, he wrote in the *Congress Bulletin*:

> Individual cases apart, the Congress produced little or no influence over either the Muslims or the Hindus in the affected areas. From the accounts received it seems that Muslim fanatics in Dacca and Ahmedabad did their worst in inflicting damage on Hindu property by looting and burning with a deliberation that showed premeditation. Hindus, instead of boldly standing up and facing the mischief makers, fled in their thousands from the damage zone. And where they did not, they were as barbarous as their assailants. These were all untouched by the Congress non-violence. And yet these are the men who form the bulk of the Congress meetings.[25]

To restore communal harmony Gandhi suggested the formation of Shanti Sevak Sangh (Peace Workers Association) in Ahmedabad and sent Mahadev Desai from Sevagram to organize it. With great courage and conviction Mahadev Desai and Narahari Parikh, president and vice-president of the Shanti Sangh, laid the foundation of the association and strove to re-energize the Congress. Two women members of the newly founded Sangh, Mridula Sarabhai and Indumati Chimanlal, went to the affected areas and spread the message of peace and harmony. On the first day of the riot, Indumati Chimanlal had showed unusual courage when she appealed to a fierce Muslim mob at Jama Masjid to stop the violence. Similarly, the noted social worker Pushpaben Mehta went through rioting mobs and was hurt when she was shepherding destitute women from an unsafe shelter home to a safer site. These women inspired the new generation with their dedicated work.

With the call of the Quit India Movement in 1942, Congress leaders and their followers were fully engaged in the freedom struggle. Later, most of the Congress leaders were imprisoned and this enabled the League leaders to consolidate their base in the major cities of Gujarat. In January 1945 Jinnah visited Ahmedabad to inaugurate the Bombay Presidency Muslim Educational Conference. He was given a tremendous reception by the local Muslims, who made substantial donations to the Muslim League.[26]

Communal riots revisited Ahmedabad on the Rath Yatra day of 1946. Concurrent with the famous Jagannath Rath Yatra of Orissa, a yatra on similar lines had been celebrated in the city since the 1890s and all Hindu communities took part in it with much fanfare. The Muslim festival of Id was also celebrated on the same day. Parallel celebrations resulted in a riot and even prominent Congress Muslims were attacked by Muslim rioters. Hindu–Muslim relations were getting increasingly complex and creating a web where it was difficult to separate religious from political, cause from effect.

Two young members of the Congress, Vasantrao Hegiste and Rajab Ali Lakhani, who were working to prevent violence were killed by a mob in the Jamalpur area of the walled city. On hearing about riots, Gandhi asked Morarji Desai, then home minister in the second Kher ministry of Bombay, to go to Ahmedabad. As Morarji recollected in his autobiography, 'Bapu told me that I should go to Ahmedabad and confront the riots personally and quench the fire of communalism without taking the help of the police and military, sacrificing myself if necessary.'[27] Morarji considered Gandhi's suggestion ideologically correct but concluded that it was not proper or useful to put it in practice. However, he went to Ahmedabad and moved around the affected areas with government officials and social workers.

Even after the intense rioting was over, stray incidents of stabbing continued in the city. Morarji again visited Ahmedabad and his account of the situation points to the growing role of Congress members in perpetrating Hindu–Muslim violence:

After I went to my Ahmedabad residence, I called in five prominent Congress colleagues and said to them plainly:

'You are paying some people to arrange for retaliatory action and this is coming in the way of restoring peace. What you are doing is wrong as nobody can justify a Hindu assaulting a Musalman in one locality because some Musalman attacked a Hindu in some other locality. You should stop such retaliatory action. If you do not promise to stop such actions, I shall have to send you to jail. If, however, you give me an assurance that you will not organize such retaliatory actions and will also not encourage them, I will be able to restore peace in Ahmedabad within seven or eight days.'[28]

The threat worked and the violence ceased within a week.

JUNAGADH AND SOMNATH

The princely state of Junagadh in Saurashtra became a contentious issue between India and Pakistan during the transfer of power negotiations. With Kashmir and Hyderabad, Junagadh was the third state that refused to sign the instrument of accession to the Indian Union. Nawab Mahabat Khan of Junagadh was a weak and eccentric ruler. In May 1947 he appointed Sir Shahnawaz Bhutto, a Muslim League politician (and father of Zulfikar Ali Bhutto), as diwan of the state. Sir Bhutto was closely associated with Jinnah and, under his influence, he manipulated the accession of Junagadh to Pakistan on 15 August. As 82 per cent of the population of this state was Hindu, this generated an uproar in the state and the neighbouring princely states of Saurashtra were alarmed. The Kathiawad Political Conference, representing the people of Saurashtra, opposed the accession and sent U.N. Dhebar (who was Congress president from 1955 to 1959) to Junagadh to negotiate with the nawab, who refused to even grant him an audience.

Unhappy at the turn of events, Vallabhbhai Patel took a cautious line. As home minister of the interim government he asked the external affairs ministry under Nehru to ascertain whether Pakistan had accepted the instrument of accession sent from Junagadh. At the same time he advised the agitated leaders of Saurashtra to start a people's struggle. The Kathiawad Political Conference called for economic boycott of Junagadh state and all the road links to the state were blocked. Only a rail link in the north and the sea route in the south remained open. In Pakistan, Jinnah too was waiting and watching. He anticipated that India would argue about a Hindu majority state under a Muslim ruler and knew he could respond with Kashmir being a Muslim majority state under a Hindu king. He delayed his response to Nehru for a month and only in mid September declared Pakistan's acceptance of Junagadh.

This intensified the resentment in Saurashtra against the Junagadh ruler and his diwan as well as against Muslims in general. In some neighbouring princely states there was even talk of retaliating against local Muslims. On 25 September 30,000 people belonging to Junagadh and Saurashtra gathered in Bombay and resolved to 'liberate' Junagadh, through an armed struggle against the nawab's regime if necessary. They also formed an Arzi Hakumat (provisional government), with Samaldas Gandhi (a relative of Gandhiji) as its president. Volunteers from the Indian side crossed the border into the Junagadh territory and the panic-stricken nawab fled to Karachi with his family and treasury in his private plane.[29] Diwan Bhutto waited for help from Pakistan till November 1947 and, ultimately, under siege of the provisional government, decided to hand over the reins of Junagadh to the Government of India. On 9 November the Indian army entered Junagadh and the soldiers of the nawab were disarmed. Bhutto had left for Karachi the previous day.

A grand reception was accorded to Vallabhbhai Patel when he arrived in Junagadh on Diwali day (13 November 1947). The next day marked the start of the Gujarati New Year and Vallabhbhai visited the Somnath temple with his cabinet colleague N.V. Gadgil. Both were 'visibly moved to find the temple which had once been the glory of India looking so dilapidated, neglected and forlorn'.[30] Patel's biographer, Rajmohan Gandhi, adds:

Gadgil felt that the temple should be renovated. He mentioned the idea to Patel, who at once agreed and publicly proposed it. The Jamsaheb of Nawanagar, who was with them, donated a lakh of rupees on the spot, and Samaldas announced that the Arzi Hakumat would give Rs.51,000. Gadgil's Ministry, responsible for public works, undertook the task and Cabinet approved, but after a discussion between Gandhi and the Sardar it was decided that a trust should renovate the temple with funds from the public.[31]

Gandhi referred to the rebuilding of Somnath in his prayer meeting in Delhi on 28 November 1947 and expressed his idea of a 'secular' government in very clear terms:

When the Sardar came here I asked him whether even though he was in the Government, he would acquiesce in its giving as much money as it liked for Hinduism from its treasury. After all, we have formed the Government for all. It is a 'secular' government, that is, it is not a theocratic government, rather, it does not belong to any particular religion. Hence it cannot spend any money on the basis of communities. For it, the only thing that matters is that all are Indians. Individuals can follow their own religions. I have my religion and you have yours to follow.[32]

As we have seen, the centres of Hindu–Muslim conflict were limited to urban areas such as Ahmedabad, Surat, Godhra and the Muslim princely state of Junagadh. Rural areas in general were incident-free and social and economic relationships continued despite political developments. The Muslim League's influence did not penetrate beyond these urban centres and there too their support base was restricted to the Muslim mercantile communities and textile workers. No area of Gujarat except Junagadh was ever a part of the League's geography of Pakistan, as Muslims were a small part of the total population. Thus, though Independence and Partition followed barely a year after the Rath Yatra riot, there was no holocaust in Gujarat as in Punjab and Bengal. Barely 2.2 per cent of the migrants to Pakistan were from Gujarat and Bombay city and of these 75 per cent went to Karachi, where traders had business interests stretching back decades.[31] Similarly, a majority of immigrants who moved across Gujarat's border with Pakistan were Sindhi and Gujarati Hindus who came from Karachi and surrounding areas of Sind.

But it has to be acknowledged that the repeated incidents of violence did result in a steady distancing of the communities and the deteriorating relationship between India and Pakistan exacerbated the situation. The rise of Hindu nationalism in Gujarat in the 1980s stretched the already fragile intercommunity relations and posed a serious challenge to the composite culture of Gujarat.

9

Social Landscape after Independence

In early 1948, in the first stage of the creation of states, the former Kathiawad area, which was divided into 222 princely states and many estates, was reorganized as the United States of Saurashtra with Class B status. Kutch state was formed as a Class C state and placed under the Central government. In the second stage in 1956 these two states became part of the larger bilingual state of Bombay and lost their separate identities.

Parallel to this administrative reorganization, there was a growing movement for a separate Mahagujarat state comprising Gujarati-speaking areas. The idea of Gujarat as a separate political unit based on linguistic considerations first found expression as early as 1920 when Gandhi set up a separate provincial Congress body for Gujarat, Kathiawad and Kutch. This sentiment was echoed during the inauguration of Saurashtra state, when Vallabhbhai Patel expressed the hope that one day all three separate administrative units would come together. The aspiration for a separate state was also accompanied by a dissatisfaction among the elite that the Gujarat area did not get sufficient attention, a feeling that was prevalent from the time of the first Congress ministry in 1937 and later during the second Congress ministry in the mid 1940s. This sense of neglect became sharper after Independence when the First Five Year Plan did not provide for any major projects on rivers such as Mahi, Narmada and Tapi.[1] These perceptions, coupled with a sense that resources were being channelled to Marathi-speaking areas, culminated in the Mahagujarat movement in 1956.

It was a popular movement centred on a linguistic assertion for a separate state where the lead was taken by students and prominent citizens who were active in the social and cultural sphere. The turning point came in August 1956 when college students of Ahmedabad went to the local Congress House with a demand for a separate state. The Congress leadership under Chief Minister Morarji Desai not only remained insensitive but responded with police repression when five students lost their lives. Indulal Yagnik came out of retirement and provided leadership to this movement and a number of members of the old guard, including Vidyaben Nilkanth, Shardaben Mehta and Dinkar Mehta, not only condemned the Congress attitude but also supported the movement. After a prolonged struggle, a separate state of Gujarat came into existence on 1 May 1960 and it included mainland Gujarat, Saurashtra and Kutch. Thus, Gujarat regained its independent status after 140 years of being merged, first with Bombay Presidency under the British and after Independence, with Bombay state.

This new political entity provided the modern Gujarati elite with an autonomous space to implement their own pattern of development. The Nehruvian model of development paved the way for new models of agriculture and industrialization based on the exploitation of natural and human resources. The slogan of the 1960s was the 'Green Revolution' of cash crop agriculture supported by new agricultural technologies such as hybrid seeds, large irrigation projects to control surface water and subsidized electricity and credit resources for farmers. This was followed by the 'White Revolution' of expanding dairy technology, milk cooperatives and the widespread marketing of packaged milk and processed milk products. The growth of the cooperatives, particularly in the sector of integrated dairy development known as the Anand Pattern was established by the Kheda District Cooperative Milk Producers' Union at Anand from 1946 onwards. It was later adopted not only by other districts of Gujarat but by other states and today the brand 'Amul' is known throughout India.

Accompanying these 'revolutions' were large public-sector initiatives in heavy industry, petroleum refineries and chemical industries. Simultaneously, the government promoted the development of small- and medium-scale industries by offering entrepreneurs land, electricity and tax holidays to set up manufacturing units in 'industrial estates' on the outskirts of cities and towns. The rallying cry was to convert Gujarat into a 'mini Japan' and by the late 1980s Gujarat was one of the most industrialized states in the country.

Inevitably, such a development model transformed the social and cultural landscape. It resulted in the intertwined processes of rapid urbanization, the rise of an entrepreneurial middle class, widespread ecological degradation and the increasing invisibilization of a large section of society which continued to live below the poverty line. These processes brought about a profound transformation in the normative framework, which set the future course of Gujarati society. The new norms of business and social life facilitated the rise of identity politics, increasing violence in private and public domains and expanding support to insular, exclusive Hindu cultural nationalism in the closing decades of the twentieth century.

URBAN GUJARAT

Rapid and widespread urbanization changed the social geography of Gujarat. The first phase of migration, which had begun in the late nineteenth century with the growth of the textile industry and the railways, intensified as a result of the Chhapaniyo famine. Land reforms initiated in the 1950s by the Congress government of Bombay triggered a second wave of migration. Realizing the limitations of being restricted to land-based activities, peasant communities of mainland Gujarat moved beyond agriculture into agro-industries and began to enter modern professions. In Saurashtra, land reforms had a different social impact as land, which was earlier largely controlled by the Rajput community, passed into the hands of the peasant communities, mainly Patidars. They began to cultivate cash crops, particularly cotton and groundnut, which was to change the political economy of the region in the subsequent decades. By 1951, 27 per cent of the population was urbanized and over a third of it was concentrated in six cities with populations over a lakh: Ahmedabad, Surat, Baroda, Rajkot, Jamnagar and Bhavnagar, the last three in Saurashtra. In the following decades urbanization grew apace with the establishment of large petroleum and petrochemical industries along the 'Golden Corridor' from south to north Gujarat and later with the setting up of mineral-based industries along the 'Silver Corridor' in coastal Saurashtra and Kutch. The prolonged drought from 1984 to 1988 set off a third wave of migration, this time from the arid zones of Saurashtra, north Gujarat and Kutch where the drought was most intense. By 1991 one in three Gujaratis lived in a city and over half of them were in twenty-one cities with populations over a lakh. Continuous growth transformed the character of cities and a glance at the four biggest cities—Ahmedabad, Surat, Baroda and Rajkot—shows the changing contours of their social geography.

By the late 1960s, there were actually three Ahmedabads. The first was the old walled city where the upper castes, Dalits and Muslims lived cheek by jowl, each community in its own pol.[2] The second Ahmedabad grew in the early twentieth century around the textile mills on the eastern periphery of the old city. In these villages-turned-industrial-townships lived Dalit and Muslim textile workers who together formed two-thirds of the labouring population. After the decline of the mills in the early 1980s, and the rise of powerlooms, chemical factories, diamond polishing units and other small-scale industries, this Ahmedabad extended southwards, attracting immigrants from Saurashtra, Hindi-speaking areas of North India and from areas as far south as the river Godavari. Separated from the first two Ahmedabads by the river Sabarmati is the third, new Ahmedabad, which began to grow after Independence. Upwardly mobile residents of the first two Ahmedabads shifted across the river, creating cooperative housing societies that replicated the caste-based residential pattern of the old city. This Ahmedabad is an elite area of upper- and middle-caste

Hindus, a few well-to-do Muslims and some Dalit colonies and slums. The institutes of higher education were established here and this part of the city is expanding northwards towards the new capital city, Gandhinagar, which came up in the late 1960s.

The contradictions of rapid urbanization first became visible in Ahmedabad with the outbreak of Hindu–Muslim conflicts from the early 1960s, culminating in the eruption of one of the worst post-Independence communal riots in 1969. These riots also saw the beginning of the partisan role of the state and the emerging nexus between political leaders and criminals. After a series of riots in the 1980s, ghettoization of Hindus and Muslims intensified, and by the 1990s there were few localities with mixed populations from the two communities. During these years Indo-Pak relations too worsened, and it was reflected in the reference to Muslim neighbourhoods of Ahmedabad as 'mini Pakistan' and the dividing spaces as 'border'.

Surat, on the other hand, followed a different trajectory of development. From being the premier trading city in western

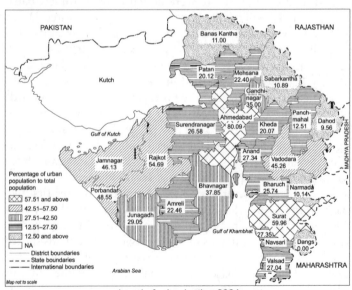

Level of urbanization 2001

India, it went into a decline and for long remained in the shadow of Bombay's prosperity. Its population steadily declined till the 1940s after which it began to pick up somewhat. The dramatic period of Surat's growth coincided with the decline of the textile industries of Bombay and Ahmedabad and after the 1970s it became Gujarat's fastest-growing city. From a population of barely five lakh in 1971, the city became a vast workplace with a variety of small-scale enterprises and the population trebled to fifteen lakh in 1991. The looms dismantled from the dying mills of Ahmedabad and Bombay were reassembled in small groups in countless work sheds and these textile enterprises account for over half the workforce. Surat contributes nearly 60 per cent of India's artificial silk, which is produced in enterprises of ten to twelve looms each, keeping the units small enough to escape labour welfare legislations. Payment is made on piece rate, as was the business practice of the textile trade several centuries ago. A majority of the textile workers are from beyond the immediate hinterland of the city: from Maharashtra, Uttar Pradesh, Andhra Pradesh and the largest number from Orissa. A small section of the migrants from Uttar Pradesh is Muslim. While this migrant population, of mainly single males in the age group of eighteen to twenty-five years, lives in slums all over Surat, areas of major concentration of migrants have developed in the outskirts of the city in industrial areas such as Udhana, Pandesara, Katargam and Limbayat.

Surat expanded on its north-eastern side to include an area known as Varachha, where the diamond polishing industry has grown since the 1980s. The city has come to be one of the world's prominent centres for the cutting and polishing of small diamonds. This industry is dominated by the Patidars of Saurashtra who moved there during the drought years of the 1980s.[3] After the communal riots of the late 1920s the city remained peaceful for about sixty years. Tensions erupted after the demolition of the Babri masjid in 1992 and the friction between the local and migrant populations transformed into large-scale communal violence.

Baroda (now Vadodara), which acquired the epithet 'sanskar nagari' or city of culture under Sayajirao, grew in its own distinct way. Before Independence, as capital city of Baroda state, its civil services attracted educated professionals from all over Gujarat as well as from other parts of the country. Kala Bhavan had attracted technocrats and teachers from Europe in the early 1900s, and after Independence students and faculty members from all over the country came to Baroda, giving it the academic ambience of a university town. The fine arts and music faculties flourished, drawing accomplished artists from all over India. Though a few textile mills and chemical industries were established in the early decades of the twentieth century, large-scale industrial development took place only after Independence. With the establishment of a refinery and giant petrochemical and fertilizer plants as well as pharmaceutical and glass industries, Baroda city began to expand rapidly. Educated professionals came to the city to manage these industries and industrial workers from the surrounding areas.

One feature which existed in all the cities but was marked in Baroda was the presence of a strong illicit-liquor underworld that had organic linkages with the law enforcement agencies as well as municipal corporators. Gujarat is legally a 'dry' state, which means that it has a flourishing bootlegging business. With the establishment of giant corporations and entry of large numbers of professionals from outside the state, the demand for liquor increased and liquor suppliers prospered. The liquor mafia could not survive without police and political patronage and, for its part, the mafia generously funded political parties and supplied muscle power during elections. This mafia was earlier controlled by the Muslims but by the early 1970s Hindus began to dominate the business. Baroda, like Surat, has a strong influence of Marathi culture and a long tradition of public Ganesh festival celebrations. Against this backdrop, economic rivalries between factions within the liquor mafia, which were already taking on 'communal' overtones, began to precipitate in large-scale violence where occasions such as Ganesh festival or Muharram procession provided the spark and emotional tinder. The first of these conflagrations took place in 1982, when, by all accounts, the police and politicians were not completely uninvolved.

Saurashtra's urban roots stretch back to the Harappan era and this trend has continued into modern times. One reason for this is that the region was divided into over 200 princely states and many of them built capital towns well before British rule. After Independence, Rajkot was the capital of Saurashtra state and it expanded as an administrative centre. After the merger of Saurashtra state with the larger Bombay state in 1956, Rajkot was of course no longer a capital city but continued to grow as the largest city of Saurashtra. It is almost a textbook example of urban growth fuelled by prosperity generated by cash crop agriculture and agro-industries. As mentioned earlier, land reforms in this region brought land to the peasant communities. The Green Revolution technologies followed and this area turned to cash crops, particularly groundnut, on a large scale. The groundnut-producing farmers of Saurashtra rose to be a powerful group which dominated the course of politics in the region and later, state politics. Within a short while, the peasant communities diversified into agro-industries and set up groundnut-oil mills, flour mills and cotton gins. Rajkot also emerged as the leading engineering industries and machine tool production centre of Gujarat. In fact, it was chosen by the Central government as the site for the first industrial estate in India, which came into existence in 1955. The thrust of this new phase of growth was towards machinery for agriculture and agro-industries: equipment to improve cultivation, extracting oil from groundnut, manufacturing groundnut-based fertilizer and, above all, pumps for drawing water for irrigation. By 1969 Rajkot was producing 50,000 diesel engines a year, a fifth of India's total production.[4] Rajkot also became a major producer of household kerosene stoves. In addition to the peasant castes, many of the artisan castes diversified into modern industries, taking advantage of the facilities and subsidies offered by the government to encourage entrepreneurship. From 1961 to 2001 the population of Rajkot increased five times from almost two lakh to above ten lakh and its area almost doubled to make space for the tremendous expansion of the city.

As cities expanded to absorb the ever-increasing stream of migrants, the competition for urban space intensified and a new, influential group emerged: the land and builders' mafia. For instance, in Ahmedabad, the early textile workers lived in chawls built on private land in the vicinity of the mills and rented out to migrants. The later migrants were labourers in the unorganized sector and they lived in urban slums, most of them on private land. Slumlords took money from migrants to settle them on such land and later, as real estate prices appreciated, evicted the occupants—through intimidation, physical violence and even slum clearances by the local government and, still later, 'communal' riots provided the cover for such land clearing. To conduct such real estate business, the land and builders' mafia built linkages with members of the underworld, bureaucracy and elected representatives. With the introduction of the Urban Land Ceiling Act the available private land decreased and the focus shifted to municipal land in the city and panchayat land belonging to villages on the margins of the expanding cities. The demand for middle-class housing also increased and land was needed for this too. Political connections were vital for illegally occupying government or panchayat land and the nexus between the builders, politicians and the underworld became stronger. Inevitably the roles coalesced and it was not unusual to find that the slumlord-turned-builder was himself (or his relative or caste fellow) a panchayat member or municipal councillor as well as member of a national political party. Members of the underworld also attempted to wield political power, as epitomized by the career of the underworld leader Abdul Latif who, while in jail in 1987, was elected from five municipal constituencies in Ahmedabad.

While Gujarat continues to be the most urbanized state in the country, unlike other states, the growth of urban centres has not divided it into antagonistic blocs of 'India' versus 'Bharat'. Unparalleled in the rest of the country, city-dwelling

Gujaratis continue to have strong social and economic links with their village of origin. Surpluses generated through economic activities in the city are invested in agriculture or small industries in rural areas, and agricultural incomes are diverted to buying property in the city. To enhance social status, wealth acquired in the city is also invested in caste-based institutions and places of worship in the village. Similarly, urban members of a caste contribute to establishing caste-based hostels and boarding houses to support the education and eventual migration of rural caste-fellows. People also move back to their villages after retirement and it would not be surprising to find that, by then, their villages had transformed into small towns.

THE EXPANDING MIDDLE CLASS AT HOME AND ABROAD

The nineteenth-century middle class was a small section dominated by educated upper-caste professionals, government officials and petty traders. We have already seen how this group fuelled the Share Mania of the 1860s and how their investments in the textile mills supported the growth of the industry. The social compositions of the middle class expanded greatly after Independence and the first to enter this group were various Patidar communities. The Green and White Revolutions had brought them wealth and as government policies exempt agricultural incomes from taxes, they received an added advantage. They steadily diverted their surplus agricultural incomes to investments in industry and in professional education for their children. Soon a significant number of Patidar doctors, engineers and industrial entrepreneurs joined the middle class.

By the 1960s, the artisan castes too began to enter the middle class. Though rooted to their traditional skills such as metal work, carpentry, textile dyeing and printing, they became entrepreneurs. This move too was facilitated by government policies which made available land, cheap credit and other subsidies for setting up small-scale industries. The government created industrial estates on the periphery of every expanding city and also offered incentives for setting up manufacturing concerns in economically less developed regions of the state and the new middle class took advantage of all these opportunities. Soon they moved beyond their traditional skills into chemical and petrochemical and other industries, thus contributing to the creation of the Golden and Silver Corridors of industrial development which made Gujarat the most industrialized state in the country.

The reservation system too had an enormous impact on the social composition of the middle class. This system of positive discrimination enabled many Dalits and Adivasis to gain access to higher education and government jobs. Of course, some Dalits and Adivasis from the progressive princely states such as Baroda and Gondal, and areas where the Gandhians had established schools from the 1920s onwards, had an early advantage as they could straightaway access higher education and acquire the qualifications to enter government service. By the 1970s there were a sizeable number of Dalits and Adivasis in the modern professions. Reservation in government jobs meant growing numbers of bureaucrats, teachers and officials in a wide variety of government institutions from these communities. It not only improved their economic status but also enhanced their prestige within their own communities. Reservation in electoral politics ensured that these communities had some degree of political power at all levels, from the state assembly down to village panchayats. Taking advantage of special government schemes for the economic advancement of these communities, some Dalits took to manufacturing and business and together established the Scheduled Caste Chamber of Commerce to advance their interests. Today they dominate the bone and raw leather industry and, most notably, the ceramic industry, within which they have formed the All Gujarat Scheduled Caste Ceramic Manufacturers Association.

A different kind of Gujarati middle class came into existence overseas. Just as the famine led people to seek work in the cities, it propelled them to move abroad in search of alternatives. The Gujarati diaspora of the early decades of the nineteenth century consisted largely of Bohra, Khoja, Memon and Lohana traders whose business activities in West Asia and Zanzibar were in continuity with the older maritime trade activities in the Indian Ocean and they kept to the East African coast. As European imperial interests in Africa expanded, the Gujarati traders moved inland, prompting Sir Winston Churchill to write:

> It was the Sikh (and Punjabi Muslim) soldier who bore an honourable part in the conquest and pacification of these East African countries. It is the Indian trader who, penetrating and maintaining himself in all sorts of places to which no white man would go or in which no white man could earn a living, has more than any one else developed the early beginnings of trade and opened up the first slender means of communications. It was by Indian labour that the one vital railway on which everything else depends was constructed. It is the Indian banker who supplies the larger part of the capital yet available . . .[5]

It was the famine that prompted people from other communities to emigrate to Zanzibar, German and British East Africa, Mozambique and Natal. A big attraction was the construction of the Ugandan Railway, where the migrants found employment. Karachi was the main centre for the recruitment of labourers who mainly came from the northern states, and Bombay became the centre for the recruitment of skilled workers drawn mainly from the Bombay Presidency. Many members of the Patidar community went to Uganda and worked on the railways; many of the newly educated from the middle castes with professional and technical qualifications went in supervisory and clerical capacities. Many returned after the completion of the project; most notable among them was Amritlal Thakkar, who went as an engineer to Africa. He returned and joined the Gandhian movement and worked among the Bhils and was well known as Thakkar Bapa. Vaishnav and Jain Vaniyas and Brahmins went overseas in greater numbers only in the early years of the twentieth century after reforms within the caste eased the social restrictions on overseas travel.

Many Gujaratis who initially went to Africa as traders and labourers became entrepreneurs, setting up cotton gins, oil mills, soap factories and saw mills. They went on to play a decisive role in the economy and politics of Kenya, Uganda, Zanzibar, Tanganyika and the different regions that made up South Africa. Doctors, engineers, accountants and other professionals continued to emigrate even after Independence till the rupture caused in the 1970s by the expulsion of Asians (a majority were Gujaratis) from Uganda by Idi Amin. There was an exodus of Gujaratis to the United Kingdom, where they arrived stripped of their assets. Most of them rebuilt their lives from scratch, running 'corner shops' and other small enterprises.

In the late 1960s, with changes in immigration policies in the United States, westward migration from Gujarat began to pick up. At first it was the professionals who migrated: doctors, pharmacists, engineers and scientists, followed by the business classes. As time went on they sponsored family members at home and, today, virtually every upper-caste, middle-class Gujarati family has relatives in the United States. While the exact number of Gujaratis in America is not known, estimates put them at between 25 and 40 per cent of the two million Indians in America. Later migrants took to entrepreneurship and today Gujaratis dominate the motel business, parking lots, laundromats and convenience stores. These non-resident Gujaratis have invested their money in property and industries in the towns and villages of Gujarat. In the big cities one can find flats, farmhouses, bungalows and commercial buildings, with names such as Uganda Park, Nairobi House, New York Tower, Minnesota Apartments, indicating the places where the resources for their creation were generated.

THE RISE OF NEW ENTREPRENEURSHIP
The early phase of industrialization was controlled by the traditional mercantile elite which had dominated trade and commerce for centuries. Mercantile society thrived on competition, though the code which governed it is encapsulated in the Gujarati proverb *kajiyanun mon kaalu,* that is, conflict

is always inauspicious. Therefore competition and conflict resulting from it was tempered and resolved by compromise. This value system had its roots in Jain and Vaishnav thought which emphasized non-violence and harmony. The institutions that maintained this system were the Mahajan and Panch which looked after the members' economic interests and negotiated as groups with each other for better terms of business. While social and economic superiority was part of the dynamics, it was essentially a 'face-to-face' relationship which strove for justice within the limitations of a traditional order. Discipline was maintained by Mahajan and Panch through a combination of economic and social control as occupational groups tended to be caste based, and invariably the head of a Mahajan or Panch was a senior member of the caste. Thus a trader or artisan who violated business norms would not only invite financial penalties but would also lose face or *abru* and could find it difficult to, say, find a bride for his son. This 'Mahajan ethos' pervaded public life and social intercourse, which is why public leadership was provided by the Nagarsheth who was not only the leading merchant of a city but also the custodian of its inhabitants. We have seen Nagarsheths who negotiated with and paid off Maratha plunderers to save their cities and fellow citizens from arson and loot.

Within the 'great tradition' of mercantilism in Gujarat, there existed a powerful stream which propelled every generation to cross boundaries and establish new frontiers. The establishment of the first textile mill, against many odds, exemplified this entrepreneurial spirit. For a while, the old mercantile ethical framework continued and tried to adapt to a new age. For instance, though Ranchhodlal Chhotalal was not formally a Nagarsheth, he continued the tradition by providing leadership to a new institution, the municipality. As the chairman of Ahmedabad municipality, he introduced modern drainage systems, public lighting and other facilities for the benefit of the general public. The early educated middle class of doctors, lawyers, teachers and literary figures also engaged with public concerns such as the spread of modern education, social reform and improvement in the status of women, revitalization of indigenous industries and, later, in the struggle against British rule. Even the attempts to create better working conditions for textile workers were made by members of this group.

But even as all this was taking place, we get the first glimpse of the new entrepreneur in the career of Premchand Raichand in the 1860s and the support he received from the emerging middle class was an augury of things to come. The systematic way in which he manipulated the law of the land, his linkages with the British state, the manner in which the quick money which he represented drew hundreds of middle-class members to his schemes, Premchand's blithe disregard for the life savings of the hundreds who were destroyed when the markets crashed and the complete absence of censure for this 'great entrepreneur' from the middle class, religious authorities and caste organizations, all made it clear that the mercantile ethos of Gujarati society was being transformed and the rules governing business and social life were being rewritten to emphasize ruthless advancement.

The Mahajan and Panch tried to adapt to modern production processes but the new entrants to the world of business and manufacturing came from diverse social backgrounds and the kind of social and economic control exercised by these traditional institutions was increasingly ineffective. The spinners, weavers and printers became 'workers' in different mill departments and the jobber probably controlled their lives more than the Panch could. Textile mill owners founded their association but mill workers from different parts of Gujarat, and indeed India, were unable to evolve a forum until decades later. Not surprisingly, the early mill owners–workers conflict in 1895 ended in violence directed at Ranchhodlal himself.

Gandhi entered the public sphere after the first wave of industrialization. Having grown up in a mercantile caste and aware of the hold of the Mahajan culture and its limitations, he was able to grasp this transition and tension. He foresaw the crises ahead and expressed his concern in *Hind Swaraj* in 1908, where he set out the challenges posed by modern technology, modern education and modern professions, which he anticipated would lead to 'life-corroding competition' and a progressive disempowerment of the bulk of the population. Comparing the modern system to the upas tree, a tree so poisonous as to destroy life for miles around, he referred to the 'parasitical professions' as its branches and 'immorality' as the 'roots of the tree'. With this understanding, he began to intervene on behalf of mill workers and small farmers, strongly advocating trusteeship of resources, intercommunity harmony, peaceful coexistence and above all the primacy of means over ends.

However, the Gandhian moral order was swept aside as the Gujarati entrepreneurial class and the middle class expanded and consolidated their economic and social control. After Independence, the pace of their expansion increased dramatically as they grew both in number and in their control over modern financial, political and educational systems. This group was no longer dominated by the upper castes, and the intermediate castes, Dalits and Adivasis who entered the fold soon began to share its aspirations and world view. Their own prosperity was their prime focus and all natural and human resources became the means to achieve it. By the 1970s, this group dominated elected institutions, the bureaucracy, the education system and the cooperative sector, including banks, dairies and agricultural market yards as well as, of course, chambers of commerce.

Just as merchants of every generation had nurtured relationships with heads of state of their time, twentieth-century merchants began by aligning themselves to the freedom movement by funding first Gandhi's ashrams, and later the Congress party and other political parties. The central idea was to ensure that the state paved the way for greater profits. The career of Premchand Raichand did not remain an isolated incident. His style was replayed and refined in the late twentieth century by other Gujarati entrepreneurs and industrialists.

ECOLOGICAL DEGRADATION

While the economy grew and people prospered, the environment went into a state of decline. The expansion in cash crop agriculture and petrochemical and mineral-based industries has been accompanied by widespread ecological degradation. Groundwater resources have declined consistently and rapidly in the last few decades. The *Gujarat Human Development Report* (2004) discloses:

> The number of 'safe' talukas, i.e. 'white' talukas, where groundwater exploitation is less than 65 per cent, has declined drastically from 162 in 1984 to 95 in 1997. That is, the problem talukas have increased more than four times, from 22 to 89 during 1984-1997 implying that more than half of the talukas of the state are in the 'unsafe' category as regards groundwater development.[6]

The recurrent hydrological droughts or intense water scarcity in Saurashtra and north Gujarat are a direct result of the uncontrolled use of ground- and surface-water for agriculture and industry. Cash crop agriculture is more water intensive and government policies granting subsidized electricity to farmers has resulted in more and more bore wells and pumps being installed, steadily depleting groundwater. As a result of falling water tables, the quality of water has also deteriorated all over the state with fluorides, nitrates and salinity levels far exceeding permissible limits, making water unfit for drinking in many areas.

Salinity of the soil has also increased due to overuse of canal water, a phenomenon which is widespread in the sugarcane-growing areas of south Gujarat. In 1997 the Gujarat Ecology Commission estimated that by 2001, 30 per cent of the land would be affected by salt.[7] The chronically drought-prone area of north Gujarat and Kutch is now turning into desert due to overuse of ground- and surface-water. In 1980-81, fifty-one talukas spread over ten districts were covered by the Desert Development Programme and Drought Prone Area Programme and by 1999-2000 this area had increased to ninety-nine talukas spread over sixteen districts.[8] Hand in hand with these processes is extensive deforestation with the result that Gujarat has one of the lowest proportions of land under forest cover: a mere 6.6 per cent[9] and the *Gujarat Human Development Report* (2004) goes on to say:

> It has been frequently argued that tribals have overused forests leading to their depletion and degradation. However, factors like timber extraction by saw mills, paper and pulp mills, and extraction of raw material by other industries as well as encroachment on forests by mines and quarries, dams and other mega infrastructure projects etc. have been largely responsible for the decline in forests in the state.[10]

Industrial waste disposal standards also leave much to be desired. According to the *Gujarat Human Development Report* (2004), eighteen industries identified by the Central Pollution Control Board as 'highly polluting' are all well developed in Gujarat. Among small-scale industries too, pollution-prone industries predominate. The Labour Commissionerate in Gujarat has identified forty-six chemicals produced in Gujarat as extremely toxic and hazardous and these are manufactured by 313 factories in the state (excluding small-scale industries).[11] The report also notes that 'water bodies in the state are highly polluted' particularly water in the rivers Sabarmati, Mahi, Narmada, Tapi, Damanganga and many others mostly located in the 'Golden Corridor'.[12]

Further west, the limestone-rich soil of fertile Saurashtra has attracted cement industries. Removal of limestone and mangroves through uncontrolled mining in the coastal areas of the Silver Corridor has led to salinity ingress from the sea, which is slowly making the soil and water saline and turning the whole belt into a wasteland. The large northern district of Kutch, which too is rich in limestone and other industrial minerals, is following in Saurashtra's footsteps. The destruction is irreversible and assumes disturbing proportions when one considers that Gujarat has a 1659-kilometre-long coastline, nearly 25 per cent of India's total coastline. In the race for industrialization, even protected sanctuaries are not left untouched: mining for limestone is taking place within the Gir Lion Sanctuary and in the late 1990s a large tract of the Chinkara Sanctuary in Kutch was denotified and handed over for limestone mining to a private cement manufacturer.

As is clear, while the state has an aggressive industrial policy, it has neither an environment policy nor a water policy to safeguard natural resources and regulate their use.

MARGINALIZATION OF LABOURING POOR

Immediately after Independence, exploitative, age-old socio-economic practices such as the *halipratha* or bonded labour in south Gujarat and *vethpratha* or forced labour in the erstwhile princely states began to wane because of state intervention. At the same time, the *grahakvati* system (traditional economic interrelations across caste groups) was on the decline due to market forces. Along with these positive developments, Gujarat came to be among the most industrialized states, having one of the highest per capita incomes in the country. Yet, paradoxically, this apparent economic prosperity has not translated into social prosperity. Between 1971 and 2001, over the period of greatest prosperity, the number of agricultural labourers grew from about eighteen lakh to fifty-one lakh and about a fifth of the population continues to lead a subhuman life below the poverty line.

At the end of the nineteenth century, the Chhapaniyo forced people from all sections of society to migrate. At the end of the twentieth century, the labouring poor are compelled to migrate in search of work because of environmental degradation and displacement due to development projects. In Saurashtra, it is expanding salinity ingress, in north Gujarat it is creeping desertification and in the eastern tribal belt it is extensive deforestation that is prompting labourers to migrate along with their families to salt pans, brick kilns, sugarcane fields and to road-building and construction sites in the cities. The conditions of work at these sites are abysmal, revealing how marginal their existence is to the entrepreneurial elite and the bureaucracy.

Gujarat produces and supplies over 60 per cent of the salt in India. The small Rann (salt flat) of Kutch and the coasts of Kutch and Saurashtra are the biggest salt-producing areas in the state, and government statistics estimate that about one lakh people work on the inland and marine salt pans. The labourer and his family migrate and live in makeshift structures of bamboo and plastic sheets on the salt pan. Recruitment is done in the village by the mukadam or labour contractor who pays the head of the family an advance. Payment is by piece rate and the entire family works so as to manufacture the maximum quantity. At the end of the season, final payment is adjusted against the original advance and on an average a family makes four to five paisa per kilo of salt produced. Most salt pan workers belong to the lower castes, untouched by and unaware of the welfare schemes of the labour department or their rights to shelter, healthcare or education. In a system where the salt pan owners, mukadams and government inspectors play their part, no records are maintained of the actual number of workers on a pan and the tragic consequences of this callous system were revealed when a powerful cyclone swept the coast of Saurashtra in 1999, washing away an unknown number of entire families of salt pan workers. The government was unable to provide any information about the casualties, prompting a senior human rights lawyer to remark on the irony that a government which conducts a census of the number of Asiatic lions in the Gir Sanctuary or the wild asses in the Little Rann of Kutch is unable to provide the number of its own citizens who lost their lives due to the cyclone!

The diamond polishing industry is another example of a flourishing sector where labourers work in the most exploitative conditions. Diamond polishing units are small workplaces which mainly recruits young men. Being all-male establishments, the incidence of HIV infections are on the rise in this industry. Doctors in diamond polishing areas of Surat were baffled by the high incidence of urinary tract infections among diamond polishers. Inquiries revealed that since payment is by the piece rate, workers try to polish the maximum number of diamonds in a working day and do not even visit the toilet, and this had led to high infection rates. Given the value of even the smallest diamond and the ease with which they can be stolen, proprietors routinely lock the workers into the premises, sometimes even overnight. When the earthquake struck on the morning of Republic Day in 2001, workers in one such site in Ahmedabad were unable to escape and were crushed to death as the building collapsed.

The situation of Adivasis in Gujarat is scarcely better and this is of some significance as they form 15 per cent of the state's population, which is double the national average. This means that one in every seven Gujaratis is an Adivasi. Tribal land alienation, a process whereby non-Adivasis take over Adivasi-owned land, is on the rise despite legislation to prevent it. A recent study conducted in 2000 for the Central government suggests that 15 per cent of land has changed hands between 1988 and 1998 and dispossessed Adivasis have become migrant labour.[13] Drought and deforestation in the forests of north-eastern Gujarat have driven Adivasis from their villages and it is common to find Bhil construction labourers in road and building construction in all the cities of Gujarat. But the most abject situation is that of tribals who harvest sugarcane in the fields of south Gujarat. Every year 1.3–1.5 lakh workers go to sugar-growing areas of south Gujarat and spend seven to eight months here. They are known as 'koyata', which is the Marathi word for the big sickle used to cut sugarcane. Fifteen years ago, 10 per cent of them were from the Dang area of Gujarat and the remaining 90 per cent were tribals from the Khandesh area of Maharashtra. Now, the social composition of sugarcane cutters has changed. The bulk of them are still tribals from Khandesh who belong to Vasava, Gamit and Bhil communities. Twenty to twenty-five per cent of them are Bhil and Kukna tribals from Dang and some groups are from the Koli community from Saurashtra and Banjaras from Maharashtra.

Sugarcane cultivation has also expanded in Saurashtra, prompting the same communities from Dang and Khandesh to migrate further afield.

All the sugar cooperatives operate through the institution of mukadam who are mainly drawn from the Khandesh and Dang area and belong to the same tribal community. It is very difficult to find out the actual names and addresses of workers because there is no such record. What is available is the total number of koyata instruments distributed by the sugar cooperatives through mukadams. As one koyata instrument goes to one koyata couple, one can at best estimate the total number of workers. Like the salt workers on the salt pans, sugarcane cutters live for most part of the year on the sugarcane field in makeshift structures of bamboo and plastic sheets, with no education or health facilities; they do not even get minimum wages. A public interest petition for koyatas' rights has been pending before the Gujarat High Court for twenty years and it is possible that the next generation of koyata may see justice done.

It is significant that many Vasava tribal sugarcane cutters are from the Uchchal and Nijhar talukas of Gujarat, which were part of the Ukai dam submergence area. They were displaced in the 1960s to make way for the dam which brought water to south Gujarat. Today, ironically, they work in semi-bonded conditions on the same sugarfields made possible by this water. Gujarat does not have a uniform rehabilitation policy for the people displaced by this pattern of development. Mining, irrigation and hydel power projects are displacing vast numbers of small and marginal farmers and Adivasis without just and proper rehabilitation. While those ousted by the Sardar Sarovar Project received a rehabilitation package, others displaced by irrigation projects over the past thirty years have not yet been fully resettled.

Thus a new structure of domination emerged where agricultural and migrant labour were ruthlessly exploited in a system which denied them minimum wages, where the payment was on piece rate, where a system of advances kept them in perpetual debt bondage and where units of manufacture and terms of employment were designed to bypass all labour welfare legislation.

Equally alarming is the increased vulnerability of women in rural as well as urban Gujarat, revealed by census data. The overall number of females per 1000 males was 942 in 1981; it fell to 934 in 1991 and 921 in 2001.[14] The Census 2001 reveals that urban Gujarat presents a picture that is still bleaker where the sex ratio is 879 females per 1000 males, the lowest in the last hundred years. The sex ratio in urban areas steadily decreased from 965 in 1901 to 896 in 1961 and 893 in 1971 with short phases of improvement in-between. In Class I cities the figure fell from 909 to 851 and 861 for the same years.[15] This suggests both greater in-migration on the one hand and increasing violence in the private sphere on the other.

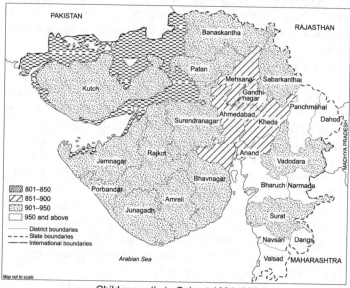

Child sex ratio in Gujarat 1991: 928

The most telling indicator is the sex ratio in the the 0–6 years category as explained by the Census 2001 report:

The overall sex ratio is prone to migration from rural to urban area in search of employment, education, etc. The sex ratio in the population category of 0–6 years is relatively immune to such bias/aberrations and can be said to be relatively secular [sic] indicator. On this account also, the State of Gujarat has fared badly as the 0–6 years sex ratio has decreased from 928 in 1991 to only 878 in 2001.[16]

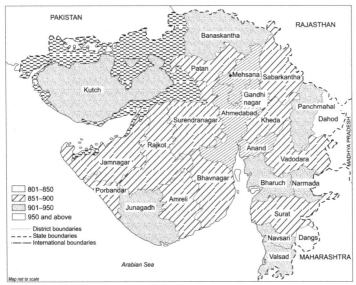

Child sex ratio in Gujarat 2001: 883

The five worst talukas in the state are Unjha, Mansa, Visnagar, Mehsana and Prantij, all in north Gujarat. Unjha tops this list with 734 female children per 1000 male children.[17]

Though female literacy has been rising it is still 58.29 per cent in 2001 compared to over 80 per cent for males. The female literacy rate among Dalit women has increased from 10.7 per cent in 1961 to 45.5 per cent in 1991. During the same period literacy rates among Adivasi women increased from 4.1 per cent to 24.2 per cent.[18] Yet, there are still many pockets where female literacy is less than 10 per cent and the state government has started special programmes to remedy this situation.

NEW POLITICAL EQUATIONS

These changes in the social landscape were inextricably linked with realignments in the political arena and the two spheres reinforced each other. The three upper castes—Brahmin, Vaniya and Patidar—continued their dominance for two decades after the formation of the state. With a combined population of about 21 per cent in the state they were able to capture either half or more than half of the total seats in the assembly elections. Among the three castes the Patidars had emerged as a dominant caste by the middle of the century. Two important Gandhian satyagrahas, in Kheda in 1918 and in Bardoli in 1928, had been focussed on farmers' rights and the two events had resulted in widespread mobilization of the peasant communities, mainly Patidars. They joined the Gandhian movement and the Congress party and occupied positions of leadership and power. With Sardar Patel's rise to national leadership and authority, this community's political clout was further strengthened. Forming 14 per cent of the population, they continued their onward march by securing a quarter of the assembly seats in five consecutive elections from 1957 onwards. But the Brahmins were not able to retain their powerful position in politics. With a 4 per cent share in the population, they won about 18 per cent seats in the 1962 assembly elections but by the elections in 1975 they had just 8 per cent of the total seats.

In the late 1940s a new political caste called Kshatriya came forward to counter the growing influence of Patidars in public life. Traditionally, there is no caste named 'Kshatriya' in Gujarati society. But, in the years just after Independence, the powerful Rajputs, who were mainly chieftains, talukdars and zamindars, were anxious to preserve their political and social status. All of them had been loyal supporters of the Raj and most of them opposed the Congress at every stage of the freedom struggle. So they were apprehensive about their future in the democratic set-up. To reclaim and perpetuate their power and prestige, they decided to organize themselves and to counter the numerical strength of the Patidar community they co-opted the Koli community,[19] which formed a fifth of the total population of Gujarat. The Rajput elite called this new combination 'Kshatriya' as both the Rajputs and Kolis were traditionally arms-bearing communities. The Kshatriya Mahasabha was formed in 1948 and later the Kolis were mobilized in large numbers with the invocation of traditional martial symbols of sword and turban. Although the Kshatriya Mahasabha could not emerge as a political force, the Kshatriya identity did evolve to become a significant factor in electoral politics and the term itself acquired a distinct socio-political resonance.[20]

In the first assembly of the state, which was carved out from the 1957 Bombay assembly, there were only thirteen Kshatriya members in a House of 132 members. Over the next twenty years their number rose to thirty-nine in the House of 182 members. In the early assemblies, Kolis were marginal as the Rajput political elite did not cede much political space to them. But with growing political consciousness, Kolis of south and central Gujarat projected themselves in the political arena and soon their caste fellows of north Gujarat too joined the race. Thus the stage was being set for the next phase of politics where Kshatriyas along with Adivasis, Dalits and Muslims played leading roles. The alchemy of this phase and its implications for future Gujarat politics will be seen in the next chapter.

10

Rise of Hindutva

Ever since its inception as a state, Gujarat's polity has passed through many turbulent phases. In the three and a half decades between 1960 and 1995 when the BJP acquired full power, Gujarat had seventeen ministries and four spells of President's rule. No chief minister, except Madhavsinh Solanki, who headed the Congress ministry from 1980 to 1985, completed the full term of five years. Six were chief ministers for less than a year. These ups and downs in the government reflected the upheaval within Gujarati society brought about by rapid urbanization, industrialization and increasing competition between various castes and communities which embarked on a quest for more meaningful identities, better social status and greater political power. The Hindutva forces rode each of these waves of discontent, turning the upheavals to their advantage and were, at the same time, shaped by them.

The Jana Sangh–Hindu Mahasabha influence became more prominent in the public sphere in the late 1960s and the Reddy Commission, which investigated into the Hindu–Muslim riot of 1969, commented on their role:

> Another noticeable feature to which we must make a reference is the definite part played in various districts which were affected, by the workers of the local Jana Sangh and Hindu Mahasabha organizations or by persons having leanings towards them. There is evidence definitely that they took a leading part in the districts of Amreli, Banaskantha, Mehsana and Baroda (vide paras 20.1, 20.17, 20.19, 20.26, 21.4, 22.36, 22.37, 24.44). In one

of the instances there is evidence to show that they were inciting the crowds to riot. One of the District Magistrates, however, stated that there was no evidence that Jana Sangh and Hindu Mahasabha workers were working under the direction of their local party or organizations.[1]

The report clearly suggests not only the involvement of the Jana Sangh and Hindu Mahasabha in the disturbances but also their area of influence in Gujarat by the end of the 1960s. Although the RSS started its branches in Gujarat by 1940-41, and the Jana Sangh a decade later, the Sangh Parivar could not emerge as a political force in the state as long as the Congress remained united and dominated politics in the state. In the 1962 assembly elections, Jana Sangh contested twenty-six seats without any success and in 1967 they contested sixteen seats but won only one. The Congress split in 1969 gave them greater confidence, though in the 1972 assembly elections they contested ninety-nine seats but won only three. Yet, their share in total votes increased fourfold during this period: from 1.8 per cent to 8.9 per cent.

In the light of its poor performance throughout India, the Jana Sangh leadership changed the direction of the party. At the 1972 session at Bhagalpur, Atal Behari Vajpayee reported to delegates that to make it 'a party of the common man' the Jana Sangh would launch a campaign to mobilize the support of 'landless labour, small peasants, Harijans, workers and employees in mills and offices, youths—particularly students, artisans, and small scale entrepreneurs'.[2] Vajpayee underlined the need to 'extend Jana Sangh's activities beyond the confines of parliamentary politics' saying, 'It is essential that our approach should not be merely reformist. Jana Sangh has to organize popular discontent and exert itself as a militant and dynamic party.'[3]

The 1974 Navnirman movement in Gujarat provided the party with a golden opportunity to mobilize support among students. This movement was directed against the Congress government on the issue of price rise of essential commodities and the protest originated in college campuses. Local students formed Navnirman Committees in every city and town, which made it easy for the Jana Sangh's Vidyarthi Parishad to participate in the popular agitation. Some college students who emerged as leaders of the movement in their towns later joined the party. Following the Navnirman movement, Jayaprakash Narayan started a mass campaign known as 'Total Revolution' movement. When the campaign developed into a national political front directed against the Congress rule of Prime Minister Indira Gandhi, the Jana Sangh joined as a constituent unit. In the 1975 assembly elections the party was able to secure eighteen of the forty seats it contested. More than seats, for the first time since Independence, Jana Sangh won wide-ranging acceptance and credibility from the middle class and upper castes because of its alliance with Congress (O) and Jayaprakash Narayan. Their standing was further enhanced among urban middle classes when, after the imposition of internal Emergency, the RSS–Jana Sangh leadership was arrested and the Sangh Parivar continued an underground struggle.

The 1980 general elections virtually changed the entire spectrum of political and social equations in Gujarat. The Congress (I) adopted a new electoral formula to counter the electoral debacle of 1977. This new formula, known as KHAM, was an electoral combine of Kshatriyas, Harijans, Adivasis and Muslims; in the numbers game these four communities formed 56 per cent of the total population of the state. The architects of the new formula, Jhinabhai Darji and Madhavsinh Solanki, were able to project the image of a pro-poor and pro-backward-class party as they had virtually eliminated the Brahmins, Vaniyas and Patidars from the core positions of the party in the post-Emergency period.

The KHAM formula was successful beyond imagination. Congress (I) won 140 seats out of 181 seats in the assembly and all but one of the twenty-six Lok Sabha seats in the general elections. The monopoly of upper castes on political power was over. For the first time in the history of Gujarat there was not a single Patidar minister with Cabinet rank. A Dalit was sent to the Union Cabinet as minister of state for home. Further, for the first time a tribal was made a Cabinet minister in Gujarat and that too with the irrigation portfolio, with which the rich and dominant Patidar farmers were directly concerned. Above all, the chief minister himself was a lower-caste Kshatriya and son of a family of landless labourers. The upper castes in the state, particularly Patidars, felt humiliated and perceived a political and economic threat to their domination. To Brahmins and Vaniyas, it appeared that their age-old political power was slipping away and was being transferred to *pachchat* or backward castes and communities.

The educated middle class—mainly Brahmins, Vaniyas and Patidars—reacted sharply and students from these communities started an agitation in 1981 against the reservation system which gave backward communities access to institutions of higher education. The Sangh Parivar once again seized the opportunity and supported the Savarna anti-reservationists, directly and indirectly. The Akhil Bharatiya Vidhyarthi Parishad (ABVP), the student wing of the BJP, was the first organization to raise the banner of protest against reservation in postgraduate medical studies. It not only initiated the agitation aimed at Dalits and Adivasis, who were the beneficiaries of the reservation system, but also took it to the middle-class localities of Ahmedabad. Extreme forms of caste violence followed and the clashes between Savarnas and Dalits which started in industrial Ahmedabad became a caste war that spread to the towns and villages of eighteen out of nineteen districts of Gujarat and the many Patidar-dominated villages of north and central Gujarat. By mid 1982, however, the BJP leadership changed their strategy because they realized this was alienating a large section of society. They did not drop their anti-reservation stance but started extensive relief and development work among Dalits and Adivasis and by 1983 they had begun to win over Dalits.

In an effort to win the 1985 assembly elections, Madhavsinh Solanki announced a hike from 10 per cent to 28 per cent in the reservation quota for OBCs in educational institutions and government jobs. The move paid dividends and Madhavsinh captured a record 61 per cent of the vote and was back in the chief minister's office. Soon the students of Morbi engineering college started an agitation against the hike and the ABVP picked up the issue, turning the local agitation into a statewide campaign. This five-month-long anti-reservation agitation degenerated into caste and communal riots when Dalit and Muslim localities were attacked in Ahmedabad and Vadodara. As violence and disturbances continued, the Congress leadership decided to change guard and Amarsinh Chaudhary replaced Madhavsinh Solanki as chief minister in 1985. The Justice Dave Commission which inquired into the agitation and the events that followed commented:

> This [Madhavsinh Solanki's] return of power antagonized the uppercaste Hindus more particularly as the evidence suggests, Patels of Khaira district and North Gujarat and the students belonging to Akhil Bharatiya Vidyarthi Parishad, the members of VHP and BJP. They all combined together to intensify the anti-reservation agitation. They also indirectly had the support of dissident group of Congress-I who too wanted Solanki's ouster.[4]

In the second anti-reservation agitation in 1985, although the hike in education and job quotas was for other-backward-but-not-'untouchable' castes (the Mandal communities), the violence was once again directed against Dalits. During these two agitations, the Brahmin–Vaniya–Patidar combine acquired a Savarna unity. But the 'Avarnas'—the Dalits, Adivasis and OBCs—could not mobilize and organize themselves as a united front. Once again, the ABVP played a significant role in spreading the agitation to many cities though the Sangh Parivar as a whole continued to solicit Dalit and Adivasi leaders in their mobilizational programmes. The BJP reversed its anti-reservation stance and, after 1985, the ABVP too seemed to favour a reservation system for the Dalits and the Adivasis. The following year, the VHP, in one of its Hindu Yuva Sammelans, asked the youth to dedicate themselves to the abolition of untouchability. They were also asked to work for the all-round development of their 'economically and socially backward Hindu brothers'.

When communal riots broke out in Ahmedabad in 1986 during the annual Rath Yatra of the local Jagannath temple, Dalits were repeatedly invited by the BJP and the VHP to join the holy war to protect Hinduism from the threat of Muslims. During these riots, a series of stabbing incidents took place; according to police reports they involved only Muslims and Dalits. The media duly reported this, conveying the impression that the Dalits and the Muslims were out for each other's blood. In such a context, the Dalits responded positively to the Sangh Parivar's overtures.

The closure of textile mills also contributed to changing social equations in Ahmedabad. By the early 1980s, about 40,000 textile workers lost their secure jobs. The textile labour consisted mostly of Dalit, OBCs and Muslim workers, and unemployment among the working population of these three communities added fuel to the fire. Most of the Dalit and OBC workers were drawn towards Hindutva forces from the mid 1980s, forgetting the earlier anti-reservation agenda of the BJP and its associates.

THE POLITICS OF YATRAS

The Sangh Parivar also tried to consolidate its social base through a series of symbolic yatras. In 1983, the VHP organized its Gangajal Yatra or Ekatmata Yatra from Haridwar in the foothills of the Himalayas to Rameshwaram in Tamil Nadu and another from Gangasagar in West Bengal to Somnath in Gujarat. Twenty-three subsidiary pilgrimages were planned for Gujarat. They were to originate from different places and merge with one of the main ones from east to west, towards Somnath. Their aim was to rise above caste, sect and denominational differences and invoke the spirit of unity among all Hindus. Signatories to the appeal to join the yatras included the ABVP, the RSS, the Arya Samaj, the Rotary Club, the Lions Club and also, more notably, the Jain Sampraday, Vaishnava Parivar, Sikh

Sampraday, Bauddha Sampraday and Bharatiya Dalit Varga Sangh.[5] The central mobilizing symbol to unite all Hindus was Gangajal, water from the Ganga, the holiest of all rivers for Hindus. The first anti-reservation riot targeting Dalits had just subsided and the local BJP–VHP leadership systematically involved Dalit leaders in this event. The symbol of Gangajal was potent and had an irresistible emotional pull to which the Dalits responded enthusiastically.

In the yatras that followed, the VHP began to use the Ramjanmabhoomi temple of Ayodhya in its mass mobilization programmes. The first organized effort was the Ram–Janaki Dharma Yatra in 1987 and it took place throughout Gujarat, including the tribal areas. The stated aim was to transcend caste and sect differences in the worship of Shri Rama and to affirm the unity of all Hindus. The second effort was the Ramshila Pujan, worship of bricks to sanctify them for eventual use at the projected Ram temple at Ayodhya. This worship organized by the VHP in 1989 turned out to be the most impressive mobilization effort in Gujarat after the freedom struggle. Even villages with no more than fifty to hundred households participated in the brick worship. Dalit localities of Ahmedabad, small tribal hamlets in far-flung areas and settlements of Kolis at the outskirts of main villages enthusiastically took part in

the programme and even offered money to the VHP. The next in the series of yatras were Ram Jyoti and Vijaya Dashami Vijay Yatras of 1990.

The fifth event was Lal Krishna Advani's Rath Yatra from Somnath to Ayodhya in 1990

Advani's Rath Yatra in Gujarat, 1990

and its chief architect was Narendra Modi, then general secretary of the BJP in Gujarat. The selection of Somnath as the starting point of the yatra was symbolic in more than one way. In the projection of Sangh Parivar, both Ayodhya and Somnath represented 'Hindu hurt' and the yatra linking these holy places represented Hindu assertion. They also wanted to bridge Shaivite and Vaishnavite traditions by linking their pilgrim centres in one yatra.

This Rath Yatra was a great political show of the BJP after their victory in the 1990 assembly elections. Together with the Janata Dal of Chimanbhai Patel, they had managed to capture 56.2 per cent of the vote and shared power in a coalition government. Nearly half the ministers of Chimanbhai Patel's coalition ministry were from the BJP and they all joined the yatra. They piloted it in their own areas and used the government's wireless service to relay information on Advani's movements. The VHP put up signboards in each city and town on the route, declaring them to be cities of a Hindu Rashtra. The event passed off peacefully in the state, mainly because the entire state machinery was on the alert and protecting the semi-government Rath Yatra.

Each yatra mobilization left behind a trail of communal clashes. The first in the series, Ram–Janki Dharma Yatra, led to violent Hindu–Muslim clashes in a number of towns of Sabarkantha and Kheda districts, including Virpur town, located on the borders of these districts, where tribals from surrounding villages attacked Muslims. It was probably for the first time in the recent history of Gujarat that Muslims were attacked by tribals. The second yatra of Ramshila Pujan precipitated Hindu–Muslim riots on a much wider scale and 180 towns and villages were affected. Even after the Amarsinh Chaudhary government banned the processions carrying Ramshila (consecrated bricks for the proposed Ram temple in Ayodhya), there was communal tension at ninety-five places in the state. The last two yatras brought in their wake clashes in the towns of north, central and east Gujarat as well as in thirty-three villages of south Gujarat, where tribals attacked isolated Muslim households.

Communal peace was shattered after the arrest of Advani in Bihar. For almost a week most cities and towns of Gujarat were affected by Hindu–Muslim clashes. Narendra Modi gave a call to observe the last week of October as 'Week of Determination' and decided to organize meetings in 1500 towns and villages of Gujarat. It was in the wake of the 'bandh' and meetings organized by the BJP–VHP that violence erupted on a large scale in many areas. In all, 220 persons were killed in the 1990 riots and though numerically it was just ten more than the 1985 riots, the divide between Hindus and Muslims had deepened. In 1985, only one high wall came up between a Patidar and a Muslim neighbourhood in the old city of Ahmedabad; by the end of 1990, residents of most Dalit chawls in the industrial areas had erected high walls around them. At places where Muslims lived side by side with Dalits, the dominant sentiment was one of fear and mistrust.

Between 1985 and 1990 the Sangh Parivar succeeded in supplanting the idea of Savarna by that of Hindutva as the binding cement for Hindus. The earlier polarization between Savarnas or upper castes and Avarnas or Dalits and tribals, which found expression in two anti-reservation agitations, was transformed into Hindu–Muslim polarization through the politics of yatras and symbolism of Ram. Earlier the ultimate symbolic target of hate was the Dalit; by the end of the 1980s it was the Muslim.[6]

The Savarna Gujarati middle class consisting mainly of upper castes began to find security within the ideology of Hindutva through which they thought they could regain some measure of power and control. Full of anxiety and apprehension in the face of the fast-changing political economy in the rapidly urbanizing Gujarat, they first tried to cling to caste organizations. When caste identities could no longer give them the power they wanted, they turned to Hindutva. For the Dalit and tribal middle class consisting of government servants, teachers and petty contractors, their journey to Hindutva was propelled by their quest for a meaningful and overarching identity beyond the traditional one offered by caste and community. In the swiftly changing socio-economic environment of Gujarat, they sought to throw off the stigma associated with their traditional identity by joining the larger 'Hindu brotherhood'. The two groups took different paths depending on their social origin but converged at Hindutva.

During the same period the VHP was able to acquire a significant following among the Gujarati migrants in the United States, United Kingdom and Africa. Encouraged by the great success of the earlier yatra model in Gujarat and India, the VHP replicated this model at the international level. A Dharma Prasar Yatra was organized in 1999 in North America to preserve Hindu dharma among the new generation. This was followed by another international yatra, Vishwa Dharma Prasar Yatra, which started in 2001 from Kenya and was devoted to the propagation of Hindu dharma. Their slogan was 'The World Is One Family', a translation of the Sanskrit *vasudhaiva kutumbakam*. It covered a number of cities in Western Europe including Copenhagen, Lisbon, Munich, Frankfurt, Paris and London. From the United Kingdom, the yatra went to various cities of the United States and, after touching Toronto, it celebrated Ganesh Chaturthi at Washington. Later it toured Guyana and Trinidad. Throughout this yatra, VHP leaders were received by various Hindu sects at their temples in Europe and America. The VHP always made it a point to stay and organize religious discourses at these temples. In cities where there were no temples, arrangements were made by various Gujarati caste organizations which offered hospitality and facilitated the programme.

THE RISE OF MODERN HINDU SECTS

Even as they were drawn to Hindutva, the upwardly mobile members of the middle class joined influential, modern Hindu sects to validate their newly acquired status and to gain entry into new networks of social security and patronage. Both the caste organizations and sect networks gave them social and psychological support as they struggled in a fast-urbanizing environment. Thus, from the late 1970s, a large number of Savarnas began to join new Hindu sects such as the Bochasan sub-sect of the Swaminarayan sect, Swadhyay Parivar and Asharam Ashram.

The Gujarati diaspora too were drawn to these new sects as many immigrants became increasingly conscious that children born in America were losing touch with their culture and the sects became the route for a cultural journey in search of their roots. The sects also fulfilled their need for a fraternity and other needs such as finding grooms and brides for their children or support for children who came back to India to study. That the Swaminarayan sect of Bochasan, known as BAPS, had built thirty magnificent temples in as many years in the United States speaks for itself. The Western connection of these sects enriched them in more than one way. They all became powerful and prestigious at home and attracted a large number of OBC, Dalit and tribal middle-class families to their fold.

Although all the fronts of Sangh Parivar have been preaching 'Hindu unity' from the beginning, in day-to-day practice they support sect, sub-sect identities making no attempt to transcend these inherent hierarchies and divisions in any manner. Thus the Sangh Parivar achieved the status of a Mahakumbh where every Hindu, with new or old sociocultural ties, finds self-validation and space in the holy congregation.

NEW FRONTS OF SANGH PARIVAR
Significantly, from the mid 1980s, the Sangh Parivar also offered new avenues to urban–rural youth and farmers in the form of two new organizations: Bajrang Dal sponsored by the VHP and Bharatiya Kisan Sangh (BKS) initiated by the RSS. The BKS was established in 1979 to mobilize farmers but started activities in Gujarat only in the early 1980s, while the Bajrang Dal was formed in 1984 as the youth wing of the VHP. As the name suggests, the Bajrang Dal projected the symbol of Hanuman, that great devotee of Lord Ram, to unify Hindu youth. Although the BKS did not incorporate any Hindu god into its name, it projected as its symbol Balaram, the elder brother of Lord Krishna who carries a plough as his weapon, in an attempt to woo farmers.

From the mid 1980s the Bajrang Dal provided muscle power to the VHP to meet the needs of agitational politics or yatra politics. The youth exercising this power were drawn mainly from the ranks of the poor, upper castes and OBCs of the smaller cities and towns. In bigger cities like Ahmedabad, Vadodara and Surat they were drawn from Dalits and OBCs. After 1990 the VHP focussed more on tribal areas and made tribal youth the vehicle of Hindutva ideology. It is not without significance that most of the kar sevaks from Gujarat who took part in the 1992 kar seva which ended in the demolition of the Babri masjid were VHP–Bajrang Dal members and volunteers.

Compared to the Bajrang Dal, the BKS remained a disciplined and cohesive force under the direct control of the RSS. They developed as a front of the Sangh Parivar, spreading the message of Hindu nationalism in general and Swadeshi in particular. By the mid 1980s, the BJP was more than eager to woo the farmers' lobby of Gujarat and within a few years they succeeded in co-opting large numbers of Patidars of north Gujarat and Saurashtra into their fold. At many places in Saurashtra they enrolled farmers of other agrarian communities like Rajputs and Ahirs to expand their social base. The BKS claims they had enrolled two lakh members by the end of the 1980s and twenty lakh by the end of 2002.

CHANGING ELECTORAL EQUATIONS

When Advani was arrested during his Rath Yatra the BJP withdrew support from the National Front government at Delhi led by V.P. Singh and the Janata–BJP government in the state led by Chimanbhai Patel. The politically shrewd Chimanbhai though continued to be chief minister. He, along with three Janata Dal MPs, lent support to the new prime minister, Chandra Shekhar, who formed the government at Delhi with Congress support. In his enthusiasm to topple the V.P. Singh government, Congress president Rajiv Gandhi went against the wishes of Gujarat Congressmen and supported the Chimanbhai ministry by entering into an alliance with the newly formed Janata Dal (G). The enervated Gujarat Congress faced the unenviable position of having to lend support to a man they had branded as pro-rich and pro-upper-caste and vehemently opposed in the 1990 assembly elections.[7]

With the politics of yatras, a series of Hindu–Muslim riots and relentless efforts to expand the social base by all Sangh Parivar fronts, the BJP reaped rich harvest in the 1991 Lok Sabha elections. People's disenchantment with Congress–JD (G) as a result of the political musical chairs they played also contributed significantly to the BJP's gain. The BJP won twenty of the twenty-six seats, up from twelve in the 1989 Lok Sabha elections. The Congress had lost rather than gained from its JD (G) alliance. Eventually Chimanbhai Patel merged the JD (G) with the Congress and continued in power by various means till his death in 1994. During the chief ministership of Chimanbhai as Congress partner, Gujarat witnessed the worst Hindu–Muslim clashes after 1990 when Surat was on fire.

In the riots following the Babri masjid demolition, Surat, with 190 deaths, accounted for more than half of the total deaths in Gujarat. However, more than the numbers, the nature and extent of violence were indicative of collective degeneracy. In many areas a number of houses belonging to Muslims were torched and scores of people were roasted alive. Even children were not spared. Women were gang raped, many in front of their family members. As many academics have reported, the city witnessed unprecedented brutality in the course of the riots.[8]

Even after such horrific incidents, there was hardly any sign of remorse among the city dwellers. Four weeks after the worst rioting, *India Today* reported:

> In spite of such horrible violence, there is no feeling of shame or sadness in anyone. The communal elements among the Hindus consisting of many traders and professionals believe that this was going to happen. One businessman said, 'Muslims will never dare to raise their heads in Surat now. They will have to learn to live in an inferior position as befits a minority.'[9]

Certainly, factors such as rapid urbanization and industrialization, large-scale in-migration and casualization of workers in textile and diamond-cutting industries as well as the nexus between police, politicians and the underworld all had a role in the spread of violence in Surat. But above all, the lack of remorse among the upper strata of the city was an index to the growth of communalism and depth of hatred towards Muslims which developed and strengthened only after the mid 1980s. In the 1985 elections, the Congress won all four assembly constituencies of Surat, two of which were represented by minority communities: one Muslim and the other Christian. The political scenario changed within five years and in the 1990 assembly elections the BJP won three seats and a new political group, Yuva Vikas Party, won the fourth seat. Moreover, of these four representatives, two were Patidar migrants from Saurashtra. Similarly, in the 1991 Lok Sabha elections Kashiram Rana of the BJP won the Surat seat with a margin of more than one lakh which increased to 1.75 lakh in the 1996 Lok Sabha elections.

CRACKS WITHIN BJP

Since 1995, the BJP has held political sway over Gujarat but this has not been without complications. The party has been ridden with factional fighting, representing not only individual egos and quest for greater power but also different socio-political support bases of caste and community. The Sangh Parivar's claim of the dominance of a particular political ideology that unites Hindu society across caste and region is not corroborated by the Gujarat political scenario. The fate of the top leadership of the six ministries that Gujarat has seen between 1995 and 2002 gives an indication of the tension within the formal politics of the BJP. Although the BJP received a thumping majority in the 1995 assembly elections, garnering 122 out of 182 seats, and projected Keshubhai Patel as the first BJP chief minister of Gujarat, he was forced to step down within a mere seven months. A fellow RSS product, Shankarsinh Vaghela, had engineered a split in the state BJP stating that the chief minister and the party general secretary, Narendra Modi, were trying to sideline him. Patel made way for a compromise candidate of the BJP, Suresh Mehta. The rift in the BJP kept deepening and Mehta was sacked as chief minister when he failed to prove his majority in the assembly. A month of President's rule was imposed on Gujarat in September–October 1996. Shankarsinh Vaghela had meanwhile left the BJP, along with forty-eight supporting BJP MLAs, and formed the Rashtriya Janata Party. With the outside support of the Congress, Vaghela became the sixth chief minister of Gujarat since 1990. Vaghela was forced to step down in 1997 over differences with the Congress leader Amarsinh Chaudhary. Despite having no mandate to rule, the Congress MLAs tried their best to regain power in Gandhinagar. Vaghela successfully manoeuvred his RJP candidate, Dilip Parikh, originally from the BJP, into the chief minister's chair. Within months the growing disaffection within the Congress–RJP alliance forced Parikh to resign.

In the 1998 assembly elections the disgruntled electorate voted out the RJP–Congress alliance: the RJP won only four seats and the Congress fifty-three seats. The BJP won a significant majority, winning 117 of the 181 seats. In the wake of several government changes and political instability, the electorate opted for the seemingly firm, well-organized and ideology-driven BJP. The poor showing of the RJP and earlier the lack of mass support for JD (G) established that a viable third-party alternative or regional party had not emerged in Gujarat. As a result, electoral politics has remained largely a two-party affair.

LOCAL POWER STRUCTURES

The BJP victory in 1995 and again in 1998 was propelled by many factors but the crucial factor was the Sangh Parivar's penetration into the local power structures of Gujarat, which began in the 1980s and continued in the 1990s. While the Rajkot Municipal Corporation was captured by the BJP in 1983, the Ahmedabad Municipal Corporation came under its sway in

1987. Moreover, they intermittently controlled the Surat and Vadodara corporations, where no party got a clear mandate. Although the BJP won only about 10 per cent seats in the 1987 panchayat elections and in the zilla and taluka panchayats, the Sangh Parivar expanded its influence in rural Gujarat by capturing various cooperative institutions like cooperative banks, credit societies, milk cooperatives and agriculture produce market committees. By 1995 the BJP made a clean sweep of elections in local power institutions ranging from municipalities to district, block and village panchayats. In the six municipal corporations of the state covering the major cities, the BJP won 395 seats and Congress only thirty-seven; the independents got thirty-three and other parties just two seats. Similarly, in the zilla panchayat the BJP won more than 75 per cent seats and in the taluka panchayat about 65 per cent seats.

It was not unusual in the Congress era for an MP or MLA to control cooperative as well as educational institutions. The leaders of dominant castes and communities could enter public life through such local institutions and then try to consolidate their power by acquiring formal positions. When KHAM politics gave more space to OBC, Dalit and Adivasi leadership, they followed the same pattern and consolidated their position and power by capturing or creating cooperative institutions and opening new educational institutions. Before the early 1990s elections in Gujarat's local self-government institutions were conducted regularly without deviating from the official schedule and the zilla panchayat and the taluka panchayat came to be important links in the power game. The cooperative banks, agricultural produce market committees and milk or sugar cooperatives turned out to be lifelines of the local power structure in cash-crop rich areas of the state.

The BJP realized the strategic importance of such institutions after the 1987 municipal and panchayat elections and started focussing first on cooperative institutions and later on educational institutions. When Chimanbhai Patel was caught up in clinging to his chief ministership, the Sangh Parivar was busy enlarging its influence on local institutions. As the Congress weakened and became directionless, the Sangh Parivar got ample opportunity to penetrate local institutions.

However the leaders who controlled the levers of power at the local level seemed uninterested in implementing the 1995 election slogan of BJP: to keep Gujarat free from *bhay, bhookh, bhrashtachar*—fear, hunger and corruption. Immediately after the BJP took over the reins of power, for the first time single-handedly, no less than a Cabinet minister was accused of oppressing Dalits—all Hindus—of his own town. The episode of Kadi town, sixty kilometres from Ahmedabad, was a testimony to the structure of domination reinforced by the BJP in Gujarat.

A minor incident involving an argument between a Dalit youth and an upper-caste shopkeeper sparked off a caste riot in the prosperous town Kadi in May 1995. During the four hours of arson and looting, allegedly at the instigation of the BJP health minister, a 4000-strong crowd of upper castes went on a rampage. Dalits were brutally assaulted, their houses and sixty-three shops and kiosks owned by them were burnt. Many Dalits reported that the police remained mute spectators to this upper-caste, mainly Patidar, attempt 'to put the Dalits in their place' and 'to teach them a lesson'.[10] Most of the houses and shops burnt were located on prime land next to the main bus stand which had once been at the outskirts of the town but had become commercially attractive due to urban expansion. The police arrested the victims of violence, imprisoned some of them and externed others from the town of Kadi, while the perpetrators of the arson and assault remained untouched. Among those arrested were a Dalit municipal councillor, a social worker and a teacher who had won a national award.

The Dalits in Kadi protested against these arbitrary arrests and demanded an investigation into the role of the health minister in instigating the violence. Irate Dalit women prevented the BJP team from visiting the area. With the Dalits of Kadi continuing their 'Satyagraha' in Gandhinagar, the issue was raised in the Rajya Sabha. The Gujarat chief minister was summoned to Delhi and asked to submit a report to the Union home minister. To press for the demands of the Kadi Dalits, more than 10,000 Dalits from all parts of the state took part in a rally in Ahmedabad, the largest since the movement to counter the anti-reservation agitation in 1981.

Under pressure from the Central government, the BJP state government accepted the demand for a judicial enquiry. But neither the chief minister Keshubhai Patel, who was in power till September 1995, nor his successor Suresh Mehta, who ruled for the next one year, officially ordered the Kadi inquiry. The controversial health minister from Kadi who was known to control key cooperatives and educational institutions was elevated to the post of minister for agriculture, small and medium irrigation in Keshubhai Patel's second ministry after the 1998 assembly elections.

That the BJP and the Sangh Parivar have been in power in the Gujarat assembly since 1998 suggests that their control over the state's politics and governance is substantial. Yet, a closer look at local election figures, as well as the internal dynamics of the party, indicates that the Sangh Parivar's dominance of contemporary Gujarati politics cannot be a foregone conclusion. Things started to go wrong for the BJP almost immediately after the 1998 assembly election victory. Some BJP legislators and ministers protested at the overbearing presence of the RSS and factionalism increased in the party, with legislators and workers divided between the supporters of Keshubhai Patel and Narendra Modi, and between the 'moderates' and those who supported the hardline politics and stances of the Sangh Parivar. Corruption and factionalism were reflected in the stunning defeat that the BJP faced in the 2000 panchayat elections when some of their own people campaigned for political rivals. The party had been unable to sustain its hold over Gujarat's politics for even half a decade. The following table representing the seat tally in district panchayat elections in 1987, 1995 and 2000 indicates the spectacular rise and subsequent downfall of the BJP in panchayat politics.

Zilla Panchayat Election Comparison by Number of Seats: 1987, 1995, 2000

Zilla Panchayat Election Year	Congress	BJP	Janata Dal	Others
1987 (seats: 683)	492	62	91	37
1995 (seats: 772)	111	599	n.a.	20
2000 (seats: 717)	513	192	n.a	12

With the BJP faring poorly in the panchayat and municipal corporation elections in 2000, Keshubhai Patel faced rebellion within his party. Despite coming to power in 1998 with a decisive electoral triumph, Keshubhai was yet again unable to complete his five-year term. In October 2001 he was replaced by Gujarat's first RSS pracharak chief minister, Narendra Modi.

CONTINUITY OF DEVELOPMENT MODEL

While the politics of Gujarat in the 1990s has been highly tumultuous and dynamic, all governments irrespective of their party affiliations have espoused the cause of the urban and rural rich in their development models. In a way, one sees continuity despite the several formal political changes in the last two decades of the century. The elite-centric development model of the Gujarat state, which was initiated at Independence, was strengthened and given legitimacy by successive governments whether run by the Congress or the BJP. The Sardar Sarovar Multipurpose project on the river Narmada is a classic example of the unequivocal stand taken by all political parties, governments and entire spectrum of elite and middle class.

While all chief ministers, irrespective of their social or

political backgrounds, projected themselves as great champions of the Sardar Sarovar project, not one attended to the problems of resettlement and rehabilitation of displaced tribals of their own state and those of Madhya Pradesh and Maharashtra. After the Narmada Water Dispute Tribunal appointed by the Central government delivered its award detailing the sharing of Narmada water and the rehabilitation package for project-affected families in 1978, the power elite repeatedly asserted that the project would change Gujarat into 'Nandanvan' and would provide a new 'lifeline' for the state through irrigation and power generation. However, for ten years following the tribunal's report, first the Janata Dal headed by Babubhai Patel and later Congress ministries headed by Madhavsinh Solanki or Amarsinh Chaudhary (the latter was himself a tribal), grossly neglected the resettlement and rehabilitation of tribal oustees of twenty villages near the dam. Pressure was generated at the grassroots level by the Gujarat Chhatra Sangharsh Vahini, which agitated for the rights of the Gujarati tribal oustees. It was only after the World Bank entered the scene and extended loans totalling 450 million dollars to help finance the construction of the Sardar Sarovar dam and canals that the tribal oustees of Gujarat received a little more attention from the state government. But tribal oustees from the neighbouring states continued to be neglected. Voluntary organizations which drew attention to social justice and human rights of the affected tribal families were branded as anti-development or anti-Gujarat, or both, by all the political parties. From 1987-88 the struggle for just and proper resettlement and rehabilitation of oustees turned into a 'no-dam' struggle under the Narmada Bachao Andolan. Concurrent to the 'no-dam' movement, the 'pro-dam' movement intensified in Gujarat, projecting the issue of water scarcity. Gujarat had passed through a severe drought from 1984 to 1987 and a number of cities of Saurashtra and north Gujarat experienced terrible water shortage. For instance, water had to be transported to Rajkot from Ahmedabad by train. Recalling that harrowing time, the plight of dam oustees was pitted against the plight of people from drought-prone areas. The power elite was quick to exploit the 'predicament' of thirsty people of parched Gujarat and the entire urban middle class started putting its weight behind the pro-dam movement with the hope of getting a permanent source of drinking water from the Narmada dam.

The anti-dam struggle received international support as it highlighted issues related to human rights and the environment which had not been addressed by the authorities. Finally, in 1993 the World Bank, which was funding the project, was compelled to withdraw support. Unfortunately, no worthwhile discussion or debate on human rights and environmental issues related to the Narmada dam ever took place in the state. The Gujarati media and academia were unable to go beyond seeing Narmada as the 'lifeline' of Gujarat. The power and economic elite and virtually the entire middle class of Gujarat perceived the Narmada Bachao Andolan struggle as a conspiracy to stop the onward march of the state.

The BJP was no exception. At the time when the tribunal report was announced Keshubhai Patel was the irrigation minister in the Janata Dal ministry and in charge of the Sardar Sarovar project. Expressing utter contempt for the tribal oustees, he suggested that with water level rising on the Satpura Hills the tribals would find their own escape routes. Throughout the 1980s the BJP in Maharashtra and Madhya Pradesh directly or indirectly raised the issue of resettlement of oustees of their own states to corner the Congress government in Gujarat but after the 'no-dam' movement they changed their position. In 1988-89, in anticipation of the assembly elections in Gujarat the BJP and the BKS intensified the campaign for the Narmada dam by organizing *padayatras* or walking tours in rural areas. After winning the elections and sharing power with Chimanbhai Patel, the BJP and the entire Sangh Parivar participated in the state-sponsored pro-dam campaign. Throughout the 1990s, first Chimanbhai Patel and then the BJP turned the 'pro-dam versus anti-dam' issue into a 'pro-Gujarat and anti-Gujarat' issue and both of them intensified and strengthened a kind of provincialism for their own political gains and the discourse around development models remained intertwined with the discourse on sub-nationalism. It was a harbinger of things to come: in the early twenty-first century the BJP leadership turned the discussion on communalism into a discourse on sub-nationalism or *asmita* of Gujarat!

This development model received further legitimacy after the Central government formally liberalized the economy in 1991. Earlier, the Madhavsinh Solanki government had been selling the idea of 'Gujarat as mini-Japan', but as the government was elected with the support of backward sections of society, welfare and development schemes such as the twenty-point programme were simultaneously announced. In the post-Congress phase after 1990, state governments have systematically withdrawn from social developmental goals. To invite more and more national and international investment in industry, various BJP governments were instrumental in easing tax laws and labour legislations.

From the early 1990s the BJP, under pressure from the BKS, has attempted to reverse some of the progressive changes brought about by land reforms from the 1950s to the 1970s. For instance, till the mid 1990s there was a ban on the purchase of agricultural land by anyone who was not residing within eight kilometres of the plot. The idea was to keep land in the hand of a tiller or a genuine farmer. This eight-kilometre clause was removed in 1995. As a result a rich farmer can now buy agricultural land and use it for non-agricultural purposes. Thus between 1995 and 1999, 14,000 hectares of agricultural land was converted into non-agriculture land in Gujarat.[11] Much of this conversion was carried out using extra-legal means and very little land conversion tax accrued to the government.[12] Another ominous trend has been the steady alienation of land from tribal ownership even in Fifth Schedule areas, where land cannot be bought by a non-tribal without the permission of the district collector. Functionaries of state—politicians and bureaucrats—as well as grassroots power brokers and industrial-entrepreneurial interests have collaborated in this Adivasi land alienation.

Over and above the continuity of the development model and structure of domination we also find continuity of an authoritarian style of leadership in Gujarat. From the time of Vallabhbhai Patel, when he was the unchallenged leader of Gujarat Congress, the notion of 'sardar' has continued despite political changes. Morarji Desai inherited the same style of functioning from Patel and was referred to as *sarvochccha* or supreme. Later Chimanbhai Patel projected the same style when he was chief minister, both in the early 1970s and in the early 1990s. This model of leadership was reinforced during BJP rule, first by Keshubhai Patel and later by Narendra Modi. Political leaders enjoying power always resented discussion and debate within the party or outside in the public sphere. During Keshubhai Patel's second term as chief minister, a Cabinet minister in charge of a sensitive department like Narmada was dropped when he called him a liar in a Cabinet meeting. In his first term as chief minister, Narendra Modi saw to it that a former minister of state in charge of the home department was not given an assembly ticket because he refused to vacate his seat to accommodate the new leader.

Gujarat has often been referred to as the laboratory of Hindutva. While the rise of Hindutva is undeniable, the metaphor of a laboratory, used by the media and academia, conjures up an image of a controlled set-up in which measured ingredients are brought together to produce a desired action or reaction. It implies that the experiment is being conducted in a hermetically sealed room, leading to an inevitable, planned result, uncontaminated by outside influences. However, this imagery does not fully capture the shifts and turbulences or the exigencies of history and Gujarati society that have shaped the rise of Hindu nationalism in Gujarat nor the cracks and contradictions which are likely to influence its future.[13]

Thus, equating Gujarat with Hindutva only would be an oversimplification of a complex web of Gujarati polity and society. Despite formal political changes, the turbulent nature of politics both in the Congress and in the BJP eras, the persisting structure of domination presided over by the upper caste, the continuity of the development model and style of leadership indicate that one cannot look at Gujarat only through the lens of Hindu nationalism. While this ideology seems to have an overwhelming hold over a substantial section of society, it also faces challenges from within its social base.

11

Hindutva and Beyond

In the collective memory of Gujarat, the opening years of the twentieth century are synonymous with the Great Famine followed by widespread plague. A hundred years later, the beginning of the twenty-first century saw the Great Earthquake and the burning of train coaches at Godhra followed by intense violence. The destruction caused by the earthquake has been etched on people's minds, but whether the subsequent years will be remembered as the time when the most horrific and shameful communal carnage took place or be commemorated as the year of 'Hindu victory' remains to be seen. While the famine and plague resulted in large-scale out-migration of Gujaratis, it was a process that led to widening horizons and new opportunities. The communal violence, in contrast, has led to intrastate migration and out-migration of urban and rural Gujarati Muslims, resulting in further ghettoization. Simultaneously, the world view of the vast majority of Hindutva-oriented Gujarati middle-class is steadily shrinking with lesser and lesser space for any kind of dialogue.

On 26 January 2001, as the country celebrated its fifty-first Republic Day, the most powerful earthquake in almost two hundred years shook north-western Gujarat. According to official estimates, about 20,083 people died, 20,717 people were seriously injured and another 1,16,836 people received less extensive injuries. About 3.7 lakh houses were destroyed and about 6.5 lakh required repairs.[1] The epicentre of the earthquake was located in the district of Kutch and the bulk of the destruction took place there and in the neighbouring districts of Jamnagar, Rajkot and Surendranagar. National and international aid poured in, in the form of specialized rescue assistance, medical aid, food and clothes. International financial agencies advanced loans to the state government to enable it to meet citizens' compensation claims and rebuild infrastructure while development aid donors, corporate houses and religious charities came forward with monetary assistance for rebuilding the devastated towns and villages.

The aftermath of the earthquake was a portent as it offered a glimpse of the partisan nature of both the state and the society in Gujarat. In the immediate relief phase, there was discrimination against Muslim communities by both the state machinery and the volunteers of the Sangh Parivar. Indeed the demarcation between the two was hardly visible as the distribution of relief materials in several towns was coordinated through local Sangh Parivar offices. The village and block panchayats would have been the legitimate structures through which to route relief and rehabilitation programmes. But in the panchayat elections held just a few months before the earthquake, the Congress had wrested power in these institutions of local self-government. Following this electoral reversal, the state government avoided these newly elected Congress-dominated panchayats, preferring instead to route the relief programme through the Sangh Parivar and its affiliates. In the rehabilitation phase, Dalits, Kolis and pastoralists faced discrimination as their damaged property was either not surveyed at all or compensation amounts were fixed at levels much lower than what the extent of damage merited. Several village sites were shifted to new venues, but in this relocation there were many instances where the dominant communities of Patidars and Rajputs saw to it that they were given sites away from the original destruction; Dalits, Muslims and other 'backward communities' were left behind, leading to the splitting of these villages. In many cases the upper-caste section of the split villages were rebuilt with monetary assistance from NGOs affiliated to the Sangh Parivar. The upper-caste sense of exclusiveness was revealed and validated by the Hindutva power elite and received tacit support from the media, which scarcely highlighted this aspect.

If the 'violence' around the post-earthquake relief and rehabilitation was invisible violence, the violence in the communal conflagration that followed barely a year later was there for the whole world to see. The last time Gujarat had experienced major communal violence had been about a decade earlier: in 1990 following Advani's Rath Yatra and in 1992 after the demolition of the Babri masjid. This time too Ayodhya was the 'epicentre'. Since early February 2002, large numbers of VHP volunteers had been going to and fro between Ahmedabad and Ayodhya for kar seva. On 27 February, a train on which kar sevaks were returning from Ayodhya was stopped near a slum on the outskirts of Godhra railway station. One of its coaches was burnt by a mob, killing fifty-nine persons. Residents of Godhra and Faizabad later reported that for several weeks, such volunteers had misbehaved with hawkers, teased women, shouted slogans at many stations and made inflammatory speeches all along the route, which may have precipitated the irate reaction of the mob. As yet, no definite picture has emerged regarding who the perpetrators were or what their motive was, and the investigations continue.

A Gujarat bandh called by the VHP on the next day turned into an anti-Muslim orgy of mass slaughter, arson and complete breakdown of law and order; the Sangh Parivar explained it as the retaliation by Hindu masses to avenge the Godhra killings. The looting and arson followed the pattern of earlier riots: Muslim shops and restaurants all over Ahmedabad were systematically ransacked and then set on fire. In the walled city, Hindu and Muslim neighbours threw stones and acid bulbs at each other, as they had been doing since 1969. All this was captured live on many television channels, making it the first communal riot broadcast live to millions of homes in India.

For the first time the capital of Gujarat, Gandhinagar, thirty kilometres from Ahmedabad, experienced communal violence. Within the precinct of the Secretariat, the offices of the Wakf

Board and Minority Development Board were burnt. This was the beginning of a series of incidents which showed that not only was the law and order situation deteriorating but the state itself was crumbling. At the main gate of the Gujarat High Court, on National Highway 8, a number of trucks, with their drivers, were set on fire. Later, the judges were evacuated under armed escort. A Muslim sitting judge of the high court was compelled to leave his official residence and take shelter in a Muslim area. Just opposite the gates of the police commissioner's office in Ahmedabad, shops were burnt and the dargah of Shah Wali Gujarati, one of the pioneers of Urdu language and literature, was razed and a temporary Hanuman temple was hastily installed. None of the symbols of the state—the Secretariat, the high court, the police commissioner's office—had any sanctity for the mob. For their part, the law enforcing authorities looked the other way. The police commissioner of Ahmedabad claimed he was helpless as the police force was but a reflection of society itself and therefore inevitably communalized. The partisan behaviour of the ruling political leaders from the chief minister and home minister downwards was obvious. Under their leadership, the law enforcing machinery indirectly supported the mobs, allowed large-scale destruction and death, and the state was subverted from within.

The most barbaric scenes were played out in industrial Ahmedabad. On the afternoon of 28 February, forty-three people, including Ahsan Jafri, a former Congress MP of Ahmedabad, were burnt alive in Gulmarg Society in the Chamanpura-Asarwa of north-east Ahmedabad. For four hours they had frantically tried to contact the police, senior bureaucrats and associates in Delhi, but the mob of over 10,000, most of them from the neighbourhood, finally set the colony on fire. That evening, in the slums of nearby Naroda area, eighty-four people were burnt alive by a 15,000-strong mob. According to those who survived, this mob consisted of people from 'outside'. As in the rest of Ahmedabad, in the industrial areas too, Muslim shops and homes were systematically wiped out.

After showing great hesitation, the government imposed

curfew in Ahmedabad and twenty-six other towns and cities by that evening. The army was called in on the afternoon of 1 March, by which time the violence had spread to Panchmahal, Dahod, Sabarkantha, Vadodara, Kheda and Gandhinagar districts. That same day fourteen people, nine of them Muslim, were burnt alive in Best Bakery in Vadodara. In Sardarpura village, near Vijapur town of Mehsana district, a mob attacked a Muslim mohalla and burnt alive twenty-nine people. On 2 March the violence spread to Banaskantha district, Surat city and Bhavnagar city. For the next three days the north-eastern tribal belt of Gujarat, from Ambaji to the Narmada, witnessed widespread looting and arson as Adivasis attacked Muslim shops and bastis. Some stray incidents were reported from bordering Adivasi areas of Madhya Pradesh and Rajasthan. It is not without significance that three months earlier the RSS had organized a large gathering of Adivasis on the theme of 'anti-conversion' presided by the RSS chief Sudarshan at Jhabua, Madhya Pradesh. Tribals from Gujarat, Rajasthan and Madhya Pradesh attended this sammelan in large numbers.

The geography of violence presents a puzzling picture as it appears that there was a spatial dimension to the way 'Hindu outrage' was felt and expressed. The areas where the most intense violence took place also happened to be the places where the assembly seats were dominated by the Congress. This appears to suggest that the violence was engineered with an eye on the forthcoming elections. The BJP strongholds of Saurashtra and Kutch did not feel the same urge to avenge the 'Godhra wrongs' even though they had displayed the capacity to practise discrimination after the earthquake. Except Rajkot and Bhavnagar which were disturbed for the first few days, all other towns and most villages were quiet. South Gujarat too remained peaceful with the exception of Surat city, which saw some unrest in the early days. There were rumours that in Surat, looking at the economic slump, local businessmen had made a deal with the Sangh Parivar to keep their city free of violence in exchange for undisclosed sums of money. Similarly, a business magnate controlling one of the country's largest business houses

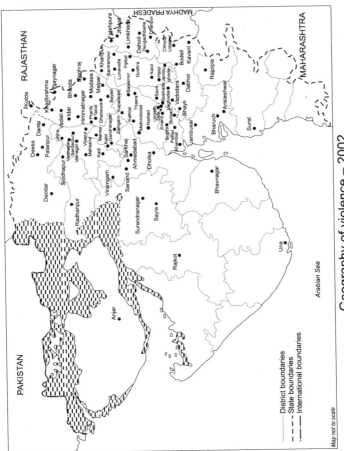

Geography of violence – 2002

Map not to scale

District boundaries
State boundaries
International boundaries

had allegedly instructed bureaucrats in Saurashtra to maintain law and order so that the company's investments in the region were not jeopardized.

The violence continued for three months at the end of which about 2000 people were killed and about 1.4 lakh were in relief camps, of which some one lakh were in Ahmedabad. The remaining were scattered in makeshift camps in the towns and villages of Sabarkantha, Mehsana, Panchmahal, Vadodara and Anand districts. The event of 27 February and the months that followed received national and international attention. The National Human Rights Commission headed by a former chief justice of India took a serious view of the episode and many human rights groups compiled citizens' reports on the extent of violence and its brutality. All pointed to the state government's inability to control the rioters and its apathy in bringing the perpetrators to book. The BJP governments at both the Centre and the state shrugged off the criticism as efforts by 'outsiders' to tarnish the image of Gujarat.

IMPLICATIONS OF 2002

The communal riots in Gujarat raise three major questions for the state. First, guarantee and protection of right to life and personal liberties and of properties of the citizens of India by the state machinery; second, provision of immediate relief to the victims and their full rehabilitation; and, third, securing justice for the victims by bringing to book and punishing all those who were involved in the carnage. These three basic rights of the citizens are not merely left to the mercy of those in power but are the solemn constitutional obligations of the state in India, in the absence or violation of which the state ceases to be a state.

The blatant and open failure of the state on the first front was, as found by the National Human Rights Commission, a clear case of res ipsa loquitor (the matter speaks for itself)— the direct participation and assistance of the law enforcement agencies, the silence on the part of the elected representatives even as a former MP was burnt alive and the mute and passive behaviour of the judiciary even though a sitting judge of the high court was forced to flee his official residence. On the second front, it is minimally expected that the state government—out of humanitarian considerations, not to speak of its constitutional obligations—will at least provide immediate relief to the victims and their families and will as early as possible rehabilitate them fully and justly. But even here it failed miserably. Echoing the experience after the earthquake, initially Hindu victims of the Godhra train-burning were promised greater compensation than those who lost their lives in the violence that followed. Most of the relief camps were organized and run by various Muslim jamaat groups, assisted by NGOs. State aid for camps came after a week but without any arrangements for water and sanitation, which the victims themselves had to organize. Despite the fear among Muslims and their inability to return to their homes due to the hostility of the neighbours, the state government was in a haste to wind up the camps to show the Election Commission that normalcy had returned and the state was ready for elections.

But when it came to the most basic, essentially sovereign function of the state—to find out the culprits, prosecute them and punish them quickly and effectively and render efficacious justice to the victims—the state was blatantly partisan. In the early phase victims were hesitant to come forward to register cases against the perpetrators who were politically well connected and in many cases they were allegedly intimidated by the police to withdraw their cases. In the relief camps, hardly any assistance was provided for victims to register claims for compensation for deaths of family members or the destruction of property. Many who had migrated from other areas to relief camps were simply too terrified to return to their homes to file cases or claims.

Finally, 4256 FIRs, or first information reports, were registered and were investigated by the same state police force which had been seen openly aiding and abetting the rioters and murderers. Not surprisingly, within a few months investigations in over half of them were closed. In the cases which came to trial, witnesses inevitably felt no confidence in such an investigating authority and despite the fact that more and more of them turned hostile, prosecutors in the cases raised no objection. The nadir was the trial of the Best Bakery Case, one of the five major cases of heinous crimes, killing and burning of Muslims during the communal carnage. Twenty-one accused were prosecuted by a 'fast track' court. As the events unfolded, one by one, all the witnesses turned hostile, repudiated their initial statements to the police and in a volte face even asserted that one of the accused actually saved their lives. As a result of these astonishing developments, the judge presiding over the case was forced to acquit the accused for lack of evidence. The silence of the higher courts was eloquent. These were not merely cases of 'miscarriages of justice' but a collapse of the criminal justice system and a total failure of the state.

In the early phase, the law enforcement agencies and the judiciary turned out to be passive and mute witnesses to the shameless outrage of the Constitution and human rights. The normally available constitutional safeguards and checks, namely the Central government and the governor (the former was led by the same political party as the Gujarat government and the latter, an old RSS hand), acted in collusion with the Gujarat government and used their constitutional powers to protect or save the chief minister of Gujarat. In this scenario the threat to the Constitution, to democracy, to the unity and integrity of India and basic rights of the people appeared real and certain. It was only in July 2003—when the Supreme Court intervened and ordered a retrial of the Best Bakery case outside Gujarat and the re-opening of cases which were wound up without complete investigation—that the possibility of justice returned.

Clearly, the state has moved far away from the standards of justice established by Siddharaj Solanki who, in the twelfth century, personally investigated the communal conflict at Cambay and punished the culprits and rebuilt the mosque which was destroyed in the violence. Subsequently, whether in the Surat incident in Mughal times or the Prabhas Patan incident at the end of the nineteenth century, both the Mughal emperor and the British government stepped in to see that justice was done and Hindu and Muslim leaders too took the initiative to resolve their differences and establish justice, peace and communal ties. Yet, after the establishment of the separate state of Gujarat, with a democratic set-up, communal and caste riots have taken place without any of the culprits or kingpins being punished by any government of the day. This trend has sent out the signal that the law can be broken with impunity and indeed that the state is there to protect wrongdoers.

There are question marks over the political future of Gujarat too. In June 2002 Chief Minister Narendra Modi dissolved the Legislative Assembly ahead of time and called for early elections. They were held in December of that year and the BJP registered a stunning victory, securing two-thirds majority. The Congress-dominated seats of north and central Gujarat were captured by the BJP, signalling that Hindutva mobilization through communal riots was successful. Narendra Modi silenced his critics because the people had chosen him through that key institution of democracy, elections, and the thumping majority was a sign of their unequivocal support. A few months later, the neighbouring states of Madhya Pradesh and Rajasthan went to polls and there too the BJP secured a majority. It appeared that Hindutva was an election-winning formula.

Yet, a glance at the voting pattern of the 2002 elections in Gujarat reveals that about 50 per cent of the electorate voted for the BJP and 39 per cent of the vote went to the Congress. In south Gujarat the difference in votes between the two political parties was just 1 per cent. Even if we presume that every Muslim voted against the BJP, and Muslims form 10 per cent of the population, it still means that 30 per cent of Hindus voted against the BJP. In the 2004 Lok Sabha elections the margin narrowed further, with the BJP securing 47 per cent of the vote share and the Congress 45 per cent. This could mean that Gujarat politics is likely to continue to be tumultuous and the see-saw between the two major parties will continue.

The events of 2002 raise questions about Gujarati society as well. The first is around the violence that was perpetrated.

Large-scale looting, arson, rape and murder of Muslims during riots have become commonplace and are internalized to such an extent that it is not uncommon to hear that 'this is nothing new for Gujarat'. All these took place during the 1969 riots and the sentiment that 'it was time the Muslim were taught a lesson' was widespread even then and it was the first time the unwritten norm that lives of women would be spared was broken and instance of attacks on women were reported. By 1986 the existence of such a norm in the past was forgotten. The first instances of mass burning took place in Surat city and Mansa town in north Gujarat in 1992. The first instances of violence on women taking the form of sexual abuse with sticks and poles were reported during this time from Surat.

While at first glance there appeared to be continuities in the patterns of violence, this riot marked significant departures from the past. Earlier, the weapons were petrol and kerosene bombs but a new development in 2002 was the use of cooking gas cylinders as explosives. Cylinders were taken from the victim's house, bundled in cloth which was set on fire, and then tossed back into the house, where it would explode like a bomb, destroying the house and setting everything ablaze. New groups joined the traditional perpetrators. From 1969 onwards the complicity of politicians and criminal gangs in communal riots was visible and mobs consisted of hired thugs and local anti-social youth. By the 1980s, the mills had closed down and the unemployed added to the lumpen groups available for recruitment. Till the 1990s, another common remark was that 'riots are engineered by politicians and violence and looting is committed by criminals and the poor'. By the riots of 1990 middle-class youths had begun to get involved in looting shops and in 2002 the mobs included larger groups of middle- and upper-class men and women who could be seen with armloads of shoes, clothes and kitchen equipment making their getaway on scooters, motorcycles and cars.

The increasing participation of large numbers of young people in such violence is also disturbing and society as a whole needs to reflect on this growing phenomenon. While the ideology of Hindutva was gaining ground, moderate voices were getting weaker and more inaudible. By the early 1990s, Hindu and Muslim community leaders reported that they no longer wielded any authority over their youth and the traditional structures of community control had crumbled. In this situation, it was not surprising to see growing numbers of young people participating in loot and arson and many youngsters from the upper and middle classes joined in the mayhem. These youngsters, in their late teens and early twenties, had grown up on a diet of anti-minority invective, and the voices of moderation, of liberal thought and tolerance had been missing from their environment and had not been emphasized or valued in their formal education. Also, since the 1990s, the social geography of Ahmedabad had gradually changed, creating Hindu and Muslim ghettos, resulting in declining social interaction between the communities. There were fewer and fewer chances for children to play together and establish any bonds. A decade ago these rampaging youngsters would have been described as lumpen youth but now it appears that there is growing anomie in the younger generation.

During 2002 there were widespread reports of the involvement of Dalits in the anti-Muslim violence in urban areas and of Adivasis in the rural areas, which points to the successful Sangh Parivar mobilization among both these groups. Till the mid 1980s, Dalits and Muslims were allies in their joint resistance to communal forces and upper-caste politics, and the two communities protected each other. The social geography of cities was such that they shared neighbourhoods and their daily lives and supported each other in times of crisis. However, taken in by the mirage of Sangh Parivar propaganda and imagining acceptance into Savarna society through the medium of Hindutva, Dalits became willing instruments in the carnage. In rural areas, on the whole, Dalits continued to support Muslims in their villages; the oppressors in this setting were Adivasis, who had been systematically wooed by the Sangh and its NGO affiliates. The challenge now is before Dalit and Adivasi community leaders as well as representatives from these communities within the BJP to think about the directions their communities are taking and the future that awaits them in a society and political system where Hindutva dominates. If the anti-Muslim and anti-Dalit pamphlets circulated after the communal violence are any indication, it appears that at the heart of the Hindutva ideology lies upper-caste dominance. Here, an analysis of the violence from the point of view of the communities involved might offer useful pointers. It is significant that the tribals of south Gujarat did not participate in the violence unlike the tribals of the north-eastern Bhil belt. Even in rural north and central Gujarat which have been the centre stage of violence, a number of Hindu communities— Dalits, Thakor, Rajput and pastoralists—have protected and sheltered Muslims, while from several accounts it appears that the Patidars were prominent among the perpetrators.

Another dimension of the 2002 carnage which is significant for Gujarati society is the role and attitude of the business community. Historically, the state's mercantile traditions have been imbued with Vaishnav and Jain values of non-violence as well as an abhorrence for conflict for practical reasons as every disruption leads to economic loss. These considerations too were cast aside as the business community chose to not speak out openly against the prolonged violence. Relief aid came but not with the same outpouring of generosity witnessed after the earthquake. Corporate houses were hesitant to come forward openly to assist Muslim victims[2] and fewer still voiced their concern even though the violence was tainting the reputation of the state worldwide and disrupting their business prospects. It appeared as if the dominance of the BJP at both the state and the Central governments deterred industrialists for fear of injuring future business prospects. However, in early 2003, two leading industrialists, speaking at a gathering of the Confederation of Indian Industry (CII) at Delhi, made critical remarks about the law and order situation in Gujarat. The industrialists of Gujarat reacted sharply and gathering under the banner of 'Resurgent Group of Gujarat' (which included leading industrialists and, significantly, a former chief justice of the Gujarat High Court) claimed that peace had returned to the state and that the CII remarks were designed to malign and mislead. The power of the ruling party was compelling enough for the CII to backtrack and make a written apology to Chief Minister Modi.[3]

An aspect that also merits reflection is that the nature of violence has been steadily getting more and more brutal. In 2002 there was not only arson, mass rape and mass burning but eyewitness accounts from the majority community confirm that young children thrown into the fire and wombs of pregnant women were ripped apart and mother and unborn child were burnt. Instances were also reported where the bodies of burnt women were sexually mutilated with sticks and rods and desecrated by the mob. One of the most numbing incidents took place in north Gujarat at Himmatnagar where a restaurant owned by a Muslim on the highway was burnt. The restaurant owner was fond of birds and fish and maintained a large aquarium and aviary on the restaurant premises with many rare species. When the mobs arrived, they not only looted the place but also poured acid into the aquarium. The birds perished when the premises was set on fire.

Till today, there has been no discussion or reflection within the community about the nature of violence that Hindu Gujarati society has shown itself to be capable of. The Sangh Parivar response to anyone who raises questions about these acts of violence is either to say that they are exaggerations of a partisan, English-language media and so-called human rights groups out to malign Gujarat and Gujaratis. They justify the post-Godhra events by selectively quoting the Ramayana and Mahabharata where *atatayee* or oppressors were eliminated by the heroes of the epics. More disturbing than their callousness was the utter silence of spiritual leaders of most modern sects in Gujarat, including the Jains for whom ahimsa is the cardinal principle. The larger ethical and moral questions raised by the epics were conveniently ignored by them. For instance, the famous dictum *ahimsa paramodharma*—non-violence is supreme religion—was preached by Bhishma after the great battle of Mahabharata.

This central principle of Hindu tradition was effectively sidestepped and the pertinent question of non-violence was scarcely mentioned. In fact, just as the lines between the state and the Sangh Parivar were blurred, the demarcation between the Sangh Parivar and the Hindu sects are equally fuzzy. This development was reflected in a newspaper announcement on the day of assembly elections in December 2002 when *Fulchhab*, a widely circulated Gujarati daily from Saurashtra, carried a prominent advertisement by the VHP which exhorted all Hindus to vote for the 'protectors of Hindu culture'. In the list of signatories to the advertisement, the local swamis of the Swaminarayan sect topped the list, followed by the local head of the Asharam sect.

And finally, the challenge before Hinduism itself. A number of currents and cross-currents, religious and social organizations including various new twentieth-century sects have contributed to the creation of a 'new' Hinduism. The nineteenth century rediscovery of classical Hinduism by sympathetic European scholars, the spread of Hindu reform movements such as Brahmo Samaj in India and Prarthana Samaj in Gujarat as well as the spread of Arya Samaj played a significant role in the evolution of new Hinduism. All of them, the orientalists and the reformers, created the impression of a 'real' Hinduism which transcended local religio-cultural traditions and 'living Hinduism' at the micro level.

This new Hinduism is primarily classical and Vedantik or Sanskritik Hinduism which is palatable to a 'Westernizing' and expanding middle class of India because they find it less obscurantist and more 'respectable' in the modern world. The redefined and rearticulated version of Hinduism created a space for those who saw the new religion more as an ideology than as a faith. In other words, using Hinduism as an instrument of political mobilization became possible. For the pioneers of 'Hindutva'—Savarkar, Hedgewar and Golwalkar—Hinduism was no more a fountainhead of spiritual, religious, cultural or ethical categories but only a national ideology to mobilize the Hindu population towards a 'Hindu Rashtra' or Hindu nation.[4]

The pioneers and the followers of 'Hindutva' in the Sangh Parivar used the 'Hindu past' in their construction of 'Hindu nationalism' by recalling great warriors like Rana Pratap and Shivaji who fought against the 'oppressive' Muslim emperors in the seventeenth century, and Rani Jhansi and Chandrashekhar Azad who fought against the British. This instrumental use of history projected 'Hindu past' in such a way that selective history became the history of Hinduism.

Yet, the political ideology of 'Hindutva' is but one dimension of this new Hinduism which has the inherent tendency of becoming more and more exclusivist and authoritarian. Not only are Muslims and Christians excluded from the discourse but also a number of syncretic communities and their contributions. By focusing more and more on classical Hinduism or Sanskritik Hinduism, the local or 'little' religious traditions and practices were either undermined or marginalized. Some of the religious streams of the bhakti tradition and medieval sects like Kabir panth, Dadu panth and Pranami sampraday, which represent syncretic elements and composite culture, were left behind in contemporary Gujarat and India as a whole. In their quest for a positive identity and upward social mobility, sections of Gujarati society, particularly those belonging to Dalit, Adivasi and other backward communities (who were traditionally associated with local sects like Kabir panth or Pranami panth), left the little traditions behind and accepted new Hinduism through the modern sects.

During the evolution of new Hinduism, neither the early reformers nor the later 'Hindutva' pioneers have offered any significant critique of modern knowledge, including science and technology. Most of the modern sect leaders generally propagate Ayurveda and Jyotish Shastra (Indian astrology) as well as yoga and meditation among their followers but hardly offer any critique of science and technology. As a result, the Hindu middle class and particularly professionals, within India or outside, do not find any difficulty in accepting some remedies of Ayurveda, yoga and meditation. On the contrary they become advocates of these traditions as part of the great heritage of

Hindu civilization. Thus, in new Hinduism, the journey of the Hindu middle class becomes smooth as they keep Western knowledge in one hand and the 'great' heritage of Hindu civilization in the other without any contradictions and simultaneously support and sustain the Western development model.

In this climate of new Hinduism, the antipathy and sometimes hostility towards Gandhi and Gandhism is hardly surprising. Gandhi's emphasis on the ethical–moral dimension of Sanatan Hinduism is not attractive to the rising entrepreneurial middle class any more. Gandhi drew strength from ahimsa and *sadhan shuddhi*, non-violence and purity of means. He also emphasized the continuity of the bhakti tradition where Ram and Rahim represent the same ultimate reality. Except to campaign for temple entry for Dalits he even resisted visiting Hindu places of worship in his long journeys throughout India. As new Hinduism and particularly 'Hindutva' has always attached greater importance to history and 'Hindu past', Gandhi's emphasis on spiritual Hinduism has been considered an obstacle in the great march of modern Hinduism. Most of the modern sects also try to bypass Gandhi by invoking philosophical Hinduism. Gandhi's critique of modern science and technology as well as of 'modern civilization' as expressed in his *Hind Swaraj* challenges the very foundation of not only the middle class but also Hindutva forces which are trying to project Hindu Rashtra as a modern nation with nuclear power and missiles with the names of Vedic Hindu gods.

While critiquing new Hinduism, it is also important to recognize that, apart from chanting the mantra of secularism, neither the other political parties nor intellectuals in Gujarat have any argument to challenge this formulation ideologically, theologically or philosophically. This intellectual vacuum has been the greatest fertilizer for new Hinduism to grow unopposed and unfettered. And while these developments have been taking place, hardly any attention has been paid to the fraying community fabric. The poet Sheikh Adam Abuwala once remarked that the 1969 riots were a turning point in Hindu–Muslim relationships in Gujarat. After this event, diyas were no longer lit during Diwali at Bohra Muslim homes, a practice which he remembered from his childhood. The process of ghettoization which set in after these riots has never attracted the attention of town planners, and physical and mental distancing proceeded apace. The shrinking space for shared childhoods leading to adult bonds of understanding and mutual respect has come to be the defining feature of Gujarati cities and, soon, of rural Gujarat too. Similar, though less emphasized, is the spatial segregation of Dalits. In the traditional layout of both villages and cities, they always had separate colonies and this arrangement continues till today and one would scarcely find a Dalit residing in a Savarna housing complex. Even during the height of 'Hindu unity', no attempts were made, from either side, to breach this *Lakshman rekha*.

WHITHER GUJARAT?

It appears that Gujarati Hindu society in the post-2002 phase is not ready to look within. A majority of them, particularly the middle class, think that 'the outsider'—English media and academia and the so-called 'pseudo-secularists'—are out to malign them and tarnish the image of Gujarat. The Gujarati media, most university teachers and literati are also not ready to look at or critically examine the issues related to development models or ecological degradation or steady marginalization of the bottom 20 per cent of Gujarati society.

For the powerful Savarna middle class, even the Indian Constitution is becoming less and less relevant because they have successfully created a system whereby they can circumvent its vision as well as legal framework to protect and perpetuate their hegemony. They draw inspiration from the 'market' and try to empower themselves through the mechanism of the market. The march towards greater urbanization and industrialization would continue and the middle class will become more powerful in the coming decades; but their outlook and future action is likely to be shaped by global–local linkages expressed through market forces. They would support Hindu nationalism as long as this ideology supports their aspirations.

Picture Credits

Notes

Preface
1. Quoted in Aakar Patel, 2003.

1. Synthesis and Continuity
1. Sundaram, 1992, p. 46. (Translations throughout the book, unless otherwise mentioned, are by the authors.)
2. Umashankar Joshi, 1981, pp. 694-95.
3. For a detailed discussion on Bhagwanlal Indraji and his contributions see Durgashankar K. Shastri, 1945 and *Bhagwanlal Indraji Commemoration Volume* of the Journal of the Gujarat Research Society, October 1939, Bombay.

2. Mercantile Ethos
1. Quoted in M.N. Pearson, 1976, p. 11.
2. *Parishadpramukhna Bhashano*. Part 2. 1974. Excerpted from quote by Rasiklal Parikh in his lecture as president of the Gujarati Sahitya Parishad in 1963. p. 349.
3. V.K. Jain, 1990, pp. 233–37.
4. ibid., pp. 237–41.
5. Quoted in ibid., p. 239 fn.
6. Hasmukh D. Sankalia, 1949, p. 156; and *Bhagvadgomandal*, Vol. 1, 1986, p. 58.
7. Dwijendra Tripathi, 1984, p. 154.
8. Krishnalal Mohanlal Jhaveri, 1933, Part 1, p.111.
9. According to popular myths, three Muslim pirs belonging to different sects are said to have converted Siddhraj himself. Bohra legends assert that he accepted their faith; Khojas claim that their first missionary, Nur Satgur, had converted him; and the Sunnis believe that he adopted their faith. While there is no historical evidence of Siddhraj's conversion to any Islamic sect, the claims of these communities suggest that they acquired honour and respectability by invoking the name of the great Hindu king as their co-religionist.
10. J.S. Mangat, 1969, pp. 20, 23.
11. Jain, 1990, pp. 187-88.

12. Pearson, 1976, p. 123.
13. Govindbhai H. Desai, 1932, p. 212.
14. Quoted in Pearson, 1976, p. 122.
15. ibid.
16. Desai, 1932, p. 211; and Shirin Mehta, 'The Mahajans and the Business Community' in Tripathi, 1984, p. 181.
17. Shirin Mehta, 'The Mahajans and the Business Community' in Tripathi, 1984, p. 179.
18. Wink, 1999, pp. 273-74.
19. Jain, 1990, p. 224.
20. Quoted in ibid. p. 226.
21. S.C. Misra, 1982, pp. 68–70.
22. Ashin Das Gupta, 1994, pp. 149-50.
23. M.S. Commissariat, 1957, Vol. 2, pp. 420-21.
24. *Bhagvadgomandal*, Vol. 8, 1986, p. 7984.
25. The Modern Gujarati-English Dictionary, 1989, Vol. 2, p. 1366.
26. Bhoola Varajbhai, '*Khedutloko kheti kare chhe te uper nibandh*', Gujarat Vernacular Society, 1852, reprinted in *Arthaat* 1(1), 1981.
27. Jain, 1990, p. 223.
28. Muni Jinvijayji was an eminent Jain monk and Indologist, professor at Puratatva Mandir at Gujarat Vidyapith and was head of the historical research section in the year Gandhi was president of the Gujarati Sahitya Parishad.
29. *Gujarati Sahitya Sammelan, Session 12: Reports and Essays*, 1936, p. 25.

3. Oppressive Encounters

1. Bhadrakali inscription of 1169 in Chaulukya section in G.V. Acharya, 1935, p. 61.
2. ibid.
3. '*Dhanpal: Shrisatyapurmandan Shrimahavirutsah*', Jain Sahitya Sanshodhak Journal Issue 3, p. 241 quoted in Durgashankar K. Shastri, 1953, pp. 195-96.
4. M.A. Quraishi, 1972, p. 10.
5. For further details see Andre Wink, 1990, p. 69.
6. ibid., p. 178. While the identification of Kambaya and Saymur is consistent with other sources, there appears to be some uncertainty as to the exact location of the other two cities.
7. Identified as Sanjan by the archaeologist–historian H.D. Sankalia in '*Sanjan: AD 980ma Ek Nhanu Surat Ke Mumbai*' in *Arthaat* 1(1), 1981.
8. S.C. Misra, 1964, p. 5.
9. V.K. Jain, 1990, pp. 78-79.
10. Term derived from Ghazni and used to refer to the ruler of Delhi.

11. A Gujarati translation of *Jagadu-carita* suggests that this could refer to the ruler of Kandahar.
12. Brajdulal Chattopadhyaya, 1998, p. 62.
13. Maganlal Dalpatram Khakhkhar, *Shri Jagadu Charit* (excerpt). Gujarati translation of the original Sanskrit by Sarvanandsuri, in Manilal Gala, 1989, pp.107–20.
14. Misra, 1964, pp. 6-7.
15. Durgashankar K. Shastri, 1953, p. 492.
16. *Padmanabh: Kanhadde Prabandh*, verse 103-04, edited by Dr Kantilal Baldevram Vyas, 1977.
17. S.C Misra, 1982, p. 69 fn.
18. S. Nawab Ali, 1926, p. 34.
19. *Mirat-i-Sikandari* quoted in Rasiklal Parikh et al., 1977, p. 396.
20. Jain sources mention the names Gadamantri and Karman Mantri.
21. Quraishi, 1972, pp. 45–49.
22. M.S. Commissariat, 1987, p. 31.
23. According to a Bull of Pope Alexander VI, published in 1493, all the territories of the east were awarded to Portugal, just as those of the Americas had been awarded to Spain. Then in 1514 Pope Leo X granted to the king of Portugal the *Padrado* or right of ecclesiastical patronage in all the conquered lands of Asia, which in effect meant that the state officially supported the work of the missions. Robin Boyd, 1981, p. 4.
24. ibid.
25. Paryushan is the annual holy period of fasting before the birth anniversary of Lord Mahavira. Akbar's farman of 1601 and 1604 to the Jains are remarkable for their comprehensive nature. They prohibited not only animal slaughter during paryushan but also hunting of birds and putting them in cages. They also prohibited entry of people of other religions into Jain temples and instructed that repair of Jain temples not be interfered with.
26. K.K. Shastri, 1977, p. 7.
27. Nawab Ali, 1926, pp. 232–34.
28. Commissariat, 1957, pp. 207-08.
29. *Maasir-i-Alamgiri* quoted in ibid., p. 189 fn.
30. ibid., pp. 207.
31. Quoted in Jadunath Sarkar, 1973, p. 96.
32. Quoted in ibid., p. 99.
33. Quoted in ibid., p. 207.
34. ibid., p. 174.
35. Anon. '*Ganimni Ladaino Pavado*' (Ballad of the Maratha Plunderer), in Manjulal Majmudar, 1963, p. 272.
36. Commissariat, 1957, p. 555-56.
37. Ratnamanirao Bhimrao Jote, 1928, p. 159.

4. Welcoming the British Raj

1. Ishvarlal Ichchharam Desai, 1958, p. 116. For more details see Lakshmi Subramanian, 'Power and the Weave: Weavers, Merchants and Rulers in Eighteenth-Century Surat' in Rudrangshu Mukherjee and Lakshmi Subramanian, 1998, pp. 52–82.
2. Douglas E. Haynes, 1992, pp. 92-93.
3. S.C. Misra, 1975, pp. 14-15.
4. *Bharuch Shaherno Itihaas* quoted in Hiralal Tribhuvandas Parekh, Vol. 1, 1935, p. 8.
5. Ranchhodji Amarji Diwan, 1978, pp. 155, 171.
6. Romesh Dutt, 1906a, pp. 331-32.
7. Quoted in Amrita Shodhan, 2001, p. 66.
8. Dutt, 1906a, p. 332.
9. ibid., pp. 336-37.
10. *Buddhiprakash* 5(1), p. 23.
11. ibid., p. 21.
12. *Gujarat Shalapatra*, 5(8), pp. 186-87.
13. Mahipatram Rupram Nilkanth, 1879, p. 8.
14. ibid., pp. 102-03.
15. Eckehard Kulke, 1978, p. 84, quoting proceedings of the Students' Literary and Scientific Society, 1856–59.
16. Hiralal Tribhuvandas Parekh, 1933, p. 39 (appendix).
17. *The Stree Bodhe and Social Progress in India: A Jubilee Memorial*, 1908, p. 61.
18. Navalram Trivedi, 1934, p. 66.
19. Narmadashankar Lalshankar, 1994, p. 56.
20. Narmadashankar Lalshankar, *Rajyarang* (1871–74) in Mahipatram Rupram Nilkanth, 1885, p. 368.
21. Hiralal Tribhuvandas Parekh, 1932, pp. 10-11.
22. Dalpatram Dahyabhai (1878) in Madhusudan Parekh, 2000, p. 615.
23. Forbes published his history of Gujarat, *Rasmala or Hindoo Annals of Goozerat*, in 1856.
24. Narmadashankar Lalshankar, 1994, p. 63.
25. Dutt, 1906a, p. 375.
26. ibid., p. 379-80.
27. Quoted in G.D. Patel, 1950, p. 73.
28. Krishnarao Bholanath, 1888, p. 65.
29. Quoted in Hiralal Tribhuvandas Parekh, Vol. 2, 1936, p. 10.
30. For more details see R.K Dharaiya, 1970.
31. Quoted in Kalyanrai Nathubhai Joshi, 1969, pp. 238-39.
32. Gujarat State Gazetteer, Part 1, 1989, p. 241.
33. ibid., p. 240.
34. British Political Resident in Kathiawad.
35. Manjulal Majmudar, et al., 1968, pp. 266–68.

Industralization and Swadeshi

1. Dalpatram, Stanzas 135 to 147 'Lakshmi Malvano Upay' (The Way to Find Lakshmi), Dalpat-Kavya-Navnit, in K.K. Shastri, 1967, pp. 192–94. English rendering of the Gujarati original by authors. This poem went into forty editions and 1.5 lakh copies were printed over the next few decades.

2. Eckehard Kulke, 1978, p. 79. A survey of the Indians staying in England for higher studies in 1884 shows that Parsis supplied 24 per cent of the Indian students; of students from Bombay presidency, 70 per cent were Parsis. When Elphinstone College was started in 1834, the majority of the students were Parsi, and by 1850 the teaching body had more Parsis than any other Indian community.

3. S.D. Mehta, 1954, pp. 3-4.

4. The most prominent of the Kanbi businessmen of this period was Ambaidas Lashkari, who was a supplier to the British army. His son went on to establish the second textile mill of Ahmedabad. For more details about the genesis and early years of the cotton textile industry see especially Makrand Mehta, 1982.

5. Makrand Mehta, 1982, pp. 10–12.

6. ibid., pp. 20–22.

7. ibid., pp. 41–53

8. Chandrika Thakkar, 'Vadna Jhadthi Taavar Sudhini 103 Varas Laambi Safar' in Yugvandana 2003, pp. 16–18.

9. S.D. Mehta, 1954, pp. 29-30.

10. Ishwarlal Ichchharam Desai, 1958, pp. 227–29.

11. ibid., p. 229.

12. Based on Census of India 1961, Vol. 5, Gujarat, Part 10-A(i) Special Report on Ahmedabad City, 1967, pp. 9-10.

13. Rusi J. Daruwala, 1986, p. 43.

14. Mulchand Varma, 'Mumbai Sharebajar: Lokshahini Niti Apnaavnari Sanstha' in Yugvandana 2003, p. 8.

15. Manju Parikh, 1988, pp. 92-93.

16. ibid., pp. 99-100.

17. Census figures quoted in Kenneth Gillion, 1968, p. 101.

18. Renana Jhabvala, 1985, p. 27.

19. ibid., pp. 26–29.

20. S.D. Mehta, 1954, pp. 124-25.

21. ibid., p. 82.

22. Makrand Mehta, 1982, pp. 100-01.

23. Mahasukhbhai Chunilal, 1925, pp. 235–40. Quote from Baroda State Gazeteer is in English and incorporated by the author in his otherwise Gujarati narrative.

24. Sorabji Mancherji Desai, 1939, pp. 572-73.

25. Ramlal Parikh, 1961, pp. 520-21.

26. E.A. Gait, Census of India, 1911, Vol. 1, Part 2, Tables, 1987 (reprint), pp. 16–20.
27. The Imperial Gazetteer of India, Vol. 15, 1908, p. 16.
28. Census of India, 1911 quoted in Howard Spodek, 1976, p. 55.
29. Bipan Chandra, 1969, p. 123.
30. Interestingly, Dalpatram's '*Hunnar Khanni Chadai*' also refers to ancient India's prosperity and this sentiment was propelled by the Indological work of Bhagwanlal Indraji, Dr Bhau Daji and others.
31. Narhari Parikh, 1966, p. 297.
32. Ambalal Sakarlal was the first Gujarati to receive a master's degree from Bombay University. He joined the judicial department of Baroda state and went on to become Chief Justice in 1886.
33. Shirin Mehta, 1981, pp. 35-36.
34. Bhavanishankar Joshi, 1889, pp. 1–3.
35. In Ahmedabad, Ranchhodlal recognized that a purely literary education was insufficient and under his guidance the Ahmedabad Municipality promoted technical education. From 1889 municipal scholarships were awarded in Ahmedabad for courses at Victoria Jubilee Institute in Bombay. In 1900 Ranchhodlal's son, Madhavlal, donated one lakh rupees for the establishment of a technical college and the RC Technical Institute was inaugurated two years later.
36. Dhruv Raina and S. Irfan Habib, 1991.

6. The Call for Swaraj

1. The Imperial Gazetteer of India: The Indian Empire Vol. 2 (Historical), 1909, p. 526.
2. S.D. Mehta, 1954, pp. 71–75. For more details see David Arnold, 1987, pp. 55–90.
3. B.M. Bhatia, 1967, pp. 1–49, 250–61.
4. Founder of the Vallabhvidyanagar University and president of the Swantantra Party in Gujarat.
5. Bhailalbhai Patel, 1956, pp. 6–8, 18, 19.
6. Robin Boyd, 1981, pp. 83-84. For more details on the role of the church during the famine see pp. 83–89.
7. David Hardiman, 1981, p. 65.
8. Quoted in Kenneth Gillion, 1968, pp. 95-96.
9. B.N. Pande, 1985, *History of Congress*, Vol. 1, pp. 546-47, 550–53.
10. Only two other Indians achieved this distinction, both Parsis. While Dadabhai was a candidate of the Liberal Party, M.M. Bhownagree represented the Conservative Party in 1895 and S.D. Saklatvala had two terms, as representative of the Labour Party in 1922 and of the Communist Party in 1924.
11. Quoted in Bipan Chandra, 1969, pp. 136-37.
12. Quoted in Annie Besant, 1915, p. 353.

13. Gujarat State Gazetteer, Part 1, 1989, p. 261.
14. Quoted in Manu Bhagavan, 2003, p. 55.
15. Dadabhai Naoroji, 1917, p. 73.
16. Saratchandra Bose, in Indulal Yajnik, 1950, pp. xiii.
17. Proceedings of the Home Department, July 1913, p. 6, quoted in Radha Kumar, 1993, p. 46.
18. Emily C. Brown, 1975, p.68.
19. *Indian Sociologist*, September and October 1907, reproduced in Vishnu Pandya and Arti Pandya, 2003.
20. Quoted in Radha Kumar, 1993, pp. 46-47.
21. Source Material for a History of the Freedom Movement in India, Vol. 2 (1885–1920), Government Central Press, Bombay, 1958, pp. 518–23.
22. Indulal Yajnik, 1967, Vol. 1, pp. 128–30; Ravishankar Raval, 1999, p. 235.
23. For further details see Y.A. Parmar, 1987.
24. Dr Sumant Mehta, 1971, p. 358

7. Gujarat, Gujaratis and Gandhi

1. Ranjitram Mehta, 1923, p. 69.
2. Ranjitram Mehta was one of the founders of the Gujarati Sahitya Parishad.
3. Pyarelal, 1986, p. 214.
4. The first trader in Natal was a Memon, Abubakar Amad, who started trade with an English partner. When the story of his prosperity reached Porbandar, his native place, and the country around, other Memons reached Natal. Bohras from Surat followed them. These traders needed accountants, and Hindu accountants from Gujarat and Saurashtra accompanied them. (*Collected Works of Mahatma Gandhi* [referred to hereafter as CWMG] Vol. 29, 1994 [reprint], p. 23.)
5. M.K. Gandhi, 2002, p. 131.
6. CWMG, Vol. 29, p. 411.
7. CWMG, Vol. 7, p. 455.
8. CWMG, Vol. 10, p. 69.
9. Gandhi, 2002, p. 443.
10. CWMG, Vol. 11, pp. 251-52.
11. For further details see M.K. Gandhi, 2001.
12. Lawyer, politician, novelist and founder of the Bharatiya Vidya Bhavan.
13. CWMG, Vol. 13, p. 9.
14. M.K. Gandhi, 2002, p. 363.
15. ibid., p. 364.
16. Politics, economic progress, etc., are not unconnected matters; knowing that they are all rooted in religion, the Controllers will make an effort to learn and teach politics, economics, social reform, etc., in a religious spirit and work in these fields with all the zeal that they can command. (Draft Constitution of Satyagraha Ashram, 1915, CWMG, Vol. 13, p. 95.)

17. *CWMG*, Vol. 44, p. 166.

18. *CWMG*, Vol. 13, p. 93 fn, 94.

19. Indulal Yagnik entered public life first as a member of the Servants of India Society and later in the Home Rule movement. He joined Gandhi, though he later became critical of the Gandhian approach to the struggle for freedom. Attracted by the Irish struggle, Indulal went to Ireland and participated in the movement. On his return to India, he became one of the pioneers of the Kisan Sabha movement, which campaigned for land reforms and the rights of poor farmers. In 1956 he came out of retirement to lead the Mahagujarat movement, which resulted in the formation of a separate state of Gujarat. His six-volume autobiography, *Atmakatha*, provides a detailed insight into Gujarati society and politics in the twentieth century.

20. Dr Hariprasad Desai, *Public Life* in Shankarrai Amritrai, 1921, p. 104.

21. Indulal Yagnik, *Atmakatha*, Vol. 2, 1955, pp. 57, 59. For further details see Mamasaheb Phadke, 1974, pp. 53–60.

22. *CWMG*, Vol. 13, p. 332.

23. ibid., p. 447.

24. Bansidhar G. Parekh, 1955, p. 89.

25. Indulal Yagnik, 1955, pp. 93-94.

26. M.K. Gandhi, 2002, p. 403.

27. ibid., p. 404.

28. Quoted in Narhari Parikh, 1996, Vol. 1, p. 92.

29. For further details see Indulal Yagnik, 1955, pp. 176–79.

30. Dinkar Mehta, 1975, p. 12.

31. Quoted in Dennis Dalton, 1993, p. 93.

32. Narhari Parikh, 1996, p. 374-75.

33. For more details see Suchitra, 1995, pp. 743–46.

34. Dhansukhlal Mehta and Ramprasad Baxi, 1953, pp. 506–08.

35. Equally distinguished was Vallabhbhai's elder brother Vitthalbhai Patel (1873–1933), who entered public life through the Bombay Council to which he was elected in 1912. He later joined the Congress and remained associated with Gandhi but preferred a 'constitutional' approach and was elected to the Imperial Legislative Council in 1918. He led the Nagpur Flag Satyagraha with Vallabhbhai and in the mid 1920s, when Vitthalbhai headed the Bombay Municipal Corporation, Vallabhbhai headed the Ahmedabad Municipality. Twice elected president (Speaker) of the Indian Legislative Assembly, he resigned the post in 1930 in protest and was arrested. When Vitthalbhai went to Vienna for medical treatment, he met Subhas Chandra Bose and they jointly issued a statement in 1933 criticizing Gandhi, even suggesting that Gandhi resign from leadership. This joint statement did much harm to Vitthalbhai's public image in India. He remained overshadowed by his younger brother's eminence.

36. Quoted in Aparna Basu, 1996, p. 69.

37. For more details about Jyoti Sangh see ibid., pp. 70–74.

38. Quoted in Dalpat Shrimali, 1970, p. 56.

39. In a letter to Narhari Parikh in 1947, Kishorelal Mashruwala reflected at length on the shortcomings of the younger generation of Gandhians trained at Vidyapith and his misgivings about whether they would be able to address future challenges. He also expressed concern about their inability to think independently and their tendency to repeat their gurus without maintaining live links with ordinary people and responding to the changing environment. Anantrai Rawal, 1985, pp. 92-93.

8. 'Hindu' and 'Muslim'

1. A miniature replica of the tomb of Hazrat Hussain, grandson of Prophet Mohammed. It is usually made of wood, bamboo, paper and tinsel and is carried in a procession on the tenth day of Muharram to mourn the martyrdom of Hussain

2. *Times of India*, 18 September 1893, quoted in Rafiq Zakaria, 1970, pp. 283-84.

3. Delhi and Etwah experienced widespread religious riots in 1886, Prabhas Patan in 1888 and Dera Ghazi Khan in 1889. In 1891 a serious Hindu–Muslim riot broke out in Palaked in the Madras Presidency. In 1893, along with Prabhas Patan and Bombay, Ballia, Bareilly, Baraich, Banaras and Azimgarh in North India and Rangoon witnessed communal conflicts.

4. Letter from the government of India to the Secretary of State for India No. 84 dated 27 December 1893, quoted in Rafiq Zakaria, 1970, p. 288.

5. Census of India 1911, Vol. 1, Part 1, Report, Calcutta, 1913, p. 118.

6. Jayanti Dalal, 1969, p. 419.

7. Quoted in C.H. Philips, 1962, p. 86.

8. Douglas E. Haynes, 1992, p. 275.

9. Narmadashankar Lalshankar, 1998, p. 63.

10. Nandshankar Mehta, 1986, pp. 328-29.

11. Quoted in Hussain B. Tyabji, 1952, p. 82.

12. Ibrahim K. Rangwala, 1984.

13. Quoted in Rafiq Zakaria, 1970, p. 293.

14. Quoted in Stanley Wolpert, 1984, p. 34.

15. M.C. Chagla, 1973, p. 25.

16. Quoted in Wolpert, 1984, p. 27.

17. Indulal Yagnik, *Atmakatha*, Vol. 2, 1955, p. 258.

18. For further details see Gail Minault, 1982, p. 194.

19. Pandit Anandapriyaji, 1924, pp. 351-52.

20. Jhinabhai Desai (Snehrashmi), 1986, p. 298.

21. M.C. Chagla, 1973, pp. 79-80.

22. Ganesh Vasudev Mavalankar and Chandubhai Bhagubhai Dalal, 1962, p. 519.

23. Dinkar Mehta, 1968, p. 191.

24. Quoted in P. Hardy, 1998, p. 231.
25. *CWMG*, Vol. 74, p. 26.
26. K.H. Khurshid, 1990, pp. 34–36.
27. Morarji Desai, Vol. 1, 1978, p. 200.
28. ibid., pp. 202-03.
29. For further details see Gujarat State Gazetteer, Junagadh District, 1975, pp. 172–79; and Rajmohan Gandhi, 1990, pp. 435–37.
30. Quoted in Rajmohan Gandhi, 1990, p.438.
31. ibid., p. 438.
32. *CWMG*, Vol. 90, p.127.
33. Pakistan Census of 1951 quoted in Zafar Imam, 1975, p. 76.

9. Social Landscape after Independence

1. Gujarat State Gazetteer, Part 1, 1989, p. 312.
2. Pols are closely packed neighbourhoods with narrow streets, high walls and a gate which can be locked. Each pol is traditionally occupied by a single caste or community, or different castes of similar social status.
3. Kiran Desai, 2004, pp. 17–20.
4. Howard Spodek, 1976, pp. 85, 86.
5. W.S. Churchill quoted in J.S. Mangat, 1969, p. 61.
6. Indira Hirway and Darshini Mahadevia, 2004, p. 80. For further details on the status of water resources in Gujarat see pp. 79–82.
7. Quoted in ibid., p. 92.
8. ibid., p. 86.
9. ibid., p. 83.
10. ibid.
11. ibid., p. 95.
12. ibid.
13. For more details see Gaurang Jani and Varsha Ganguly, 2000.
14. Indira Hirway and Darshini Mahadevia, 2004, p. 183.
15. Census of India 2001, Series 25 Gujarat, Provisional Population Totals (Paper 2 of 2001) Rural Urban Distribution, 2001 p. 16.
16. ibid., p. 18.
17. ibid., p. 19.
18. Quoted in Indira Hirway and Darshini Mahadevia, 2004, pp. 190, 192.
19. Kolis are divided among a number of communities, mainly Talpada Koli, Chunvariya Koli, Dharala, Baraiya and Patanvadiya who are mainly engaged in farming and work as agricultural labour. Kolis living on the coast are fishermen and boatmen. In 1907 Kolis were classified by the British as a Criminal Tribe, ascribing to them a range of anti-social activities such as highway robbery and theft of animals, cattle and standing crops. They were also alleged to be blackmailers and hired assassins. (M. Kennedy, 1985, pp. 97–107). Stigmatized thus, Kolis became a socially neglected group and, today, the majority of Kolis from Kutch, Saurashtra

and bordering areas have the lowest female literacy rate in the whole of the state. Along with the bulk of tribal and rural Dalits, they constitute the 'Other Gujarat' of the twenty-first century.
20. For further details see Ghanshyam Shah, in Francine R. Frankel and M.S.A. Rao, 1990, pp. 59–114

10. Rise of Hindutva

1. Justice P. Jaganmohan Reddy Report, 1971, p. 306.
2. Walter K. Anderson and Shridhar D. Damle, 1987, p. 185.
3. ibid.
4. Justice V.S. Dave Report, Vol. 2, 1990, p. 9.
5. VHP pamphlet, published by the Mehsana branch of the VHP, Mehsana, no date.
6. For further details see 'Hindutva as Savarna Purana' in Ashis Nandy, et al., 1995, pp. 100–23.
7. Ghanshyam Shah, 1996, pp. 165–70.
8. Jan Breman, 1993, pp. 737–41; and Lancy Lobo and Paul D'Souza, 1993, pp. 152–54
9. Quoted in Jan Breman, 1993.
10. *Times of India*, Ahmedabad edition, 18 May 1995.
11. Department of Agriculture, Government of Gujarat, quoted in *Gujarat Samachar* 18 August 2003.
12. *Gujarat Samachar* 2 December 2002.
13. For further details see Achyut Yagnik and Nikita Sud, 2004.

Hindutva and Beyond

1. http://gujarat-earthquake.gov.in/final/rehab_build.html
2. Raveen Thukral, 2002.
3. 'Gujarat Inc throws weight behind Modi, takes on CII', *Indian Express*, 21 February 2003; and 'A Sorry Episode', *Economic Times*, 8 March 2003 (editorial).
4. For further discussion on this see Ashis Nandy, et al., 1995.

References and Select Bibliography

GUJARATI

Books

Acharya, G.V. 1935. *Gujaratna Aitihasik Lekho*. Part 2. Mumbai: Shri Farbas Gujarati Sabha.

Banker, Shankarlal. 1967. *Gandhiji Ane Rashtriya Pravrutti: Sansmarno Ane Anubhavo*. Ahmedabad: Navajivan Prakashan Mandir.

Bhatt, Nanabhai. 1983. *Ghadtar Ane Chantar, Ek Kelavanikarni Anubhavkatha*. Parts 1 and 2. 3rd edition. Ahmedabad: Shravan Trust Ahmedabad. (First edition 1954.)

Dalpatram. 1887. *Jnatinibandha*. 4th edition. Ahmedabad: Gujarat Vernacular Society.

Dalal, Jayanti (Ed.). 1969. *Shri Navin Dahyabhaina Natako*. Part 3. Ahmedabad: Gujarat Sangeet Nritya Natya Akademi.

Desai, Govindbhai H. 1898. *Gujaratno Arvachin Itihas*. Ahmedabad: Gujarat Vernacular Society.

———. 1929. *Vadodarama Chalis Varsha*. Vadodara: Pustakalaya Sahayak Sahakari Mandal Ltd.

Desai, Ishwarlal Ichchharam. 1958. *Surat Sonani Murat*. Surat: Published by Ishwarlal Ichchharam Desai.

Desai, Jhinabhai (Snehrashmi). 1986. *Safalyatanu*. 2nd edition. Ahmedabad: R.R. Sheth and Company. (First edition 1983.)

Desai, Shambhuprasad Harprasad. 1965. *Prabhas Ane Somnath*. Prabhaspatan: Narendra Bhaishankar Trivedi.

Desai, Sorabji Mancherji. 1939. *Tawarikhe Navsari*. 2nd edition. Navsari: S.M. Desai Memorial Fund Committee. (First edition 1897.)

Dharaiya, R.K. 1970. *Gujarat in 1857*. Ahmedabad: Gujarat University.

Diwan, Ranchhodji Amarji. 1978. *Tarikhe Sorath Va Halar*. Translated from the Persian into Gujarati by Shambhuprasad Desai. Junagadh: Prabhas Publication. (First published in 1830.)

Gala, Manilal (Ed.). 1989. *Prarambhik Kshitijo*. Ahmedabad: Rachana Publishers.

Gandhi, Ramdas. 1967. *Sansmarano*. Ahmedabad: Navajivan Prakashan Mandir.

Jhaveri, Krishnalal Mohanlal (Trans.). 1933–36. *Mirat-i-Ahmadi*. Vol. 2. Parts 1–4. Ahmedabad: Gujarat Vernacular Society.

Joshi, Bhavanishankar. 1889. *What Measures Are Necessary to Be Taken for the Introduction of Foreign Industries into India*. Ahmedabad: Gujarat Vernacular Society.

Joshi, Kalyanrai Nathubhai. 1932. *Sir Vitthaldas Damodar Thakersey*. Mumbai: Published by Madhavji Damodar Thakersey.

———. 1969. *Okhamandalna Vagher*. Vadodara: M.S. University.

Joshi, Umashankar. 1981. *Samagra Kavita*. Ahmedabad: Gangotri Trust.

Jote, Ratnamanirao Bhimrao. 1928. *Gujaratnu Paatnagar-Ahmedabad*. Ahmedabad.

Kalarthi, Mukul (Ed.). 2000. *Shrimad Rajchandra Ane Gandhiji*. Reprint. Ahmedabad: Gujarat Vidyapith. (First published in 1964.)

Khori, Adalji Jamshedji. 1884. *Dukal Vishe Nibandha*. Ahmedabad: Gujarat Vernacular Society.

Krishnarao Bholanath. 1888. *Bholanath Sarabhainu Jivancharit*. Ahmedabad.

Maganlal Vakhatchand. 1977. *Amdavadno Itihas (San 1850 Sudhino)*. Reprint. Ahmedabad: Gujarat Vidyasabha. (First published in 1851.)

Mahasukhbhai Chunilal. 1925. *Visnagar Ane Vadodara Rajyani Toonk Hakikat*. Visnagar.

Majmudar, Manjulal (Ed.). 1951–55. *Diwan Bahadur Kru. Mo. Zaveri Lekhsangrah*. Parts 1 and 2. Mumbai: Shri Farbas Gujarati Sabha.

——— (Ed.). 1963. *Gujarati Loksahitya Mala*. Part 3. Ahmedabad: Gujarat Rajya Loksahitya Samiti.

Majmudar, Manjulal, et al. (Eds). 1968. *Gujarati Loksahityamala*. Part 9. Ahmedabad: Gujarat Rajya Loksahitya Samiti.

Mangaldas, Lina. 1979. *Akhand Divo*. Ahmedabad: Shreyas Prakashan.

Master, Karim Muhammad. 1969. *Mahagujaratno Mussalmano*. Parts 1 and 2. Vadodara: Prachyavidya Mandir, M.S. University.

Mavalankar, Ganesh Vasudev, and Chandubhai Bhagubhai Dalal. 1962. *Rashtriya Chalvalman Ahmedabad Municipalityno Falo*. Ahmedabad: Ahmedabad Municipal Corporation.

Mehta, Dhansukhlal and Ramprasad Baxi (Eds). 1953. *Narsinhraoni Rojnishi*. Ahmedabad: Gujarat Vidyasabha.

Mehta, Dinkar. 1968. *Parivartan: Atmakatha*. Ahmedabad: Lokayat Gyankendra Trust.

Mehta, Nandshankar. 1986. *Karan Ghelo: Gujaratno Chhello Rajput Raja*. Reprint of 9th edition. Ahmedabad: Gurjar Granth Ratna. (First published in 1866.)

Mehta, Ranjitram. 1923. *Ranjitramna Nibandhon*. Part 1. Mumbai: Sahitya Prakashak Company Ltd.

Mehta, Dr Sumant. 1964. *Samajdarpan*. Ahmedabad: Gurjar Granthratna Karyalay.

———. 1971. *Atmakatha*. Ahmedabad: Mahakavishri Nanalal Smarak Trust.

Narmadashankar Lalshankar. 1994. *Mari Hakikat by Narmadashankar Lalshankar*. Edited by Ramesh Shukla. Surat: Kavi Narmad Yugavart Trust. (First published in 1866.)

———. 1998. *Narmakosh*. Edited by Ramesh Shukla. Surat: Kavi Narmad Yugavart Trust. (First published in 1873.)

Narsinhrao Bholanath. 1926. *Smaranmukur*. Mumbai: The Sahitya Prakashak Company Ltd.

Nilkanth, Mahipatram Rupram. 1879. *Mehtaji Durgaram Manchcharam Charitra*. Part 1. Ahmedabad.

——— (Ed.). 1885. *Narmagadya*. Mumbai: Government Central Book Depot.

Panchal, Shirish, Bakul Tailor, and Jaidev Shukla (Eds). 2002. *Vismi Sadinu Gujarat*. Vadodara: Samvad Prakashan.

Pandya, Kamalashankar. 1974. *Veran Jivan*. Vadodara: Shri Kamalashankar Pandya Sanman Samiti. (First edition 1973.)

Pandya, Vishnu, and Arti Pandya (Eds). 2003. *Azadi Jangnu Patrkaratva: Londonma Indian Sociologist*. 2nd edition. Ahmedabad: Samantar Prakashan.

Parekh, Bansidhar G. 1955. *Sheth Mangaldas Girdhardas: Jeevan Ane Karya*. Ahmedabad: Published by Mathuradas Mangaldas.

Parekh, Hiralal Tribhuvandas. 1932. *Gujarat Vernacular Societyno Itihas*. Part 1. Ahmedabad: Gujarat Vernacular Society.

———. 1935–37. *Arvachin Gujaratnu Rekhadarshan*. Vols 1–3. Ahmedabad: Gujarat Vernacular Society.

——— (Ed). 1933. *Granth Ane Granthkar*. Vol. 4. Ahmedabad: Gujarat Vernacular Society.

——— (Ed). 1936. *Lady Vidyabahen Manimahotsav Abhinandangranth*. Ahmedabad: Gujarat Vernacular Society.

Parekh, Madhusudan (Ed.). 1999-2000. *Dalpat Gadya, Dalpat Granthavali*. Parts 4 and 5. Gandhinagar: Gujarat Sahitya Akademi.

Parikh, Narhari (Ed.). 1966. *Navalgranthavali*. Ahmedabad: Gujarat Vidyapith, Ahmedabad. (First published in 1937.)

Parikh, Ramlal (Ed.). 1961. *Gujarat Ek Parichay*. Published to mark the Sixty-sixth Session of the Indian National Congress in Bhavnagar by Thakorebhai Desai, Chairman of the Reception Committee.

Parikh, Rasiklal, Hariprasad Shastri, and Pravinchandra Parikh (Eds). 1972–87. *Gujaratno Rajkiya Ane Sanskrutik Itihas*. Vols 1–9. Ahmedabad: Sheth Bholabhai Jeshingbhai Adhyayan-Sanshodhan Vidyabhavan.

Patel, Bhailalbhai. 1956. *Gamdanun Vastav Darshan*. Vallabhvidyanagar: Charotar Vidyamandal.

———. 1970. *Bhaïkakana Sansmarano*. Ahmedabad: Sastu Sahitya Vardhak Karyalay.

Patel, Ravjibhai Manibhai. 1949. *Gandhijini Sadhana*. Revised and enlarged edition. Ahmedabad: Navajivan Prakashan Mandir. (First published in 1939.)

————. 1963. *Hindna Sardar*. Ahmedabad: Navajivan Prakashan Mandir.

Phadke, Mamasaheb. 1974. *Mari Jeevankatha*. Ahmedabad: Navajivan Trust.

Raval, Ravishankar. 1999. *Gujaratman Kalana Pagran*. 2nd edition. Ahmedabad: Kala Ravi Trust & Archer.

Rawal, Anantrai (Ed.). 1985. *Prasangik Patro: Kishorelal Mashruwala*. Ahmedabad: Shravan Trust.

Sandesara, Bhogilal, G. (Ed.). 1956–59. *Varnaksamuchchaya*. Parts 1 and 2. Vadodara: M.S. University.

Shah, Chunilal Vardhaman (Ed.). 1948. *Prajabandhu Suvarnaank*. Ahmedabad: Lok Prakashan Limited.

Shah, Kantilal. 1972. *Saurashtrama Gandhiji: Asha Ane Purti*. Rajkot: Rajkot Jilla Sahakari Prakashan ane Mudranalay.

Shah, Purushottam and Chandrakant Shah (Eds). 1954. *Charotar Sarvasangraha*. Nadiad Charotar Sarvasangraha Trust.

Shankarrai Amritrai (Ed). 1921. *Amdavadno Jivanvikas*. Ahmedabad.

Shastri, Durgashankar K. 1945. *Pandit Bhagwanlal Indrajinu Jivancharitra*. Ahmedabad: Gujarat Vernacular Society.

————. 1953. *Gujaratno Madhyakaalin Rajput Itihaas*. Vols 1 and 2. Ahmedabad: Gujarat Vidyasabha.

————. 1977. *Aitihasik Sanshodhan*. Ahmedabad: Gujarati Sahitya Parishad.

Shastri, K.K. 1977. *Shri Vallabhacharya Mahaprabhuji*. 2nd edition.Vadodara: Prachyavidya Mandir, M.S.University. (First published in 1954.)

———— (Ed). 1967. *Dalpat-Kavya-Navnit*. 2nd edition. Ahmedabad: Gujarat Vidyasabha.

Shrimali, Dalpat. 1970. *Sevamurti Parikshitlal*. Ahmedabad: Navajivan Prakashan Mandir.

Sumro, Adam. 1982. *Karachi: Kaal Darpanman*. Mumbai: Sindhu Prakashan.

Sundaram. 1992. *Utkantha*. Mumbai and Ahmedabad: R.R. Sheth & Company.

Trivedi, Chimanlal (Ed). 1999–2001. *Dalpatkavya: Dalpat Granthavali*. Parts 1–3. Gandhinagar: Gujarat Sahitya Akademi.

Trivedi, Navalram. 1934. *Samaj Sudharanun Rekhadarshan*. Ahmedabad: Gujarat Vernacular Society.

Vakil, Keshavlal Motilal. 1886. *Sthanik Swarajya*. Ahmedabad: Gujarat Vernacular Society.

Vyas, Dr Kantilal Baldevram (Ed.). 1977. *Padmanabh: Kanhadde Prabandh*. Mumbai: N.N. Tripathi Pvt. Ltd.

Yajnik, Indulal. 1955–73. *Atmakatha*. Vol. 1, 1967, 2nd edition, Ahmedabad: Ravani Publishing House; Vol. 2, 1955, Ahmedabad: Navchetan Sahitya Mandir; Vol. 3, 1956, Vatrak, Kheda District: Vatrak Khedut Vidyalay; Vol. 4, 1969, Ahmedabad: Gurjar Granthratna Karyalaya; Vol. 5, 1971, Ahmedabad: Gurjar Granthratna Karyalaya; Vol. 6 (Dhanvant Ojha, Ed.), 1973, Ahmedabad: Mahagujarat Sewa Trust.

Zakaria, Hashim. 1970. *Memon Komno Itihas*. Karachi: Memon Youths Organisation.

Articles

Anandapriyaji, Pandit. 1924. '*Gujaratma Hindu Sabha*'. *Yugadharma* **4**(5). Samvat 1980.

Periodicals

Arthaat **1**(1). Centre for Social Studies, Surat, October 1981.
Buddhiprakash **5**(1). Gujarat Vernacular Society, Ahmedabad, April 1858.
Gujarat Shalapatra **5**(8). August 1866.
Puratatva, Vol. 5, Gujarat Vidyapith, Ahmedabad, 1927.
Gujarat Samachar.
Yugvandana, Mumbai Sharebajar Visheshank, Mumbai, 2001 and 2003.

Others

Bhagvatsinhji (Ed.). 1986. *Bhagvatgomandal*. Parts 1–9. Reprint. Rajkot: Pravin Prakashan. (First published 1944–55.)
Parishadpramukhna Bhashano. Part 2. Ahmedabad: Gujarati Sahitya Parishad. 1974.
The Stree Bodhe and Social Progress in India: A Jubilee Memorial. Mumbai: The Stree Bodhe Office. 1908.
Gujarati Sahitya Sammelan, Session 12: Reports and Essays. Ahmedabad, 1936.
The Modern Gujarati-English Dictionary, Vol. 2, 2nd edition, Director of Languages, Gujarat State, Gandhinagar, 1989.

ENGLISH

Books

Anderson, Walter K., and Shridhar D. Damle. 1987. *The Brotherhood in Saffron: The Rashtriya Swayamsevak Sangh and Hindu Revivalism*. New Delhi: Vistaar Publication.
Arasaratnam, Sinnapah. 1994. *Maritime India in the Seventeenth Century*. New Delhi: Oxford University Press.
Baird, Robert D. (Ed.). 1981. *Religion in Modern India*. New Delhi: Manohar Publishers.
Banga, Indu (Ed.). 1992. *Ports and Their Hinterlands in India 1700–1950*. Delhi: Manohar Publishers.
Banga, Indu (Ed.). 1994. *The City in Indian History: Urban Demography, Society and Politics*. Delhi: Manohar Publishers.
Basu, Aparna. 1996. *Mridula Sarabhai: Rebel with a Cause*. Delhi: Oxford University Press.
Besant, Annie. 1915. *How India Wrought for Freedom*. Madras and Mumbai: Theosophical Publishing House, Madras, and Indian Book Depot, Bombay.
Bhagavan, Manu. 2003. *Sovereign Spheres: Princes, Education and Empire in Colonial India*. Delhi: Oxford University Press.

Bhatia, B.M. 1967. *Famines in India: A Study in Some Aspects of the Economic History of India (1860–1965)*. 2nd edition. New York: Asia Publishing House. (First edition 1963.)

Borsa, Giorgio (Ed.). 1990. *Trade and Politics in the Indian Ocean: Historical and Contemporary Perspectives*. New Delhi: Manohar Publishers.

Boyd, Robin. 1981. *A Church History of Gujarat*. Madras: The Christian Literature Society.

Brown, Emily C. 1975. *Har Dayal: Hindu Revolutionary and Rationalist*. New Delhi: Manohar Publications.

Campbell, James M. 1988. *Hindu Castes and Tribes of Gujarat*. Vols 1 and 2. Reprint of 2nd edition. Gurgaon: Vintage Books. (First published in 1901.)

———. 1990. *Muslims and Parsi Castes and Tribes of Gujarat*. Reprint. Gurgaon: Vintage Books. (First published in 1899.)

Chagla, M.C. 1973. *Roses in December*. Mumbai: Bharatiya Vidya Bhavan.

Chakravarti, Ranabir (Ed.). 2001. *Trade in Early India*. New Delhi: Oxford University Press.

Chandra, Bipan. 1969. *The Rise and Growth of Economic Nationalism in India*. Reprint. New Delhi: People's Publishing House. (First published in 1966.)

Chandra, Satish (Ed.). 1987. *The Indian Ocean: Explorations in History, Commerce and Politics*. New Delhi: Sage Publications.

Chattopadhyaya, Brajdulal. 1998. *Representing the Other: Sanskrit Sources and the Muslims (Eighth to Fourteenth Centuries)*. New Delhi: Manohar Publishers.

Chaube, J. 1975. *History of the Gujarat Kingdom*. New Delhi: Munshiram Manoharlal Publishers Pvt. Ltd.

Commissariat, M.S. 1938 and 1957. *A History of Gujarat (With a Survey of Its Monuments and Inscriptions)*. Vols 1 and 2. Mumbai: Orient Longman.

———. 1987. *Studies in the History of Gujarat: The Thakkar Vassonji Madhavji Lectures of the University of Bombay for the Year 1930-31*. Reprint. Ahmedabad: Saraswati Pustak Bhandar.

Dalton, Dennis. 1993. *Mahatma Gandhi: Nonviolent Power in Action*. New York: Columbia University Press.

Daruwala, Rusi J. 1986. *The Bombay Chamber Story: 150 Years*. Mumbai: Bombay Chamber of Commerce and Industry.

Das Gupta, Ashin. 1994. *Indian Merchants and the Decline of Surat c.1700–1750*. New Delhi: Manohar Publishers. (First published 1979.)

Das Gupta, Ashin, and M.N. Pearson (Eds). 1987. *India and the Indian Ocean 1500–1800*. New Delhi: Oxford University Press.

Desai, Govindbhai H. 1932. *Hindu Families in Gujarat: Being an Account of Their Domestic, Social and Economic Life*. Vadodara: Baroda State Press.

Desai, Morarji. 1978. *The Story of My Life*. Vols 1 and 2. New Delhi: S. Chand and Company.

Dutt, Romesh. 1906a. *Economic History of India under Early British Rule.* 2nd edition. London: Kegan Paul, Trench, Trubner & Co. Ltd. (First published in 1901.)

———. 1906b. *Economic History of India in the Victorian Age.* 2nd edition. London: Kegan Paul, Trench, Trubner & Co. Ltd. (First published in 1903.)

Eaton, Richard M. 2003. *India's Islamic Traditions 711–1750.* New Delhi: Oxford University Press.

Forbes, Alexander Kinloch. 1924. *Ras Mala or Hindoo Annals of Goozerat.* Vols 1 and 2. London: Oxford University Press.

Frankel, Francine R., and M.S.A. Rao (Eds). 1990. *Dominance and State Power in Modern India: Decline of a Social Order.* Vol. 2. Delhi: Oxford University Press.

Gandhi, M.K. 1958–94. *The Collected Works of Mahatma Gandhi* Vols 1– 100. New Delhi: Publications Division, Government of India.

———. 2001. *Satyagraha in South Africa.* Reprint. Ahmedabad: Navajivan Publishing House. (First published in 1928.)

———. 2002. *An Autobiography or The Story of My Experiments with Truth.* Reprint. Ahmedabad: Navajivan Publishing House. (First published in 1927.)

Gandhi, Rajmohan. 1990. *Patel: A Life.* Ahmedabad: Navajivan Publication House.

Gillion, Kenneth. 1968. *Ahmedabad: A Study in Indian Urban History:* Ahmedabad: New Order Book Company.

Gopal, Lallanji. 1965. *The Economic Life of Northern India, c. A.D. 700– 1200.* Varanasi: Motilal Banarsidass.

Gopal, Surendra. 1975. *Commerce and Crafts in Gujarat: 16th and 17th Centuries.* New Delhi: People's Publishing House.

Guha, Ranajit (Ed.). 1987. *Subaltern Studies.* Vol. 5. New Delhi: Oxford University Press

Habib, Irfan. 2002. *The Indus Civilization.* New Delhi: Tulika.

Hardiman, David. 1981. *Peasant Nationalists of Gujarat: Kheda District 1917– 1934.* Delhi: Oxford University Press.

Hardiman, David. 1996. *Feeding the Baniya: Peasants and Userers in Western India.* Delhi: Oxford University Press.

Hardy, P. 1998. *The Muslims of British India.* New Delhi: Cambridge University Press, Foundation Books. (First published in 1972.)

Hasan, Mushirul. 2002. *Islam in the Subcontinent: Muslims in a Plural Society.* New Delhi: Manohar Publishers.

Haynes, Douglas E. 1992. *Rhetoric and Ritual in Colonial India: The Shaping of a Public Culture in Surat City, 1852–1928.* Delhi: Oxford University Press.

Hirway, Indira, and Darshini Mahadevia. 2004. *Gujarat Human Development Report.* Ahmedabad: Mahatma Gandhi Labour Institute.

Imam, Zafar. 1975. *Muslims in India*. New Delhi: Orient Longman.

Jackson, A.M.T., and R.E. Enthoven. 1989. *Folklore of Gujarat*. Reprint. Gurgaon: Vintage Books. (First published in 1914.)

Jain, V.K. 1990. *Trade and Traders in Western India (AD 1000–1300)*. New Delhi: Munshiram Manoharlal Publishers Pvt. Ltd.

Jhabvala, Renana. 1985. *Closing Doors: A Study on the Decline in Women Workers in the Textile Mills of Ahmedabad*. Ahmedabad: Setu.

Jinnah, Fatima. 1987. *My Brother*. Karachi: Quaid-e-Azam Academy.

Jordens, J.T.F. 1998. *Dayananda Sarasvati: Essays on His Life and Ideas*. New Delhi: Manohar Publishers.

Kennedy, M. 1985. *The Criminal Classes in India*. Reprint. New Delhi: Mittal Publishers. (First published in 1907.)

Khurshid, K.H. 1990. *Memories of Jinnah*. Edited by Khalid Hasan. Karachi: Oxford University Press.

Kooiman, Dick. 2002. *Communalism and Indian Princely States: Travancore, Baroda and Hyderabad in the 1930s*. New Delhi: Manohar Publications.

Kripalani, J.B. 2004. *My Times: An Autobiography*. New Delhi: Rupa & Co.

Kulke, Eckehard. 1978. *The Parsees in India: A Minority as Agent of Social Change*. New Delhi: Vikas Publishing House.

Kumar, Radha. 1993. *The History of Doing*. New Delhi: Kali for Women.

Lokhandwalla, S.T. (Ed.). 1971. *India and Contemporary Islam*. Simla: Indian Institute of Advanced Study.

Majmudar, M.R. 1968. *Gujarat: Its Art Heritage*. Mumbai: University of Bombay.

Mangat, J.S. 1969. *A History of the Asians in East Africa c. 1886 to 1945*. London: Oxford University Press.

Mcdonald, Hamish. 1998. *The Polyester Prince: The Rise of Dhirubhai Ambani*. St. Leonards, New South Wales: Allen & Unwin.

Mehta, Ashok, and Achyut Patwardhan. 1942. *The Communal Triangle in India*. Allahabad: Kitabistan.

Mehta, Kapilray. 1950. *Ahmedabad Directory*. Ahmedabad: Gujarat Publishers.

Mehta, Makrand. 1982. *The Ahmedabad Cotton Textile Industry: Genesis and Growth*. Ahmedabad: New Order Book Company.

———. 1991. *Indian Merchants and Entrepreneurs in Historical Perspective*. Delhi: Academic Foundation.

Mehta, S.D. 1954. *The Cotton Mills of India 1854 to 1954*. Mumbai: The Textile Association of India.

Metcalf, Thomas R. 1965. *The Aftermath of Revolt: India 1857–1870*. New Jersey: Princeton University Press.

Minault, Gail. 1982. *The Khilafat Movement: Religious Symbolism and Political Mobilization in India*. Delhi: Oxford University Press.

Misra, S.C. 1964. *Muslim Communities of Gujarat: Preliminary Studies in their History and Social Organization*. Mumbai: Asia Publishing House.

———. 1982. *The Rise of Muslim Power in Gujarat: A History of Gujarat from 1298 to 1442*. 2nd edition. New Delhi: Munshiram Manoharlal Publishers Pvt. Ltd.

————— (Ed.). 1975. *Qissa-i-Ghamgin by Munshi Abbas Ali*. Vadodara: M.S. University.

Mookerji, Radhakumud. 1912. *The History of Indian Shipping and Maritime Activity from the Earliest Times*. Mumbai: Longmans, Green and Company.

Mukherjee, Rudrangshu, and Lakshmi Subramanian. 2003. *Politics and Trade in the Indian Ocean World*. New Delhi: Oxford University Press. (First published in 1998.)

Nandy, Ashis, Shikha Trivedy, Shail Mayaram, and Achyut Yagnik. 1995. *Creating a Nationality: The Ramjanmabhoomi Movement and Fear of the Self*. Delhi: Oxford University Press.

Naoroji, Dadabhai. 1917. 2nd edition. *Speeches and Writings of Dadabhai Naoroji*. Madras: G.A. Natesan & Co.

Nawab Ali, S. (Trans. and Ed.). 1926. *Mirat-i-Ahmadi by Ali Muhammad Khan Bahadur*. Vadodara: Gaekwar Oriental Series.

Nizami, Khaliq Ahmad. 2002. *Religion and Politics during the Thirteenth Century*. New Delhi: Oxford University Press.

Pande, B.N. (Ed.). 1985. *A Centenary History of the Indian National Congress*. Vols 1–3. New Delhi: AICC/Vikas.

Parel, Anthony. 1997. *M.K. Gandhi: 'Hind Swaraj' and Other Writings*. New Delhi: Cambridge University Press, Foundation Books.

Parikh, Narhari. 1996. *Sardar Vallabhbhai Patel*. Vols 1 and 2. Reprint. Ahmedabad: Navajivan Publishing House.

Parikh, Rasiklal C. 1938. *'Kavyanusasana' by Acharya Hemchandra* Vol. 2. Mumbai: Shri Mahavir Jaina Vidyalaya.

Parmar, Y.A. 1987. *The Mahyavanshi: The Success Story of a Scheduled Caste*. Delhi: Mittal Publications.

Patel, C.N. 1981. *Mahatma Gandhi in His Gujarati Writings*. New Delhi: Sahitya Akademi.

Patel, G.D. 1950. *Agrarian Reforms in Bombay*. Published by the author in Mumbai.

Pearson, M.N. 1976. *Merchants and Rulers in Gujarat: The Response to the Portuguese in the Sixteenth Century*. New Delhi: Munshiram Manoharlal Publishers Pvt. Ltd.

Philips, C.H. (Ed.). 1962. *The Evolution of India and Pakistan 1858–1947: Select Documents*. London: George Allen and Unwin Ltd.

Pocock, David F. 1972. *Kanbi and Patidar: A Study of the Patidar Community of Gujarat*. London: Oxford University Press.

Pyarelal. 1986. *Mahatma Gandhi Vol. 1: The Early Phase*. Reprint. Ahmedabad: Navajivan Publishing House. (First published in 1965.)

Quraishi, M.A. 1972. *Muslim Education and Learning of Gujarat (1297–1758)*. Vadodara: M.S. University.

Ratnagar, Shereen. 2001. *Understanding Harappa: Civilization in the Greater Indus Valley*. New Delhi: Tulika.

Ray, Baren. 1996. *Gandhi's Campaign against Untouchability 1933-1934: An Account from the Raj's Secret Official Reports*. New Delhi: Gandhi Peace Foundation.

Sachau, Dr Edward. 1989. *Alberuni's India*. Vols 1 and 2. Delhi: Low Price Publications. (First published in 1910.)

Sankalia, H.D. 1949. *Studies in the Historical and Cultural Geography and Ethnography of Gujarat*. Poona: Deccan College.

———. 1977. *Aspects of Indian History and Archaeology*. Delhi: B.R. Publishing Corporation

Sarkar, Jadunath. 1973. *Shivaji and His Times*. Reprint. Orient Longman.

Seal, Anil. 1968. *The Emergence of Indian Nationalism: Competition and Collaboration in the Later Nineteenth Century*. London: Cambridge University Press.

Shah, Ghanshyam, and D.C. Sah (Eds). 2002. *Land Reforms in India Vol. 8: Performance and Challenges in Gujarat and Maharashtra*. New Delhi: Sage Publications.

Shah, Ghanshyam, Mario Rutten, and Hein Streefkerk (Eds). 2002. *Development and Deprivation in Gujarat*. New Delhi: Sage Publications.

Shinoda, Takashi (Ed.). 2002. *The Other Gujarat: Social Transformations among Weaker Sections*. Mumbai: Popular Prakashan.

Shodhan, Amrita. 2001. *A Question of Community: Religious Groups and Colonial Law*. Calcutta: Samya.

Siddiqi, M.H. 1985. *The Growth of Indo-Persian Literature in Gujarat*. Vadodara: M.S. University.

Spodek, Howard. 1976. *Urban-Rural Integration in Regional Development: A Case Study of Saurashtra, India—1800–1960*. University of Chicago Department of Geography Research Paper No. 171.

Stokes, Eric. 1989. *The English Utilitarians and India*. Delhi: Oxford University Press.

Tripathi, Dwijendra (Ed.). 1984. *Business Communities of India*. New Delhi: Manohar Publishers.

Trivedi, A.B. 1943. *Wealth of Gujarat*. Published by the author in Mumbai.

Tyabji, Hussain B. 1952. *Badruddin Tyabji: A Biography*. Mumbai: Thacker & Co. Ltd.

Varma, Ganeshi Lal. 1993. *Shyamji Krishna Varma: The Unknown Patriot*. New Delhi: Publications Division.

Weber, Thomas. 1997. *On the Salt March: The Historiography of Gandhi's March to Dandi*. New Delhi: HarperCollins Publishers India Pvt. Ltd.

Wink, Andre. 1990. *Al-Hind The Making of the Indo-Islamic World Vol. 1: Early Medieval India and the Expansion of Islam 7th–11th Centuries*. Delhi: Oxford University Press.

————. 1999. *Al-Hind The Making of the Indo-Islamic World Vol. 2: The Slave Kings and the Islamic Conquest 11th–13th Centuries*. Delhi: Oxford University Press.

Wolpert, Stanley. 1984. *Jinnah of Pakistan*. New York: Oxford University Press.

Yajnik, Indulal. 1943. *Gandhi As I Know Him*. Delhi: Danish Mahal.

————. 1950. *Shyamji Krishnavarma: Life and Times of an Indian Revolutionary*. Mumbai: Lakshmi Publications.

Zakaria, Rafiq. 1970. *Rise of Muslims in India Politics*. Mumbai: Somaiya Publications Pvt. Ltd.

Government Publications

The Imperial Gazetteer of India, Vol. 15. Oxford. 1908.

The Imperial Gazetteer of India. 1909. The Indian Empire, Vol. 2 (Historical). Oxford: Clarendon Press.

Gujarat State Gazetteer, Parts 1 and 2, Government of Gujarat, Gandhinagar, 1989–91.

Gujarat State Gazetteer, Government of Gujarat, Ahmedabad
  Ahmedabad District, 1984.
  Broach District (Revised Edition), 1961.
  Junagadh District, 1975.
  Kheda District, 1977.
  Surat District (revised edition), 1962.

Dracup, A.H., and H.T. Sorley. Census of India, 1931 Vol. 8: Bombay Presidency. Parts 1 and 2. Reprinted by Usha Publications, New Delhi, 1987.

Census of India, 1961 Vol. 5, Gujarat Part 10 – A (i) Special Report on Ahmedabad City, Delhi, 1967.

Gait, E.A. Census of India, 1911, Vol. 1: India. Parts 1 and 2. Reprinted by Usha Publications, New Delhi, 1987.

Census of India 2001, Series 25 Gujarat, Provisional Population Totals (Paper 2 of 2001) Rural Urban Distribution, Directorate of Census Operations, Ahmedabad, 2001.

Singh K.S. (Ed.). People of India—National Series Vol. 7: Identity, Ecology, Social Organization, Economy, Linkages and Development Process: A Quantitative Profile. Anthropological Survey of India, Oxford University Press, Delhi, 1996.

Singh K.S. (General Editor). People of India—Gujarat Vol. 22. Parts 1–3, Anthropological Survey of India, Popular Prakashan Pvt. Ltd, Mumbai, 2003.

Source Material for a History of the Freedom Movement in India, Vol. 2 (1885–1920), Government Central Press, Bombay, 1958.

Report of the Commission of Inquiry into the Communal Disturbances at Ahmedabad and other places in Gujarat on and after 18th September 1969 by Justice P. Jaganmohan Reddy, Government Central Press, Gandhinagar, 1990, Conclusion and Observations.

Report of the Commission of Inquiry into the incidents of violence and disturbances which took place at various places in the State of Gujarat since February, 1985 to 18th July, 1985 by Justice V. S. Dave, Vol. 2, Government Central Press, Gandhinagar, 1990.

Articles

Arnold, David. 1987. 'Touching the Body: Perspectives on the Indian Plague 1896–1900', in *Subaltern Studies*. Vol. 5. Edited by Ranajit Guha. Oxford University Press.

Jones, Kenneth W. 1981. 'The Arya Samaj in British India 1875-1947', in *Religion in Modern India*. Edited by Robert D. Baird. New Delhi: Manohar Publications.

Bhatt, Anil, and Achyut Yagnik. 1984. 'The Anti-Dalit Agitation in Gujarat.' *South Asia Bulletin* (4)1.

Breman, Jan. 1993. 'Anti Muslim Progrom in Surat.' *Economic and Political Weekly* 17 April.

Chandra, Sudhir. 1993. 'Of Communal Consciousness and Communal Violence: Impressions from Post-Riot Surat.' *Economic and Political Weekly* 4 September.

Desai, Kiran. 2004. 'Workers and Communal Riots: A Case Study of Surat.' *Labour File* May–June.

'Gujarat Inc Throws Weight behind Modi, Takes on CII.' *Indian Express* 21 February 2003.

'A Sorry Episode.' *Economic Times* 8 March 2003 (editorial).

Lobo, Lancy, and Paul D'Souza. 1993. 'Images of Violence.' *Economic and Political Weekly* 30 January.

Mehta, Shirin. 1981. 'Social Background of Swadeshi Movement in Gujarat 1875-1908.' *Vidya* 24(1).

Patel, Aakar. 2003. 'Gujarat: A State of Unrest'. *Mid Day*, 2 November.

Raina, Dhruv, and S. Irfan Habib. 1991. 'Technical Institutes in Colonial India: Kala Bhavan, Baroda (1890–1990).' *Economic and Political Weekly* 16 November.

Shah, Ghanshyam. 1990. 'Caste Sentiments, Class Formation and Dominance in Gujarat.' In *Dominance and State Power in Modern India*. Vol. 2. Edited by Francine R. Frankel and M.S.A. Rao. New Delhi: Oxford University Press.

———. 1996. 'BJP's Rise to Power.' *Economic and Political Weekly* 13–20 January, pp. 165–70.

Suchitra. 1995. 'What Moves Masses: Dandi March as Communication Strategy.' *Economic and Political Weekly* 8 April.

Thukral, Raveen. 2002. 'No Direct Aid from Corporates for Gujarat Riot Victims.' *Hindustan Times* 12 June.

Periodicals
Journal of the Gujarat Research Society, *Bhagwanlal Indraji Commemoration Volume*, October 1939, Bombay.
Times of India, Ahmedabad edition.
Economic Times, Ahmedabad edition.
Hindustan Times, Delhi edition.
Indian Express, Internet edition.

Websites
http://gujarat-earthquake.gov.in/final/rehab_build.html
http://onlinevolunteers.org

Others
Bhatia, Bela. 1992. *Lush Fields and Parched Throats: The Political Economy of Groundwater in Gujarat*. United Nations University-World Institute for Development Economics Research, Working Papers No. 100.
Janaki, V.A. 1969. *Gujarat as the Arabs Knew It: A Study of Historical Geography*. Research Paper Series No. 4. Vadodara: M.S. University.
Jani, Gaurang, and Varsha Ganguly. 2000. 'Problem of Land Alienation among Tribals of Gujarat.' Setu: Centre for Social Knowledge and Action, Ahmedabad.
Mehta, Dinkar. 1975. Oral History Transcripts. Nehru Memorial Museum and Library.
Parikh, Manju. 1988. Labour-Capital Relations in the Indian Textile Industry: A Comparative Study of Ahmedabad and Coimbatore. Unpublished Ph.D. thesis, University of Chicago.
Rangwala, Ibrahim K. (Ed.). 1984. *Anjuman-e-Islam (1884–1984) Centenary Celebration Volume*. Ahmedabad.
Yagnik, Achyut and Nikita Sud. 'Hindutva and Beyond—Political Topography of Gujarat' presented at the seminar 'State Politics in India in the 1990s: Political Mobilisation and Political Competition' organized by Developing Countries Research Centre, University of Delhi and London School of Economics at New Delhi, 13–17 December, 2004.

Index